Ken,

Great connectin,
certain there's at least one chapter here
that you certainly enjoy.
All the best!

Dan Purdy

Billy Kl

THUNDER SNOW OF BUFFALO

THE OCTOBER SURPRISE STORM

DON PURDY & BILLY KLUN

Archway Publishing books may be ordered through booksellers or by contacting:

Archway Publishing
1663 Liberty Drive
Bloomington, IN 47403
www.archwaypublishing.com
844-669-3957

Scripture taken from the King James Version of the Bible.

ISBN: 978-1-6657-0619-3 (sc)
ISBN: 978-1-6657-0618-6 (hc)
ISBN: 978-1-6657-0620-9 (e)

Library of Congress Control Number: 2021908268

Print information available on the last page.

Archway Publishing rev. date: 6/4/2021

CONTENTS

Thunder Snow of Buffalo
The October Surprise Storm
By Don Purdy & Billy Klun

WHEN IT'S TOO TOUGH FOR THEM, IT'S JUST RIGHT FOR US

A FOREWORD BY MARV LEVY
WITH THE HONORABLE MAYOR BYRON W. BROWN

First, it was so nice to hear from Don, and to admire his energy and the progress he has been making on the book now that he has finally finished shoveling away all that snow from the 2006 October Storm. I imagine he's still got fourteen more years of shoveling to do before he catches up with the next inevitable and swiftly approaching winter, but, with his energy, I'm placing my bet on you, Don.

When I first was offered the job as head coach of the Buffalo Bills back in 1986, team owner Ralph Wilson cautioned me that there were just two seasons a year in Buffalo. They were:

1. The Fourth of July
2. and Winter

Over my coaching years there, I learned that at times it could seem to be that way, but I also jumped on the fact that we could adapt and that we could turn adverse weather to our team's advantage during those *stormy January* type days - inspired by our fantastic fans. We savored when we could play some games during that kind of weather, and it, in addition to our fans, inspired me to say, as

I pointed across the field at our opponent's bench just before the kickoff on many of our game days when the snow was pelting down, *when it's too tough for them, it's just right for us.*

As I've often said, "Football doesn't build character, it reveals character." During those most unusual and treacherous mid-October days in 2006 (my first year back as General Manager), rather than lending itself to a competitive home-field advantage, the weather instead posed extraordinary operational and logistical trials. We, as an organization and community, faced an unexpected, uninvited, and unconventional opponent. But not surprisingly, the special challenges presented by this massive storm did indeed reveal great things about the collective character of the Buffalo Bills organization and the proud citizens of Buffalo. Readers are certain to enjoy learning about the details behind these efforts as well as the accompanying insightful "supporting stories."

It was also very thoughtful of Don to offer to donate some of the proceeds from this collection to a charity of my choice; if that all does workout, I happily mentioned the St. Jude's Children's Research Hospital as a worthy recipient, which Don and Billy were more than in agreement with as well, in addition to plans for other local community organizations.

> *"Hi Don,*
>
> *So great to hear from you again. I hope all is going well for you and Amy during this horrendous coronavirus pandemic fiasco. I am happy to report that Fran and I and all of our family members have been able to do the necessary "broken field running" needed to avoid contracting it. There is some benefit in flying past that 95th birthday (for me; not Fran. She's still a young chick).*
>
> *Your progress in getting that exciting book out to the public sounds exciting, and I sure will look forward*

to receiving it and reading it. If I have any trouble
with the big words, I'll give Thurman Thomas a call.
Best wishes to you, Amy, and all from
both Fran and Me, Marv" - email from
Marv Levy on March 25, 2021.

Shortly before finalizing *Thunder Snow of Buffalo*, we were contacted by Lorey Schultz, Deputy Director of Communications for the office of the Mayor of Buffalo, the Honorable Byron W. Brown. We had reached out initially a few weeks earlier, as he in his capacity as mayor played a critical role in the response and recovery for Buffalo from this storm and as well as the continuing renaissance and revival of the Greater Buffalo Region. Given the demands on his time, especially during the Covid-19 pandemic, we would have completely understood not receiving a response, but during the call, Lorey asked if there was still time for the Mayor to contribute a statement as the October Storm, particularly about how the response by the city's citizens, businesses, and government, remains a deep source of pride and meaning for Mayor Brown. Lorey and the Mayor were relieved to learn we hadn't yet gone to print - and naturally, we were equally enthusiastic to hear his level of excitement for the memories and experiences of the Western New York community to be compiled collectively, including his own.

15TH ANNIVERSARY OF THE OCTOBER STORM CONTRIBUTION FROM THE HONORABLE MAYOR BYRON W. BROWN

When I think back to the "October Surprise", I am reminded that every storm and every challenging circumstance has a way of bringing people and communities together. 15 years ago, I was just settling into my new role as Mayor of the City of Buffalo when this powerful early Lake Effect snowstorm snuck up on all of us, toppling trees, bringing down power lines, and leaving 70% of our residents without electricity for days. It was a severe situation and the first major storm emergency for my Administration.

I'll never forget that first morning, driving into work and seeing the extensive damage and later urging residents to remain calm and patient, reassuring everyone that we would get through this together. The approach that helped me lead our community through this was realizing that, in situations like this, clear, consistent communication was critically important.

Public safety was our first priority. Buffalo's dedicated employees worked around-the-clock in the early days of the recovery. It was all hands-on deck, with various city crews removing the hundreds of trees that were blocking streets, or plowing our main roads, secondaries and residentials.

We learned many lessons from this storm, including the importance of collaboration. Thousands of residents, businesses, and organizations volunteered to assist every step of the way. Nowhere was this more evident than in the rebuilding of our tree inventory. We lost hundreds of trees in this storm and had to work through years of lingering effects. Today, I'm pleased to say that, in partnership with Re-Tree of WNY and the Buffalo Green Fund as well as a coordinated effort between City agencies and our local, state and federal partners, surviving trees have returned to full growth, and the overall street tree population is now the same as it was before the Storm.

As we reflect on the 15th anniversary of the "October Surprise Snowstorm", I encourage all of our residents to think about the tremendous progress we have made, while remembering the ways we came together, helped each other, and revealed the best in our people, reinforcing Buffalo's reputation as the City of Good Neighbors.

ONE
JUST ANOTHER DAY...?

It was a dark and stormy night...

Time out.

Nope.

Cue the record scratch.

That tired cliché will not begin *this* story. Despite the epic weather event that began on Thursday, October 12, 2006 and continued through the dark morning hours of the imminently ominous Friday the 13th, this story began instead most innocently...

So, let's start over as we, along with many other Western New Yorkers both near and far, share the remarkable events and their experiences surrounding the October Surprise Storm of 2006, one that actually crippled the tough, resilient city of Buffalo, New York, at least temporarily.

Late on a Friday afternoon in October 2007, one year after the Storm, my friend Anthony had just landed at the Buffalo Niagara International Airport on a flight from Tampa, Florida, where I picked him up for our third annual "Guys' Weekend" or ironically, "The October Weekend," as we dubbed it. Shortly after we pulled onto the New York State Thruway, Anthony looked out his passenger side window and remarked, "Oh my gosh... Wow."

Turning to look out his side of the car, I expected to see perhaps a deer or an accident, but I saw only green grass and lightly falling leaves – a normal, Buffalo autumnal scene. That normalcy alone was the reason for his amazement because, as Anthony remarked, "The last time I saw this place, it looked like Mad Max," a fact I had forgotten about. He was now witnessing the mundane remnants of what he had last viewed as a post-apocalyptic waste land: a few crooked trees that nature had chopped off at the knees surrounded by an otherwise normal landscape, at least to the locals who had adapted after recovering leaps and bounds from what Anthony had seen just one year before. Despite what we as locals saw as progress and normality, scars remained as Anthony then said, "You can *still* tell that *something* happened."

Like other Buffalonians, I'd become acclimated to the slow, gradual recovery over the past year, so my "wow factor" had faded. But Anthony's reaction to the simplicity of seeing grass or just the repaired building roofs made me further appreciate what an amazing, collective job the citizens of the Greater Buffalo area, its businesses, and local governments did to regain this level of recovery.

As a teenager, I too often recall ending up in an emergency room after breaking a bone, dislocating a joint, getting stitches, or suffering some other nasty sports injury and reflecting at day's end, "When I woke up this morning, I had no idea that my day would end up *here*." On October 12, 2006, the people of Greater Buffalo experienced that same scenario on a collective, grand scale. That is – they simply had no idea that their day (and the several days after) would end up like *this*.

That Thursday was a fairly typical autumn morning in Western New York (WNY). Our daughter, Anna, then twelve-years-old, woke up first. I went downstairs at about 6:30 am for the much-needed dose of morning coffee, soon to be joined by our then seven-year old, Claire. If lucky, there was a ten-minute window when the three of us intersected at the breakfast table. On an average day, this was trimmed down to about four minutes, as most families can relate to. My wife, Amy, a West Seneca elementary school teacher, never sat down in the mornings as she somehow got herself *and* the girls - including hair, clothes, and lunches - ready for school every single day. To suggest this morning routine always went smoothly would be disingenuous. Surely, when the house windows opened in the spring, some of the shouting matches, usually about borrowing clothes, often prompted neighbors to nearly dial 9-1-1. While my role perhaps should have been to play judge and jury, I usually opted for pretending that I (somehow) didn't hear it. The local news was always on TV in the background where we caught the weather and whatever else may have been happening. For the most part, it served as pleasant ambient sound, but we'd catch snippets of some actual helpful news.

The only notable thing about that Thursday morning was the TV weather forecast mentioning a "chance of snow" later in the day as that in itself was definitely unusual for mid-October. Despite Buffalo's snowy reputation, this was many weeks before we usually saw any of the white stuff - at least any that would stick on the ground. It's not unheard of for the upper elevations of the Southern Tier, like the great ski village of Ellicottville, to receive some that early, but not in the suburbs like West Seneca or the City of Buffalo proper. For us, we've had some Halloween nights with costumes covered by heavy winter jackets or worn a little tighter because of the sweatshirts stuffed underneath them, but even that is rare; typically there's a fifty-fifty chance that the ground will be white on Thanksgiving as well as a fifty-fifty chance of finding someone who wants it to be.

When thinking about the month of October in Western New York, to famously quote Buffalo Bills Hall of Fame Coach Marv Levy, "Where would you rather be than right here, right now?" The foliage is spectacular, like God's coloring book. The air feels and smells crisp. Everything good that one could associate with autumn, Buffalo has an abundance of it. When my Southern friends, who are almost all originally from the north, come up for "The October

Weekend" or other visits, the moment they step out of the Buffalo airport, they take a moment to, as Pink Floyd's David Gilmour lyrically wrote, *"Breathe. Breathe in the air."*

On that Thursday morning of October 12, the local TV and radio weather forecasters did boldly predict that temperatures would be colder than usual. Anna had a school modified soccer game that afternoon, so I told her to pack a long-sleeved shirt to wear under her jersey. I always *loved* watching Anna's games (and Claire's in later years). Most would agree that watching your own kid play a sport evokes a more personal level of interest as compared to watching your favorite professional sports teams which only makes sense when you've invested in your child's hopes, dreams, and passions - in addition to the fees, fundraisers, drives to practices, and countless other expenses and time that go into it. It can be difficult for parents to truly know whether their kids *really* love to play themselves at such an early age. Some kids, perhaps even most, play "just to play," and it's we, the parents, who impose *our* dreams and ambitions onto them. Just as team sports offer most valuable life lessons about winning and losing, so too do activities like music and the arts. I've found myself overwhelmingly moved by some West Seneca school plays or concerts that our daughters weren't even participating in. Amy and I felt strongly that testing the waters of these activities held only an upside, however, when any became a disproportionate demand on their time at the expense of grades or even their sanity, we tried our best to support the restructuring of their schedules. For Anna and Claire, their participation in sports and music, along with the life lessons and lifelong friendships that accompanied these, ended up being a strong net positive to their quality of life.

Here's one quick story that certainly made me appear overzealous to my fellow parents. In 2012, I was away with the Bills for nine days as we suffered an *ugly* loss to the 49ers in San Francisco and then stayed, for logistical reasons, in Arizona for the week before playing the Cardinals on the following Sunday, which turned out to be a much-needed win in overtime. Upon our landing back in Buffalo on Monday morning, I quickly checked into my office before heading straight to Claire's JV soccer game. When I arrived at halftime, one parent told me that we were up 1-0. Claire saw me arrive and flashed her grin full of metal braces with a rapid wave. With neither team scoring in the second half, her West Seneca team held on to the 1-0 win. Post-game, when Claire saw me walking across the field she bolted from her sideline and leaped into my arms as I swung her around. She then opted out of the bus to drive home with me. Once in the car, Claire asked, "Dad, did you see my goal?"

I responded, "Wait, *you* scored the goal?"

"Sure did!" she said.

"So," I said, "That means when you sprinted halfway across the field to jump in my arms and I swung you around, all the parents who didn't know I'd been away for nine days must have thought, *Wow, that goal really meant a **lot** to that family!*" We laughed so hard, and little did the parents know that she'd be more excited about us stopping at Arby's on the way home than her scoring the only goal of the game.

So, that Thursday morning, as with any other morning, Anna caught her bus at the end of our street, Hi View Terrace, at about 7:50 am. My cousin, Bob Van Wicklin, who served as a Legislative Director in Congress for fourteen years always told us that Hi View would get that elusive "gh" to become "High view" someday when we paid enough in taxes. Claire attended the same elementary school where Amy taught, so they left together at 8:15 a.m. I left at the same time for my front office job at the Bills, at One Bills Drive in Orchard Park; my commute was a mere six miles from home or, depending on how you caught the world's longest traffic light at the five-corner intersection of Southwestern Boulevard, Union, and Lake, a twelve-to-seventeen minute drive away. I took that light "orange" more times than I'm comfortable admitting in print. And to those of you from Buffalo familiar with that light, don't even try to tell me you haven't either.

The scattered "water cooler talk" at One Bills Drive was about the possibility of flurries or even *some* snow sticking on the ground that night. Other than that, it was business as usual and little attention was paid to anything outside the building. Regular football season was well underway with plenty to do, as one can imagine!

Shortly after returning to my office from lunch in the team cafeteria, an excellent perk offered to the staff during the season, some oddly colored clouds began emerging to the north and west over Lake Erie. There was ample foot traffic in my office as players picked up their weekly paychecks just inside my door, an interaction since lost to the automation of direct deposit. Their pay was very complex with many NFL-specific deductions, dues, charitable contributions, garnishments, and taxes from every state they played in, except for Florida or Texas. Picking up their paychecks upstairs also provided the players, especially rookies, an opportunity to ask me questions privately, behind closed doors. My office, because it faced west, would often get very warm in the afternoon with the mid-late afternoon sun pounding in. In fact, the window frame on the inside would get *so hot* that I (too often) wondered if an egg could fry on it. (For the record, I never *actually* tried it; imagine walking in on such a stunt! Or worse, how would the "reason for dismissal" be phrased on my termination letter?)

The opposite was true of the east side of the building that received the morning sun, which **Joe Frandina**, VP of Stadium Operations, who shared an office with his long-time friend, and (pre-Bills) work partner, **Perry Dix** would often remind me. One hot summer morning, with Perry's large frame already in the office and the sunlight beating in, Joe remarked, "I walked in and smelled ham."

Joe and Perry's engineering company designed the Bills Fieldhouse/Indoor practice facility in the mid-90's which became the envy of the league. Long-time VP Bill Munson, one of Team

Owner Ralph Wilson's most trusted advisors, was so impressed that he convinced Mr. Wilson to hire Joe and Perry full-time with the Bills.

Anyway, on that Thursday afternoon, clouds developed that were *so blue* they didn't even make sense; like a crayon called, "The Deep Blue Sea." If you saw clouds of this color in a painting, you would think the artist overdid it; they were simply not believable.

These clouds were northwest – directly over the City of Buffalo. It was still sunny and crisp in Orchard Park, but one could see a distinct line that resembled a "wall of weather" - a phrase all too familiar to Buffalonians who have experienced traveling through weather elements polar opposite to conditions often just a few miles or even yards away. This weather phenomenon comes courtesy of Lake Erie - the "last" Great Lake that hugs Western New York's shore line as water moves from the west towards the St. Lawrence Causeway and then the Atlantic Ocean. It also serves as the catch-point of the Erie Canal, the 2nd longest canal in the world, that originates at the Hudson River near Albany, built to transport goods from New York City to the Great Lakes region. Buffalonians have been thrilled in recent years to see long-awaited commercial redevelopment of restaurants and bars on the Lake Erie coast line that transitioned from the original grain mills and docks that covered the area for the first half of the 20th Century, and sat abandoned like ruins of a forgotten past for the latter half. Not only has it provided an economic boon, but as John Fogarty wrote years ago but has grown to be more and more true, *"If I had my way, I'd shuffle off to Buffalo to sit by the lake and watch the world go by."*

Within minutes of my noticing the crazy-colored clouds, two things happened that verified what I was seeing:

First, a car pulled into our parking lot with several inches of snow on its roof. Clearly, this car must have come from the land of the ice and snow, just north, where those most ominous clouds loomed, but this was still a truly odd sight for October;

Secondly, I just happened to be on the phone with Roger Edel, our team's New York State Workers Compensation attorney, whose office was in downtown Buffalo. Before the conversation even started, he said, "Don, you would NOT believe the weather here in the city. It's like a *blizzard*." Now, when a Western New Yorker uses the term *blizzard*, it is not taken lightly. Someone from the South who might see just a couple of inches per year is more likely to toss out the word much more liberally, but in Buffalo we reserve *blizzard* for something truly extraordinary, an event that occurs maybe every few years when snow accumulates several inches per hour for several hours or even days. What exactly was this thing happening so early, two full months, before winter? Strange things afoot, indeed.

Soon, a buzz began around the office about the snow. Others had started to hear from colleagues or relatives who were in the city or the northern suburbs and the news was all the same – the city was getting belted and we, in the towns south of Buffalo, or the "Southtowns" as Western New Yorkers call them, were likely to be next. My thoughts turned to Anna's soccer game down in Hamburg, which was firmly in the Southtowns and right along Lake Erie, in hopes that it would not be cancelled. At this point, it seemed possible that they would still play as long as those clouds stayed north.

At about 3:00 pm, **Pete LaForce**, our next-door neighbor and good friend, received a phone call from Buffalo State College where he served on their Security Staff:

"Pete, we need you here right away. It's an all-hands-on-deck situation. We need to round up the students and help them back to their dorms."

"What for? What's going on?" Pete asked, worriedly.

"This storm. The roads. There are tree limbs and live electrical wires down all over the place. Don't you see it?"

Pete was stunned. "It's bright, sunny skies here in West Seneca. Wow. But OK. I'll be there as soon as I can."

With my most important work of the day finished, and reachable by phone, I left the office for the soccer game to at least catch the 2ⁿᵈ half. Upon my arrival, I found Amy and Claire sitting near the parents who we'd gotten to know the best. Our 7-year-old, Claire, usually wasn't a big fan of watching Anna's games. She normally could at least move around and possibly play with a younger sibling of one of Anna's teammates, but today she found refuge in only one place: on Amy's lap, wrapped up tightly in a blanket.

The "word on the street" amongst the parents was almost exclusively about the snow falling in Downtown Buffalo. As was the case in my office building, seemingly everyone was sharing accounts of relatives or friends experiencing the unexpected snowfall up in the city. As we watched the game, we continued to marvel at those incredibly nasty clouds to the north. The air was cold, but there was still no snow and it was still bright and sunny. The clouds didn't appear to be moving down upon us. At least not yet.

We didn't know it at the time, but as our cars exited the parking lot after the game, even though there were still four games left on the schedule, there would be no more soccer that season because of what was about to happen in a few hours.

It began flurrying on the drive home, but flurries were a far cry from the stories we'd been hearing from the Northtowns. After pulling into our driveway, I made a quick detour into the garage to grab some firewood; we were actually kind of excited to have an early, cozy night by the fireplace and as luck would have it I had just bought two cord of wood from a local guy our neighbor recommended. He delivered it just a week earlier, on an 80° day. In fact, we were dripping with sweat as we unloaded the wood neatly along the back wall of the garage where the air was thick and still.

Needless to say, it felt strange to now have weather, just a week later, when having an indoor fire actually made sense.

Before going in the house, I asked Anna to briefly stop and pose for a picture while still wearing her soccer uniform. She was always, and understandably, eager to rush inside and eat dinner after games. Somewhat annoyed, she sighed but ended up being a good sport, actually hamming it up with a happy face and arms up in the air as if to shout, "Look at me! I'm wearing shorts - in the snow – Woo Hoo – *now let's get our butts inside and eat dinner!*"

Co-author and contributor to this book, Billy Klun, was a fourteen year-old freshman at Canisius High School, less than two months into a new school and new routine having been in public school for his education up to that point. While his memory is far from perfect, he was able to share a bit of what he remembered from that day, too:

> *I wish I could recall the morning of October 12th as clearly as others do - but I think that's the wonderful proof that this was supposed to be just an ordinary day. Like an ordinary Thursday I got up at an early hour to go catch the public school bus that would take me to the public middle school where I would change to another bus to then proceed to my actual high school - a joyful perk of attending private school against your will. The Fall of 2006 was my first semester at Canisius High School and the first time I had not attended public school - a fact I was still struggling to grapple with, but realize in hindsight was one of the best decisions that ever happened to me. Ironically, some of my contentment with this came this day, along with the pounds of snow that I was about to be buried in - metaphorically speaking, of course.*

The night before the storm, October 11th, my Mom, Kate, had told me that two cord of wood was being delivered during the day and that I would need to bring it into the garage as we were planning on having a birthday party for my uncle on Friday the 13th - I would, presumably, have other chores at that time that would take priority. Being the brilliant and free-spirited teenager I was, I strongly and boldly said, "Yeah, ok - no problem." (I was bold, but not an idiot.) During the school day, I'm sure I complained about the need to stack wood like a pioneer at some point to my new friends, but as the day progressed we all saw the snow as it started to come down - Canisius High School is right downtown and was some of the first to see the snow as it rumbled in off Lake Erie.

The drive home that day, including bus changes, was longer than normal, but again, nothing terrible by Western New York standards - accidents were starting, but all the reports were saying the snow would die down and clear up by morning as it was supposed to get warm again. When I arrived home, the two cord of wood - that I had definitely forgotten at this point even existed - was now buried under, at most, two inches of snow, but certain parts of my memory also recall it as a bit of a dusting. (Perhaps that was just what I was telling myself and what I planned to tell my Mom when she came home that night!) Either way, my highly motivated teenage attitude decided that it could wait until the next day after school when it would be dried off from the sunny day that was forecasted, as I still did not believe there would be very much snow... Oops!

At about the same time, Bills punter, **Brian Moorman,** recalls:

> *I remember my wife and I were at Blockbuster on Thursday evening when the storm began to roll in. We really had no idea what was about to come, and because it was so early in October, we figured all we were going to get were the little snow pellets that were coming down in sheets as we ran out to our car. They reminded us of the Dip'n'Dots ice cream you can get in the mall- and they covered the ground pretty quickly. By the time we got home, however, they had already changed to snow. We spent most of the evening wondering if it was going to stop until our power went out and created more concerns than how much snow we were going to get. Being from Kansas and getting the storms we get there, we are both used to going without power, but with the amount of moisture we had, we were getting worried about our sump pump. Luckily, and I have no idea why we were so lucky, our old sump pump had gone out a few days before and we had just had it replaced. Where the luck comes in, is our plumber had talked us into putting in a backup battery "just in case." A few days later it became more of "Thank goodness"!!*

Mike Schopp, along with Chris Parker, aka "The Bulldog", was hosting their regularly-scheduled, popular Sports Talk program on WGR 550 AM that afternoon:

> *My leading memories from that storm start with the starkness of the weather difference between the Northtowns (heavy snow) and Southtowns (little to*

*nothing). I remember a caller from maybe Orchard Park responding to someone reporting some of the devastation with how he was out in his yard – **grilling**! Meanwhile, someone from the City [Downtown Buffalo] around that time called in to say they had just seen a woman electrocuted [presumably from a downed power line].*

Wait. What?

The split screen visual here from places only ten miles apart was mind-blowing, even for locals. It's certainly worth noting that folks were calling into Buffalo's premier Sports Radio Station to talk about *the weather* on a Thursday during Bills and Sabres season rather than about their upcoming games.

What Mike had been hearing from callers all afternoon shortly became personal on his drive home. As Mike finally pulled into his driveway, after a treacherous, scary, and unusually long drive, he saw his wife, Carolyn, and neighbors outside helping to remove a fallen tree from the road.

As evening came at the One Bills Drive Offices, Vice President of Player Personnel **John Guy**, was in mid-season "grind" mode which routinely kept him in his office late. He remembers long-time Coach Chuck Lester popping into his office strongly advising him to leave as Chuck had been with the team since the 80's and was very familiar with Buffalo weather. Chuck's word of caution was driven from a strong sense that something very odd was happening, but while he noted Chuck's warning, John marched to the beat of his own drum.

John was hired in 2001 by Team President and General Manager, Tom Donohoe, after having served as a high-level scout with the Raiders and Steelers. He was a distinguished gentleman like Denzel

Washington with the humor and laugh of Eddie Murphy and his tastes in clothes and food were first class. Once at a Christmas party Amy and I hosted at our home, he showed Anna, then 11, and Claire, then 6, a magic trick that required a champagne bottle, a silk tie, and a match - made possible because he brought the items, not because I had them laying around. They *loved it*.

John also had excellent connections around the league. For instance, when the great Chiefs linebacker Derrick Thomas passed away prematurely, he became the Godfather of Derrick's son. An avid reader, John constantly yearned to learn more about every topic. On the morning of September 11th, 2001, I found myself in his office within minutes of the second plane crashing into the towers. While commentators were still reluctant to speculate on the cause, John muttered one word, "Jihad." This, as we know, turned out to be true.

After Chuck came by to warn twice more, John finally obliged and left the building… Trouble was, he could no longer find his car.

He retreated back inside, deciding to spend the night in the office - something that would become a common theme amongst many Western New Yorkers that night and much like the rest of WNY, his adventure had just begun.

Perhaps in retrospect it was actually fortunate that John couldn't find his car as long-time Bills Public Relations Director **Denny Lynch** was able to describe what John's commute north from One Bills Drive might have looked like: En route home to Williamsville, Denny found himself stranded on the NYS Thruway for several hours. Finally, just past the Exit 53 ramp (towards Downtown Buffalo), he saw a car back up on the right shoulder just enough to swerve onto the ramp. With other cars following suit, Denny did a U-turn from the far left lane to drive the wrong way over three lanes of traffic to try the backtrack to that exit. Once on I-190 North, he pulled up to the toll booth and fumbled to find the required fifty cents as the attendant became increasingly annoyed. After finally scraping the coins together, he politely asked the attendant, "Why are you even working tonight?" which prompted a shoulder shrug. Denny completed his normal twenty minute commute in just over *four hours* with his primary reflection being (other than backtracking on the thruway), "Thank Goodness I'd gone to the bathroom *just* before leaving One Bills Drive!" .

Tim Wenger, Operations Manager for News Radio 930 WBEN, happened to be in downtown Buffalo during this time attending a meeting inside the FBI Buffalo Headquarters, sitting in the conference room as the Storm began to make its presence felt to all attendees in that room. As Tim listened to the presentations at the Citizens Academy, he could hear the crackling of ice on power lines outside and the constant patter on the giant windows as the sleet blew sideways. Tim recalls Maureen Dempsey of the FBI looking to him and asking, "You think this is going to get bad?"

The FBI academy session was cut short and they all went into the streets to retrieve their cars to make their way home. Tim remembers, "By the time I left downtown and made it to the Village of Orchard Park, I recall noticing power was out in numerous spots and the road conditions had deteriorated to mid-winter condition."

As the manager responsible for programming at Western New York's most listened-to News Radio station, Tim was faced with the extraordinary challenge of how to best serve the region with the most helpful, emergency information possible. With massive power outages seeming likely, radio was about to become the "go to" form of media like never before.

While Tim was challenged to decide what people would *hear*, Police Commander **Mike Nigrelli** would soon be charged with deciding where and when people could *drive*. Mike recalls:

> *By October of 2006, I was already twenty-one years into my career with the New York State Police. I*

*was the Zone Commander for the Western Region
of the New York State Thruway Operations. At
that point in time, I firmly believed that I had seen
it all. Nothing could have prepared for the events
that began to brew on the 12th day of October and
continued well into Friday the 13th. My wife and
I went out for dinner on the evening of the 12th in
the Southtowns of Buffalo. It was raining when we
entered the restaurant. When we left the restaurant
about an hour and a half later, my windshield was
covered in ice and it was hailing. After digging out my
windshield scraper and cleaning off the windshield,
we drove home in icy road conditions. We talked
about how unusual it was to have this type of weather
in mid-October. When I got home, I thought that this
"freak weather" episode would quickly pass without
any significant problems. How wrong I was!*

At about 11:00 pm, Mike would receive the first of many calls
from supervisors under his command reporting on the highway
conditions and associated traffic problems.

~~Houston~~, *Buffalo*, we have a problem.

Billy's Mom, in the same conversation about the wood, had also
told him that after school - she was a Buffalo Public School teacher -
she was going to go grocery shopping for the party and to not expect
her home right after work as normal:

So I didn't.

 *Later that night, I was on the couch watching
TV and doing my homework - a combination I still
don't fully understand how I managed - when I*

heard the garage door open and some loud revving outside but didn't think much of it. Then more revving. And more revving. Finally, I got up to look out the front door to a new winter wonderland that I did not know was happening outside, including my Mom attempting to plow her Buick Rendezvous into our driveway that now had significantly more snow and a pile of wood in it. Thankfully, my Mom saw the cord of wood in the upper corner of our driveway but could only manage to get about halfway up our two-car length driveway. I ran out without a jacket to help with what I assumed would be groceries to only be told to go back inside via hand signals interpreted through the windshield of her car - she had not gone to the grocery store.

I would come to find out that the snow began getting worse just in time for buses to arrive at her school and as one could imagine, it did not go as planned leading to many delays which she decided to stay and help out with. One of the perks of being a teacher that many do not know is that in cases of emergencies where the safety and well being of a child is at risk, teachers may be asked to transport kids home in their own personal vehicles, something my Mom had done in the past and was dreading she may have to do again, however thankfully did not need to. As such, and hearing the same weather reports we all did, she came straight home - turning her normally twenty minute commute into 45 minutes, in addition to how long she stayed after school that day, all assuming she would have time to "quickly run over" to the grocery store after school and before the party on Friday. Once in, we began

*baking a chocolate cake and frosted half of it with
vanilla frosting - we only had enough for half the
cake, but figured she could just buy more the next
day and we would finish it then. We lit our gas
fireplace - a household favorite activity, and watched
as the snow continued to come down. At some point,
probably around 10:00 pm or so, I went up to bed
and - being the heavy sleeper I was - would not wake
up until the morning when my alarm would go off,
followed by Mom yelling from her room, "Go back
to sleep - there's no school and we're gonna have some
shoveling to do."*

Understatement of the century.

Back home, Anna and Claire were content to spend the evening on the rug in front of the fire with their homework. Little did we know that the fireplace was about to transform from ambiance to necessity. Other than the season's inaugural fire and "some snow" on the ground there didn't appear to be anything else unusual about it. The girls went to bed at about 10:00 pm, as usual. Then, just before 11:00 pm, the lights began to flicker. We hadn't paid much attention to the weather outside - we hadn't really felt a need to. A little snow and pretty cold, but no big deal, right? Maybe it had been all over the radio or TV for the past few hours and we were just unaware, but when we looked out the window into the dark, we were shocked by the sight of heavy snow that was pulling down and even snapping tree limbs that still had all their leaves. No sooner than we had looked outside, at exactly 11:00 pm, the electricity died with a loud, fading hum.

This time, it was for good. None of us at that point could predict what the next week would hold.

"Outside's the rain, the driving snow
I can hear the wild wind blowing
Turn out the light, bolt the door
I ain't going out there no more"
- "Cover Me", Bruce Springsteen (1984)

TWO
THUNDER SNOW AND BLUE LIGHTNING

Given that the power outage that Thursday night occurred at exactly 11:00 pm, we'll never know if the Television Meteorologists were *just about* to sound the alarms about the current and forthcoming wreckage during their regularly scheduled 11 O'Clock News broadcasts.

Or maybe we will, because meteorologists from the <u>all three</u> local TV Channels enthusiastically agreed to share their memories, mind-blowing weather facts, and mea culpas in an upcoming chapter.

Until then, buckle up. Or, as the iconic radio voice of the Bills Van Miller famously said, *Fasten your seatbelts, everybody!*

We reluctantly went to bed at about 11:30 pm, though the difference between "going to bed" and "going to sleep" was a canyon. At that point, it would have taken more than a little Nyquil to knock us out due to the chaos outside.

At about the same time, a Bills team doctor and his staff were stuck in their downtown Buffalo office building. As the snow had gotten a head start in the city that afternoon, the doctor and his staff did not realize the severity of the weather during their daily, busy course of serving patients. By the time they thought to flee, it was too late. Many downtown offices found themselves in the same predicament, it all just snuck up on them and by late afternoon, most simply could not leave as over <u>two feet</u> of the heaviest, wet snow blanketed the streets without plows having yet been called into action. They, like so many, sat helplessly in their cold, dark, powerless building until about 2:00 am when one doctor informed the staff he had an SUV that *should be able* to cut through even this heavy snow. At that point, they ventured out and while this seemed like a good idea, they would soon be saying to themselves, as *Anchorman's* Ron Burgundy did after descending into the bear pit (thus seeing how massive the grizzlies appeared from ground level) to save Veronica, "I <u>immediately</u> regret this decision."

Back home on Hi View, our futile attempts to sleep were negated by the deeply unsettling and unforgettable cracks and booms. Anna perfectly described them as gunshots with the one difference being while a gunshot is sudden, these bangs started with a cracking sound, then grew and grew to deafening decibel levels, even through our closed windows. Each boom echoed through the night for several seconds, sometimes bleeding into minutes, one followed by another and another. *Relentlessly.* A perpetual concert of thunder and lightning made it increasingly difficult to discern between cracking trees that threatened our house and the scary, but innocent booms of thunder. Every time we got close to sleep, hyper-sensory overload said "no."

Perhaps, most spectacularly, the lightning was blue. That's right, *blue*. Bills linebacker **Angelo Crowell**'s memory that night was the same, saying:

> *Oh man, trying to sleep was impossible. I practically gave up. Finally, I just called my Mom in North Carolina (which I realize probably scared the heck out of her for the phone to ring at that hour) to try to describe what was going on. I mean, it was snowing and thundering and the lightning was BLUE! I'd never seen anything like it!"*

But Angelo wasn't alone in seeing the blue lightning that night. Apparently there were two reasons for it: First, the highly abnormal combinations of conditions in the sky created an odd hue. Secondly, and the reason the power outage was so widespread, was because entire transformers were being struck by lightning, crashing to the ground, being crushed by limbs or trees, and ***exploding*** causing a greenish glow that still haunts Billy's mom, Kate, and is what she remembers most from that night.

Over at One Bills Drive, John Guy found himself alone, along with just the overnight security guard, in a vast, empty office building, reminiscent of *"The Shining."* Fortunately, given his propensity for long hours, the free-spirited John had a strong familiarity and comfort level with the building, for example:

One day, after a regular meeting with Trainers, I was cutting through the locker room en route back to my office when I ran into John. While on the phone with someone, he said to me, "Come with me for a minute." John put his arm on my shoulder and we started walking. To where? I had no idea.

To the person on the other end of the phone, John said, "I've got Don Purdy with me. You trust him, right?" There was a pause as he awaited an answer - "Good. Hang on then, cuz we're gonna do this."

As we continued to walk, John started taking off his dress shirt. I, in turn, tried to employ some social distancing, but John would have none of it. He pulled me back and said, "I really need you to do this."

"Do *what*?" I nervously asked.

"You'll see," he said, "This *has* to happen." as he then removed his dress pants down to his boxers.

"Whoa. Whoa, seriously now," I asked. "What are we doing here?"

To the person on the other end of the phone, John said, "Hang on. We're almost ready."

I turned my head on a swivel to survey the locker room wondering if others were watching because this had to be some sick prank. There were a few players and Equipment guys around, but nobody was looking at us. *What the heck?*

Finally, as we reached the far corner of the locker room, John let go of my shoulder and told the person on the phone, "Here we go" as he stepped up onto a scale.

John handed the phone to me. On the other end was Rob Hanrahan, our Pro Scouting Director, who said, "OK, Purdy. Shoot it to me straight. What does it say?"

Relieved, I relayed the digital number on the screen to which Rob replied, "Crap (or he might have employed some stronger "locker room talk"). OK, thanks. You can put John back on."

John grinned and thanked me for verifying his weight for the personal weight-loss bet they'd been waging; I had just experienced my own *My Cousin Vinny* "initial jail meeting scene" moment.

So, at about 2:00 am, John went down one floor to the Training Room to find *anything* that could pass for pillows and blankets. Towels were the closest thing he could find. After attempting to create a makeshift bed on his office floor, he concluded that it was a failure. The thin carpeting on the concrete floor was too hard. After tossing and turning for about an hour, he went back down to the Training Room to try sleeping on a training table that the players get taped and treated on daily by the trainers. Another fail. Once again, it looked more comfortable than it really was.

At about 2:30 am, Amy and I were actually afraid to look outside. Our instincts were too right - we should have been afraid. Very afraid. What we saw outside the window was simply unbelievable.

The girls heard us talking and walking, so they woke up too.

Or perhaps they had, understandably, not even fallen asleep in the first place. The last time the girls woke to such a startling noise at that time of night was my celebrating Aaron Boone's walk-off home run versus the Red Sox in Game Seven of the ALCS three years earlier. The whole family, all four of us, peered out of Claire's upstairs window at our front yard. The lightning was so frequent, almost continual, that it provided plenty of (blue) light to survey the scene. We could barely speak, and that was still the early stages. Tree limbs that just that afternoon had been horizontal, were now hanging vertically or even broken off onto the ground.

Helplessly, we returned to bed. But at about 3:00 am, Amy nudged my shoulder and said, "We have to do something."

I said, "Ame, let's at least try to get *some* sleep. There's nothing we can do right now. Tomorrow is going to be a very long day. We'll need as much energy as possible." She reluctantly agreed.

At 3:30 am, any attempt to sleep vanished as the mother of all crashes took place. The entire house shook. I seriously feared that the actual foundation of our house had been fractured. A 100-foot Oak tree in our front yard split, then crashed onto our roof. We wouldn't know until later the next day, but it went right *through* our roof into the attic.

In the early morning hours of October of 1983, my hometown of Speculator, NY, and the entire Adirondack region was rudely awakened by an earthquake measuring a 5.2 on the Richter Scale. Though there was no real damage, the sound and feel of this foreign phenomenon rocked our worlds for a few terrifying seconds. Upon arriving at Wells High School later that morning, we all initially believed that our furnaces had inexplicably exploded. On this night in 2006, our house shook even more violently than during that earthquake.

For some reason, my next instinct was to call my boss, Jim Overdorf; I knew I would only get his office voicemail as I paced back and forth in our family room. I obviously didn't want to call his cell or his home at 3:30 am, I just wanted to leave a message that he'd hear in the morning since my periodic glimpses of the street, courtesy of the blue lightning, signaled that driving anywhere in four short hours from then would be impossible. My message went something along the lines of:

> *Jim, it's Don. It's 3:30 in the morning and we're experiencing an apocalyptic scene. A huge tree just crashed on our house and I can see many more trees down across the road. Not sure how I can make it to the office tomorrow, but I'll be at the airport Saturday to go to Detroit [for our team's charter plane to play the Lions]. Hope you made out OK. This is unbelievable.*

I'm sure the actual voicemail came across WAY more disjointed and panicked than that, but guessing how long and challenging the day would be once the sun rose, I needed to bank on that message to Jim so as to not forget.

Work-wise, traveling to Detroit on Saturday for our game at the Lions was my greatest concern - every NFL road game requires a great deal of preparation. My responsibilities included drafting the Seating Chart in coordination with the Head Coach, preparing the per diem (meal money) for each traveler, and finalizing the flight manifest with our Travel Coordinator and independent "hired gun" Airline Coordinator, Bill Harpole. This required me to be the first team executive at our private Airport Hangar to, first and foremost, verify that every traveler was authorized to be on the team plane. This helped things flow more quickly than if the airline representative, not knowing every traveler, had to ask everyone to present their ID. If TSA made a random appearance, which they were certainly authorized to do, then we were still fully compliant with ID's even though I knew each traveler. On the return trip, ID was far more often required as it was not our, pun-intended, "home turf." Having this storm impede these responsibilities in any way was my greatest fear during these next few hours - aside from the tree on our house, of course.

At about the same time, our neighbor directly across the street, Jason Millard, was nowhere close to sleeping either so he went out to his front porch for a smoke and to reconcile what he was hearing with what he could see first-hand. At nearly the exact moment the match lit his cigarette, a bolt of lightning lit up the transformer across the street (yes, in *our* yard) which exploded into a multi-stream of blue sparks that would have made the Fourth of July envious. If this book was a movie, a close-up of his face as he watched, with the cigarette falling out of his mouth, would be a must. Earlier that evening, Jason had mocked friends from North Buffalo who'd tried to explain why they were unable to travel down to his house for a planned (and expensive) seafood dinner and to see his house for the first time as he'd just moved in the year before, all thwarted because of "some snow." He now completely understood what held them back and all was forgiven.

The sounds of the destruction, especially the ones that we could not yet fully see but for now could only hear, were playing out most dangerously on the roadways. And Police Commander, Mike Nigrelli, was forced to make some important life and death decisions:

> *I provided guidance and direction as I continued to assess the level of response needed for this emerging event. Around 3am, I realized through the feedback from my support staff, that the roadway had become impassable in large stretches from the Rochester area to the Pennsylvania border. I directed my staff to call in additional State Police personnel and request more Thruway Authority resources to battle the storm. It*

*was at about this time that we lost power at our house.
I decided to return to work to take direct command of
the emergency operations. The storm had other plans
though. My take home car was a Ford Crown Victoria.
And it was encased in thick ice. That was problem #1.
Problem #2 was that my driveway had almost two feet
of snow topped with a thick icy glaze. Problem #3 was
that I just sent my snowblower in for annual service the
previous week. To further compound my dilemma, my
street was impassable. The Highway Department, like
the rest of us, was not in full winter operations mode,
and the streets were covered in heavy snow and ice. In
short, I was going nowhere fast!*

Meanwhile, about thirteen miles north, up at Buffalo State College, our next-door neighbor, Pete LaForce, was dealing with major security challenges during this madness. Pete's first major hurdle was simply reaching campus earlier in the afternoon after being summoned by his colleagues to help. His normal route was blocked by downed trees, live power lines, not to mention nearly two feet of heavy, unplowed slush. His second, third, and fourth alternate routes all dealt him the same. Having finally arrived, Pete and his crew, over the course of several hours, were able to eventually usher all the students safely back to their dorms. But his work wasn't done. While surveying a Main Campus Center building, he noticed something - soon he would realize was actually some*one* - laying on a bathroom stall floor. Alarmed, Pete prodded the man who then awoke, very annoyed, basically telling him to "get lost."

"Sir, don't you have anywhere to go?" Pete asked.

The man responded angrily, "I tried a bunch of times to get home, but couldn't. Had to bail out of my car. I just want to sleep so leave me alone. Besides, I should be able to sleep wherever I want since I'm a major donor here. My name is even on a building, so beat it!"

Even more perplexed, Pete called the College President who instantly knew who the man was and came over to the building to diffuse the situation, then escorted the man to a guest house on campus to sleep for the rest of the night.

Back home, Amy and I knew that the only thing we could do was to *try* to get a couple hours of sleep in order to have as much energy as possible for the next day, even though we still had no clue of the enormity of the situation.

As I laid there, I was trying to play out the next day in my head: *Would it be possible to get the big things fixed before the Detroit trip? What about "The October Weekend" - the one weekend of the year when ten friends come from all over the country to my house - just eight days away?* All of these travel arrangements have been made. These thoughts consumed me even before we laid eyes on the actual severity of the damage in daylight.

Amy drifted in and out of sleep. I tried, but just couldn't. We both knew that something was bizarrely wrong out there – to the point of being historic. The booms, cracks, and blue lightning continued. As tree limbs snapped; the echos lingered.

THREE
"NO WAY THAT JUST HAPPENED"

In the 1995 movie *Tommy Boy* - surely you expected a *Friday the 13ᵗʰ* reference here, just keeping you sharp! - the two main characters, Tommy Boy and Richard played by Chris Farley and David Spade respectively, hit a deer at night while driving in unfamiliar territory in Iowa. Unsure of how to properly dispose of the carcass, they throw it into the back seat to figure out later. After resuming their drive, the deer that they thought was dead unexpectedly rises in the back seat. They screech to a stop, bust out of the car, sprint frantically to a safe spot, only to then watch the deer kick the windows out, tear through the car roof, and run away. With mouth and eyes wide open, Richard exclaims, "No way that just happened." Tommy, bizarrely, responds, "That. Was. *aaaaww*esome."

When the sun rose - though never had I been less sure that it would - on Friday, October 13ᵗʰ, 2006, the Buffalo area awoke, surveyed their landscape, and collectively thought, "No way that just happened." Perhaps from Mother Nature's perspective it was awesome, but our reaction was definitely the former.

At about 6:00 am, we made our way downstairs. It was time to lay eyes on reality and prepare ourselves for a cleanup unlike anything we'd ever faced. Visually, it was nearly impossible to digest the landscape. Tree limbs the size of cars dangled, seemingly hanging

by a thread, referred to by many as "widowmakers" until they were
brought down safely. Even longer limbs and entire trees laid across
the street in every possible direction like a giant game of Pick-up
Stix. Intermingled was an imploded spaghetti factory of downed
power lines and beneath that were the remnants of cars, lawns, and
whatever else was naively left outside assuming it would survive *a
little bit of snow.*

Anna and Claire awoke with full knowledge that there was
obviously no school – a realization that usually for kids that age is
a treat, but it was clear from their bewildered looks that they knew
there was something much different about this "snow day." Almost
simultaneously, they peered out their window and gasped what we
would all keep saying for the rest of the day: *Wow.*

On our way downstairs, we noticed the living room was darker
than usual. Before we even hit the last step, we found our normally
bright and sunny living room to be in the shade. One big shadow.
Our entire front window was blanketed by a forest of tree - not
trees, **tree.** It was like our living room became a fort in the woods.
Miraculously, the tree branches had fallen in such a way that they
ended up with a few small branches *against* the windows and,
fortunately for us, not *through* the windows. At first glance, it looked
like an animated tree monster from a fairy tale movie that was trying
to claw its way into the house. Had the tree fallen just a couple of
inches closer to the house, the branches would have crashed through
the glass – much like in the movie *National Lampoon's Christmas
Vacation* when Clark Griswald chops down the beautiful Spruce that
falls the wrong way and it crashes into the chic, modern living room
of his neighbor, portrayed by Julia-Louis Dreyfuss. We chalked that
near miss up as a *big* blessing.

Because we were unable to open the front door, we were forced
to use the back door to make our way toward the front yard. There,
on our roof, sat about one-third of an enormous oak tree which we
instantly knew was the one that so violently rocked our world at

3:30 am. *No wonder it shook the house,* I thought. At this time, I was unaware that much of this tree was not only *on* the house, but also *in* the house. Looking in the attic, which requires opening a small door to access, didn't even cross my mind at that time.

We shifted our attention toward the backyard and pool area: it looked like another horizontal jungle. Several trees had sliced through our fence in about a dozen different places like a hot knife through butter. Thankfully, none landed on the pool cover we'd just paid $1,500 for. (And yes, to my friends in Florida, we must cover our pools for half the year.)

Where to begin? **Should** *we begin? How dangerous was it?*

From what Billy remembers of the morning of Friday the 13th:

> *I started outside, after sleeping in of course as any teenager would do, only to find most of my neighbors within a three or four house radius on either side slowly wandering into the street, if they weren't already there, looking around in shock and awe. I can remember walking to the end of my driveway, wearing boots and long pajamas, and looking up at the sky, feeling warm, like it was warmer than it should be. I can then remember turning to my Mom and talking about the plans that we had made for tonight for Uncle Tim's birthday - plans that none of us knew if they would still happen now. If nothing else though, my Mom and I agreed that we needed some basics in the house because we had nothing. No milk. No eggs. No breakfast foods. No food really at all, and not that the pantry was always bare, but knowing that we would have to be doing "party shopping" anyways, it wasn't a big deal and we made it work up until that point.*

We went back into the house to make a list when I realized our kitchen was noticeably darker than usual - it was not uncommon on cold nights for my Mom to draw the retractable curtains in the kitchen down but when I looked up I wasn't looking at the curtain with a Forest Green design, but rather an entire Forest Green colored tree blocking the window! We had a large oak tree in the rear corner of our backyard that had come down in the night - interestingly, my Mom has always said, "I heard every tree that came down that night except for the one in our yard - by that point I must have been so exhausted from being up and worried that I fell asleep and slept through it. I didn't get much sleep, but that's when it must have happened." She told me that when she came down that morning, she noticed it was darker too, only to open the curtain (which she had in fact drawn because it was cold and snowing) and look out the window to then see a squirrel looking right back at her, both wondering what the other was doing so close to "their" house.

Meanwhile, when our Bills team doctor and his crew had ventured out of their downtown Buffalo offices at about 2:00 am, they soon realized that many others attempted the same escape idea. A commute home that normally took fifteen minutes took *six hours* as they encountered car after car either abandoned or disabled in their pathway. While we were assessing the severity of the Storm, they were assisting as many vehicles as possible by manually pushing them to the side of the road, to clear a path for plows and to allow the good doctor and his office mates to pass through. Certainly the thought of 'which of my colleagues is going to treat my hernia' passed through their heads.

Over at One Bills Drive, **Deb Driscoll**, a most trusted Personal Assistant to Head Coach, Dick Jauron, had just experienced a ride she'll never forget. Deb lived up in Grand Island, about twenty-five miles north of the stadium. Grand Island was grazed by the Storm and although she had heard about the weather event in the City and Southtowns, she was unaware of the true severity. By the time her commute on I-190 South reached the Buffalo State College area, she found herself as one of only three cars on the road. At one point, the two cars in front of her came to a complete stop without any rhyme or reason. After those two cars finally accelerated forward, she realized they'd driven over live electrical wires laying across the road which, as if that weren't dangerous enough, were **on fire!** Seeing the two cars successfully pass through, Deb said a quick prayer, gripped the steering wheel, stomped on the gas pedal, and did the same.

But her drive wasn't over…

Let's pause here to address what many, after reading Deb's account, might reasonably ask, *Why wouldn't she turn back at that point?* Having served twenty-seven years in the NFL myself, one mantra that is fully understood and reigns supreme is: "The ball WILL be kicked off at 1:00 pm on Sunday." The level of preparation needed to ensure this to be true every Sunday (or Thursday or Monday) is difficult to explain. This is true even during normal circumstances, much less an epic storm. During the 2020 Covid-19 pandemic, "essential" became a commonly-used, household word. In the context of an NFL team during the regular season, Deb was truly essential. Her office was just outside the Head Coach's *and* the General Manager's – Command Central for the entire Buffalo Bills organization. During the week preceding a road game, Deb coordinated operations, including drafting the trip itinerary, right up until Friday afternoon, when she passed the torch to staff like me, and others, who managed the trip itself, a challenge that would only become more difficult in the hours and days to come. It should be noted that away game preparation was just one small part of Deb's critical role and the same can be said for the Team President's Administrative Assistant, Toni Addeo, who actually worked with Deb at the Sabres before joining the Bills.

Having just driven Evil Knievel-like over flaming, live electrical wires, Deb's own recreation of *Mr. Toad's Wild Ride* took her to the Skyway on Route 5 in Downtown Buffalo. For those not familiar, the Skyway earned its name for the reason its name suggests: it's *way* up there, like a long, isolated bridge that is precariously perched on pillars that seem to push it at an unnatural angle up into the sky, just high enough to see the top of the hockey arena where the Buffalo Sabres play and over the ruins of Buffalo's Beloved "Aud", former home to both the Buffalo Sabres and Buffalo's short lived NBA team, the Braves. Because of its unique shape and height as well as placement directly on the waterfront, it's usually the first road to close in inclement weather, but because this storm was such a surprise, it hadn't yet been closed - our Police Commander friend Mike Nigrelli was dealing with these challenges in real time. Deb had resorted to prayer earlier to pass over the fire wires which she now dialed up once again for help making it up the ramp and over the elevated highway. As she describes it, she prayed, "God, if you help me over the Skyway, I won't ask you for anything. For a while. Or… I probably will, but *please* still help!"

He did. And Deb finally reached the base of One Bills Drive. But being amongst the earliest to arrive, she still needed to drive about two-hundred yards - the length of two football fields and the same length that Andy Dufresne needed to crawl through that sewer pipe in the *Shawshank Redemption*. (As an aside, quite honestly, there should be no need for a spoiler alert for *Shawshank*: if you've never seen it, put down this book immediately and watch it, but then come right back. We'll be here, waiting.) These two-hundred yards weren't an easy feat - it was going to be through two feet of heavy, wet snow to reach the building which had not yet been plowed or cleared. So, unable to make it to the building via her car, Deb abandoned it as far on site as she could and trudged her petite self through the snow and into the Security office where Marty McLoughlin awaited (though I'm sure she'd admit it was better than what Andy Dufresne crawled through). She hastily threw her keys to him and said, "Marty, my car is the one blocking the roadway in. Could you have Stadium Operations move it, please?" as she raced upstairs to her office.

One Bills Drive had no power; this included the kitchen that was charged with feeding the players a very specific, high-nutrient diet under the direction of the Strength Coaches. Inside the building, the odor was most pungent - to quote Ron Burgundy (Will Ferrell) from *Anchorman,* "It stings the nostrils" - but this was not "in a good way" as the kitchen's exhaust ventilator was down as they prepared the collard greens.

Retired police officer and team driver **Bob Schultz** recalls, "Driving through the snow felt like trudging through wet cement." Bob's stay in the building that day would be brief as what the players might eat paled in comparison to the players' safety on the roads. Being only October 13th, most of the rookie players had not yet been educated in or tested by winter driving let alone Buffalo winter driving and nothing compared to what WNY just experienced.

Bob's primary duties with the Bills were to drive injured players to and from surgery and treatment, picking up potential Free Agents at the airport, but worst of all, taking players that were cut by the team to the airport. *Awkward indeed.* Some "special" calls to action include, as Bob explained, "being instructed, with graphic profane suggestions, to locate a player who either was not at the airport at departure time or failure to arrive for the 8:00 am Players' meeting, or worse, not appearing for mandatory weigh-in on Thursday mornings." On this day Bob was presented with a new directive as

Head Coach Dick Jauron asked Team Security Director Chris Clark to send Bob on a mission to as many players' and coaches' homes as possible to bring them in. Bob recalled:

> *Well, away I went with a list of players and coaches to pick up in the frozen slushy mess. It took us about two hours to accomplish this task. Of course, as we found the private residences of coaches and players, nobody's driveways were passable. So it was the slide for life trying to power through the slush and pick up our "packages"without those high- priced bodies injuring themselves.*

In the office, a backup generator served to provide essential power to Deb's area in Command Central. Here, as per Head Coach Dick Jauron, a rapid-fire phone chain was about to spring into action to alert players that practice was postponed - an extremely rare occurrence.

Before he knew it, John Guy awoke to the few staffers, ones who lived in unaffected areas several miles from the Storm, who were all starting to arrive at the building shortly after Deb did. Fortunately, in addition to having access to locker room showers, complete with a full range of toiletries (for which I regularly paid the invoice, so trust me: they had *everything*), John was also spotted a fresh set of clothes by an equipment staffer. Aside from not having slept, he was ready for another day of work, and *another* night at the office, as his home was still not accessible according to a phone call placed to a neighbor.

John was no stranger to office misfortune, though it would stand to reason that spending so many hours there increases chances of such bad luck. One day he came to my office and said, "Hey Purdy, I was told to see you about an auto claim."

"Yeah sure, what happened?" I responded quizzically. Typically, the only auto claims I processed were when one of our traveling scouts, driving for work purposes, hit a deer while navigating their designated part of the country, so naturally I was curious to find out what happened to John as he was based here in Buffalo.

"A Port-A-Potty got me." he said.

"WHAT?!" I asked.

"Yup. Smashed right into my car."

Sitting up in my chair, I braced myself for the details behind this bizarre claim. Apparently, it happened on a Monday morning after a home game, before the portable bathrooms in the parking lot had been picked up by the independent contractor. The wind was so strong that it picked one up, sent it topsy turvy across the parking lot and landed onto John's car. When I called the claim into our insurance carrier, Berkley Specialties based in Dallas, Texas, they admitted they'd never heard that one before, but it was certainly a work-related claim that would be covered.

On that Friday morning, as the employees who were able to make it started arriving, John turned the page. Being the consummate pro, he shared his overnight experience with his closest colleagues, then worked as hard as he always did for the duration of the day.

As it turned out Billy's next-door neighbors, the Costanzas, also needed a few things so their daughter Anne Marie decided to take a walk to our local Wilson Farms - a local mini mart that was very popular for many years. He also remembered:

> *Thankfully Mrs. Brown, who lives across the street from my Mom to this day, had the phone number for the family who owned that particular branch of Wilson Farms and was able to call down and find out that they were in fact opening up within the next ten minutes due to demand.*

Anne-Marie was a few years older than me so we didn't know each other well, other than the basics and the frequent "Hi, how are you?" as we were hopping into cars or going wherever we were going. Little did I know that someone who I barely knew would become a critical part of a story that I often tell people when I reflect on the October Storm. Anyway, we began down our street, which on a normal day wouldn't have been a big deal: both sides of the street had sidewalks and it was a beautiful suburban street, lined with large oak trees, two in almost every front yard... at least until October 12th, 2006.

I must add a caveat in here – as much as my Mom and I both knew that I needed to go to the store, she was not a big fan of me going. She could see the power lines were down everywhere, however she trusted me to use my best judgment and genuinely thought Anne Marie would be there to help me should I need it. (That would be where my Mom was wrong for the first time in her life, as she would tell you.) We started walking down the street and within a few houses realized walking on where the sidewalks were (albeit under some deep, frozen, slushy snow was not going to be an option the whole way as trees were scattered all over the place. The further and further down the street we got, the more and more chaos we still saw. In fact about halfway down there were two large trees that had fallen into each other into the middle of the road, and one of my poor neighbors thankfully saw the trees before colliding with them in the snowstorm the night before, leaving their car behind to go retrieve once the trees had been cleared. We kept walking to Wilson Farms which, when we had to make a choice: right to go down the steep, possibly icy hill of Mill Road which was more familiar and shorter, but no sidewalks and no idea what state the bridge over Cazenovia Creek was in; or, to the left down another suburban street towards a main road (Union Road) only to then maybe have to walk down that as, again, the conditions were unknown. We decided for the former, and began the (small) walk up, to then go down the hill of Mill Road towards a blind quick turn and then over a bridge.

Now, under normal conditions, the bridge is over a very slow, trickling part of Caz Creek, but that particular day, however, what was running underneath that bridge was more of a surge as the inches and inches of wet snow started to melt and rush the larger frozen blocks towards the bridge. It was not unheard of for large chunks to come crashing into (and over) this bridge when the storm surges get bad during a melt or heavy rain in the wintertime - this often would lead to an icy covering - which, incidentally my Mom would manage use to do an impromptu 540° spin in the center of the bridge in our Dodge Caravan many years earlier. This flooding would become a big issue for many people as the storm progressed, including Don and the many people who lived on his street that abutted this creek. The walk to Wilson Farms was normally no more than fifteen or twenty minutes as it was exactly a mile. Round-trip, if you weren't back in 45 minutes, your Mom knew you stopped somewhere else and were up to something. (Or maybe that was just my experience...) That particular day, because of the snow, the trees, the power lines, and not being able to cut through the yards as I often would, it took us closer to thirty-five minutes just to get there. While

*I am not a fast man, that's the slowest minute-mile
I've ever done.*

Back at home in West Seneca, any attempt to leave was futile. Our cars were buried in snow and the street was 100% impassable. Anything short of a helicopter was useless.

It was unspoken and understood that we needed to start the cleanup. Almost robotically or zombie-like, people began emerging from their homes to survey the landscape, each with the same bewildered look. They, much like us, were wearing any mismatched clothes they could throw together as nobody had even thought of busting out their winter clothes yet. Plus, as the morning went on, it began to get warmer almost as if it hadn't just snowed the night before. None of us had ever seen anything remotely like this, nor had the region in exactly 100 years, and we were reasonably certain that we never would again in our lifetimes. I kept thinking to myself about hurricanes and the similarities in devastation: *How do people get through them?*

The view of our street once we emerged was even worse than it had appeared from our living room window: the piles of downed power lines blended with broken trees with even more power lines still dangling over the road with loose, live ends sparking and hanging just about eye level. A feeling of devastation began to settle in.

I quickly called my parents who lived up in the Adirondacks (I didn't wake them up at 2:00 am, Angelo). It was a struggle to describe the scene. My words, hopefully unlike this written telling, were doing it no justice so I snapped a couple of quick pictures of the front of our house and sent them while we were talking. While Angelo Crowell felt a need to tell his Mom what was happening, I needed my parents to **see** it. Taking and sending pictures in 2006 was not as natural as it is today, but upon receiving the picture, my Mom's whole tone changed. It's not that she didn't believe me, but there is always something about *seeing* an image that really drives home a point.

Moments later, my long-time friend Chris Edwards (another "Weekender") called from Ellicottville, about 45 minutes south of Buffalo. He asked, "What the heck is going on up there? I turn on the TV and see all this devastation. I assumed they were talking about Colorado or something. Is this really happening in Buffalo?" This simply amazed me. How could Ellicottville, which is a prominent ski area of Western New York where it's most likely to snow, not only escape the Storm but have conditions so tranquil that they couldn't even believe it was Buffalo that they were watching on TV?! How isolated was this?

After surveying the front yard and the street, I came back inside to a great surprise: Amy had whipped up some eggs. For starters, it was great to be reminded that we had a gas stove so no matter how long the electricity was to be out, which clearly it would be for a *very* long time, that we had the capacity to cook with a stove. Good protein, long-term energy for what was clearly going to be a physically challenging day. It would prove huge because I don't recall ever eating again the whole day.

On our street, impromptu "cleanup parties" were well underway, which we would find out later was happening all over WNY, as neighbors came together to help each other clear the wreckage from the Storm. The common goal for everyone became making clear paths for emergencies. No bullhorn announcement or phone tree was necessary for folks to understand this need; it was obvious to all that the most pressing problem was the lack of electricity and no power truck, or any other vehicle for that matter including fire trucks, ambulances, police, or otherwise, could come or go until we cleared our street. With so many power lines down, it was understood that each and every one would have to be fully restored before *anyone* got theirs back. When everyone started coming out, we began to tell stories, but then we all quickly realized: *We'll have plenty of time to chat about our storm experiences later. Let's go.* And that's exactly what happened, including the telling of "storm stories" over the coming weeks, months, and even years.

Two large groups of neighbors formed, one at each end of the street, and simply began dragging trees from the street onto the nearest lawn - anyone's lawn, it didn't matter. Anyone with a chainsaw started cutting what couldn't be moved because it was too big. Up until that point, I had no idea how many of our neighbors owned chainsaws. Our street had morphed into an Oregon Logging and Forestry outfit, except we didn't look like cool lumberjacks - rather more like poorly dressed zombies on a mission. In fact, given our shock, some of us could have passed for White Walkers (of Game of Thrones notoriety), but not my beautiful wife, of course.

The problem was that these were not just the limbs of trees, they were in many cases *entire trees*. They also were deeply embedded knee deep under the heaviest snow I've ever felt. Growing up in the Adirondacks, I know my snow. Every type of snow imaginable from ultra-fine to corn snow to heavy flakes. This snow was probably the closest to pure water as I'd ever seen: with your eyes closed, you probably couldn't feel the difference carrying a 5-gallon bucket of this snow and one of pure water. While my *feel* and *weight* tests were subjective, most people who had to shovel it and move it would more than likely agree with me.

(In the midst of all this, my boss, Jim Overdorf, called to let me know he got my message and hoped that I was ok - his concern was and still is much appreciated.)

Anna and Claire were confused about why they couldn't help. Looking back, I wish I had taken a few more minutes to explain how dangerous the situation was. I have always loved the fact that they wanted to help. They were seeing our neighbor kids, Andy and Megan LaForce, who were high school and college age helping to drag the trees off the street. Giant limbs and dangling power lines, some that were sliced in half where you could actually see the thick metal wiring sticking out of the ends, were still lurking above our heads and wildly strewn about on the ground. There was no way we could chance them being out there. Billy, being just two years older "and a year wiser", was one of those high school aged kids that Anna and Claire were jealous of, but his Mom, Kate, didn't mind having him help. In fact she insisted - though she set limits on the "fun" things he was allowed to do, including trekking over those downed lines and through the broken branches to get them some of the essentials they would need.

While on their adventure to Wilson Farms, Billy can actually remember he and Anne Marie gleefully cheering, though it didn't last long as they saw the groups of people beginning to pile into the small convenience store:

> *Once we were in, we realized our problems weren't over. We were clearly not the first people who thought to run to Wilson Farms and we **definitely** did not get there early enough. Thankfully I was able to grab the essentials that we wanted: a gallon of milk, a loaf of bread, two 2-liters of Diet Pepsi (an absolute essential in my house at the time), and I grabbed myself an extra treat: a box of small donuts. The last box. After cashing out, as I was loading my goods into a small leather Disney backpack with a Mickey Mouse emblem stitched onto it that I had used for Kindergarten (as it was the only backpack I had available since my school bag was a side bag that would have been too heavy when full), a mother in her mid-30s walked up to the counter and asked the cashier if they had any donuts left, "Are you sure? That's all my kids will eat on snow*

days and I can't seem to find them anywhere." Cue the guilt trip.

As I kept trying to shove these donuts into the bottom of my bag so that no one would see me I heard someone else walk up to the counter,

"Do you have any donuts?"

"No, sorry, we're all out - the delivery was supposed to come today, but clearly that's not gonna happen."

I look to my right and I see a construction worker: clearly poorly caffeinated due to the several large coffees in his hand, not to mention the weary look on his face that suggested he had already been up all night working. Not only was I taking these donuts away from some kids, now I was stopping the actual people who were just trying to dig us out from their own donuts. Now, it's at this point that I'd love to tell you that at 14-years-old I was bright enough to turn to the guy, hand him the box, and thank him for all his hard work - it is also at this point I will admit that I was not. All my companion for this journey had grabbed was a bottle of Evian and a loaf of bread - which amazed me at the time as she seemed to wander every aisle and not find anything, but now I can confirm this is a common sight if I'm the one sent grocery shopping for my household -amazing what a few years of hindsight can change!

As we began our trek back, still with snow covered sidewalks and dodging traffic as we cut into the streets where we couldn't pass, the trip was now uphill as; you might remember I said we went down the hill to Wilson Farms. I had carried all of it until the point where we hit the bridge and the blind curve - I had walked this path a lot, but never in these conditions or with what I was bringing back. Needless to say, we made it back up the hill, through the snow into our houses safely, though perhaps a little more frustrated and tired than I had been at the beginning. By the time I returned, my Mom and some neighbors had surveyed our backyard and found that the tree that had fallen, thankfully, was not quite tall enough to have landed on our house, but the upper branches were just long enough to brush along and rest on part of it. The neighbors with saws were triaging and, after trimming those branches to make sure they didn't do any damage, we got bumped to near the bottom of a list that was being kept only in a collective "hive mind" as we were not going to be a priority - something we agreed with as well at that point.

Police Commander Mike Nigrelli, was still in the midst of administering painstaking decisions. Mike recalls:

Around 5:00 am, I made my first request to on duty staff to send a patrol car to come pick me up. I continued to manage the emergency remotely from my residence staying in close contact with State Police Headquarters in Albany as well as the Buffalo Division of the Thruway Authority. I received several calls from my staff with updated information. It turned out that picking me up was not going to be easy. The first patrol car got stuck on the I-90 heading in my direction. The second patrol car got stuck helping the first patrol car (you can't make this stuff up). Finally, at around 8:00 am, I was told by the officer assigned to desk duty that a car would be headed my way. I explained that my street was impassable and I would start walking from my cul-de-sac street to the main road. As I walked from my house in the cul-de-sac up the street, it was surreal how much snow had fallen in the overnight hours of October. When I got to the main road, I saw all of the power lines that were down laying on the ground. I continued my trek down the main road. Eventually, the patrol car picked me [up] after I had walked almost a mile in deep snow.

When I got to the State Police Headquarters on the Thruway, we were in full emergency operation mode. A stretch of roadway over one-hundred miles on the New York State Thruway was closed. Every available Trooper and piece of equipment was in use. There were stretches of highway with stranded motorists. We were deploying snowmobiles from law enforcement and volunteer groups to render assistance. The Thruway Authority was working feverishly to clear the roads and ramps to allow the safe passage of traffic. We escorted many convoys of utility trucks that were dispatched to Western New York to help restore power to the thousands of homes who had lost service. The media was calling constantly, searching for any new information. I was doing live radio and television interviews to provide much needed information to the general public.

By late in the day on the 13th of October, the roadways had been cleared of stranded motorists. The Thruway Authority was coordinating the removal of scores of disabled vehicles. Thankfully, there were no fatalities or serious injuries sustained on the Thruway as a result of this catastrophic weather event. It was really a total team effort from State Police members,

Thruway Authority, Volunteer Fire Departments, Tow Truck companies, and the list goes on.

Back at Hi View Terrace, our collective efforts hardly felt like we were putting a dent in our cleanup mission, but we were about to catch a huge, unexpected break. As dozens of us were feverishly struggling to manually pull trees off the road, we heard a loud rumble behind us, different from the sound of generators which had been humming incessantly since the power went out the night before. As we turned to look toward the dead end of our street, we saw one of our neighbors, Russ Jandreau, sitting atop a tractor slowly trudging our way. Now, this was no garden variety tractor: this was an excavator, like the ones used on construction sites with a mechanical "arm" that could scoop up trees and drop them to the side. The only way he could have appeared more heroic to the weary eyes of our neighborhood was if he had been wearing a cape.

What a break! Who lives on a suburban street and has such a tractor? Russ did, that's who. He worked for National Fuel, the primary gas company in WNY who thought it best that he keep this type of machinery at home and we couldn't have been more lucky and grateful. What we all could have imagined being several days of isolation turned out to be just hours. This move also benefited Russ's employer as he enabled *himself* to drive off our street and to his National Fuel headquarters, thus now personally able to serve the larger community and provide those essential services during what was still the peak of the emergency calls coming in.

It's impossible to quantify, but the number of limbs that Russ and his tractor moved off the street was easily five times more and faster than what the dozens of us could have removed during the same time, not to mention how much safer. We, as a street, took a cash collection for Russ - the only way at the time we could think of to express our gratitude; he helped us regain access to our street.

In fact, within the hour of Russ removing enough trees and limbs to make the street passable, a car came flying down and peeled into a driveway, right next door, where the elderly mother of the driver lived. She received medication that, without Russ and his tractor, she would have had to wait much longer to receive.

The cleared (enough) street also provided a pathway for our neighbor, Pete LaForce, to return home after spending the night herding Buffalo State Students back to their dorms and dealing tactfully with a frustrated donor who attempted to sleep in a bathroom stall. There's a funny phrase I've heard used that describes someone who shows up *after* the work is done - *a blister*. Pete was the opposite of a blister, always the first to help someone out, and in this case, despite having not slept a wink, he would have been the first to start hauling trees if he had been home that morning.

Russ was the hero of Hi View Terrace, but we were just one street, in one town, in one county, all within a region populated with about one million people who were all impacted in one way or another by this storm. Many others like the great people on our street continued to work tirelessly to lift Buffalo out of this dangerous mess and work towards whatever level of normalcy was possible. Many like Russ, not only that day but in the days to come, are one of the biggest reasons Buffalo rebounded so quickly after this storm.

As of noontime on Friday the 13th, however, many
more like Russ would still be needed.

FOUR
YES, THAT JUST HAPPENED

As much as he tried to convince himself that it would pass, WBEN 930 AM Radio Broadcast Program Manager Tim Wenger knew the situation was bad when he left the downtown FBI meeting early on Thursday evening. "It's October after all," he kept telling himself. Tim also felt an awesome responsibility to utilize WBEN's radio platform and tremendous local reach to keep the Buffalo community informed at the expense of the lost advertising revenue built into the regular programming business model but, thankfully for Buffalonians, he did just that. Tim noted:

> *Power was out to tens of thousands by morning and the number continued to grow. Roads were impassable due to downed power lines. Schools and businesses were closed and panicked residents were flooding open stores to get necessary supplies. I quickly made the determination that WBEN needed to be **live** and **local** and **on air continuously** until at least power was restored to most. Our regular hosts and news team were on the air and we added in all our ancillary staff to fill out the night, overnight and weekend hours. Hour after hour, we took calls from residents who were in the dark and troubled by being stranded in their homes or work place.*

Back at home, thanks to our great neighbors and the heroics of Russ with his super-tractor, Amy and I could now turn our attention to possible problems inside the house, still unaware that the tree that had fallen on our roof was also in our attic; worse, it didn't even occur to us to look. It was nice to have the sun shining brilliantly that morning, as strange as it seemed. Even though there was over two feet of snow on the ground, it was somehow rather warm - just one more element of this whole storm that didn't make any sense.

On the flip side, we were about to find out that the melting snow, combined with a non-operational sump pump due to the absence of electricity, was no friend of our basement. Our first glimpse down the basement stairs provided a *terrible, horrible, no good, very bad* surprise. Trying to make sense of this visual, Amy first thought, "Why is the floor so close and how is it moving?" Watching household objects float by in knee-deep water with a continuous, unstoppable flow of water pouring into the basement was sickening. The relief and joy of having our street (mostly) cleared was instantly replaced by a new dread.

We didn't have a concept of what it meant to have a failed sump pump. We had just moved into the house a year earlier and never paid much attention to it - never needed to before. To us, the sump pump was simply that thing in the corner by the washing machine that made noise when it rained and had something to do with water. It never crossed our minds that one of our problems, maybe our biggest problem, would be a flooded basement. It now also meant that our major appliances – the boiler, hot water heater, washing machine, and dryer – were all in jeopardy. Of less importance, but of significantly higher sentimental value, was a vintage 1950's Coca Cola machine that our parents had given us, along with other furniture.

Amy and I immediately grabbed buckets and started bailing.

We opened the bilco hatch doors from which there are ten stairs up to ground level, with our driveway another fifteen feet to the right. Like robots (except robots don't get sore), we scooped up what we could, then carried bucket after bucket up the bilco door stairs, and dumped water onto the driveway which carved out a stream through the two-feet of snow.

Repeat.

Repeat.

Repeat.

But our efforts were futile. Every time we went back down, in a nightmarish way, the water level had *risen*. The intake of water was exceeding our manual outtake, putting those aforementioned appliances at risk. We conceded that the air hockey table, foosball table, bookshelves, carpets, and other furniture were lost - but if we lost those essential appliances, we knew we'd have issues far beyond the length of this storm.

Fortunately, we had an unexpected, but extremely appreciated gift in the form of three young neighbor friends who stopped by and asked if they could help bail. Derek Bajdas and his sister Haley, who had come down earlier to joke about playing football in the snow, which we often did, with Billy and Tom Cavanagh (the same Tom who, almost fifteen years later, would produce the awesome cover of this book) as all were friends of Anna's, via her friendship with Haley. Haley, the youngest "voice of reason" I've ever known, nixed the football idea exclaiming, "C'mon! Not now – can't you see how much there is to clean up?" I couldn't have accepted their offer faster. Tom and Derek helped me move two wooden pallets from the garage to the basement so we could prop them underneath the washer and dryer which brought the bottoms of the appliances up from two inches above ground to about eight inches and surely bought us some time. That move alone saved about one-thousand dollars. We then inserted some cinder blocks underneath other items to keep them dry. However, the immovable hot water heater and furnace were another story.

Our frustration was mounting as the basement was drowning. The more light-hearted moments earlier in our morning of eating eggs, taking pictures, and Amy joking with a friend and fellow teacher, Lori, about spending their "snow day" grabbing lunch at a restaurant seemed like a distant memory. Any novelty about the fascinating landscape had completely faded. Adrenaline was being overtaken by lactic acid as my legs and back grew more and more sore from hauling buckets upon buckets of water up those stairs after our "warmup" of dragging trees all morning. Amy, between bucket trips, was calling businesses that sold generators and might still be open that day. Between the soreness and discouragement at our inability to control the inflow of water into our basement, I was actually considering paying up to $800 for a small, basic generator to start our sump pump. (Yes, Amy, that is an admission that I was really close to spending that kind of money that day.) We started to fade and ultimately hit a wall. This was in addition to not having our morning coffee for probably the first time since high school... *the horror.*

In the 1982 comedy classic sequel *Airplane II: The Sequel,* when the flight attendant takes the microphone to inform the passengers that the shuttle was off course by a half-million miles, hit by an asteroid, and lost its navigational system, the passengers remain relatively calm. One passenger stands up to ask the flight attendant, "Ma'am, are you telling us everything?"

The flight attendant, played by Julie Haggerty, nervously responds, "Not exactly. We're also out of coffee," which sends the passengers into full panic mode – running around screaming and beating each other up. So, there you go, supported scientifically by *Airplane II,* we were operating at a severe physical, emotional, and psychological deficit due to our lack of coffee.

While standing in knee deep water in the basement, my

cell phone rang. It was Kevin Meganck from our Pro Personnel Department at the office who asked, "How ya doing, man? Heard [from Jim] your place got rocked."

"Hey, yeah, we did. Took a tree to the roof and I'm bailing water out of the basement but we'll get through. How'd you make out?"

"It was pretty bad, but was eventually able to make it in. Hey listen, we're signing Jason Jefferson to the active roster this afternoon."

"Oh crap. The ECRS (Electronic Contract Reporting System)," I responded.

Any time a player signed a contract, our most excellent Administrative Assistant, Gail Zielinski, typed it up based on terms and language negotiated by Jim Overdorf. Then, an electronic version of the contract must be sent to the National Football League (NFL) Office in New York City by 3:59:59 pm Eastern time. 4:00:00 pm was too late for an official transaction; this was almost exclusively my responsibility. While Kevin had the system on his computer as an authorized backup, he hadn't done one before. He was, however, plenty sharp enough that I could walk him through it by phone and at that point we had no other choice.

Kevin, as a result of being bright and savvy, remains a key figure in the Personnel Department of the Bills today. I'm proud to have been part of his NFL journey and we remain good friends. A few days after my release in 2017, he came to my house with a couple items I'd forgotten in my office. When I then visited Training Camp in 2018 for a business meeting with my new company, Avrij Analytics, Kevin made a point to meet up and gave me the nameplate that appeared above my office all those years - something I still reflect on as genuine and thoughtful. I wouldn't be surprised to see Kevin as an Assistant General Manager or even a General Manager in the NFL - so much so that on my last day, I looked him in the eye and said, "When this happens, remember me."

"OK, let's do this," I said, while pacing back and forth in the driveway.

I talked Kevin through the step-by-step instructions. Much credit to him, and not surprisingly, he fully and properly executed the electronic contract – even receiving acknowledgement via an email notification from the League while we were on the phone. A huge wave of relief washed over both of us. Had we failed, the player would not be officially signed and could not practice or play; our Coaches and Personnel would have been very upset - and justifiably so. That was a scare, but a comfort to have resolved a very important business matter.

Around this same time, Billy was returning home from his trek for food rations… or donuts and pop, however you'd like to look at it:

> *It was about this time that my Mom finally got a hold of my Gramps, her dad, who lived in South Buffalo in the house that he and my grandmother raised my Mom and her siblings in. Gramps was a wonderful man who was very prideful, but also had a very, very strong Irish stubbornness to him. Little did we know, but in the middle of the night, during the heart of the storm his heat cut out - because he had electric heat - so when the electric went out so did his only source of warmth. Being the MacGyver that he was, he instead decided to huddle around his stove, which was gas, all night trying to keep warm. It goes without saying that at this point my Mom was devastated and so upset that her father had spent the night sitting upright in a hard wooden chair just trying to stay warm. She was frustrated with him that he never called to ask, but I*

think if you asked her, she'd tell you that she was more frustrated with herself that she didn't even think to call him first. In any case, she immediately told him that he needed to come over and that if anyone gave him any hard times about driving, because there was a driving ban at this point, that he should play the "old man card" and say that he was going to his daughters for warmth. He wasn't super comfortable with it as he did not like to take help from anyone, but she said to him, "Don't forget you wouldn't actually be lying - that is what you're doing." That must've been about the fastest that man ever drove - one must take into consideration that his baseline was only slightly above a tortoise's pace. Nonetheless, he was at our house pretty quick even despite the road closures, tree damage, and downed power lines. Thankfully by this point our street has been cleared enough for cars to travel, presumably much to the hard efforts of my neighbors similarly to the ones like Don talked about on his street.

Once my grandfather arrived, we settled in and began what we knew would be several days of backbreaking work. As I started shoveling the driveway, we started also taking that pile of wood that was under, what I thought was only going to be a mere dusting of snow, and spreading it out across the whole driveway to start drying out. We had to rotate the wood as it dried to prevent having wet tops or bottoms as we didn't want our house filled with smoke as we tried to use it; this monotony made the task tedious and thus it became assigned to me, the youngest of our ramshackle crew. Again, the weather was actually pretty nice that day, and it was getting pretty warm so a lot of people weren't even wearing jackets; between *us sweating from working and moving around and the sun that was beating down, it didn't feel **that** cold. That became the part I remember so many people talking about in the immediate aftermath: we got through this crazy snowstorm only to turn around and clean it up in T-shirts.*

The next task we knew we were going to have to work on was, what my Mom to this day still calls, the Widowmaker Fight. Above our sidewalk was a large branch, probably about ten feet long, that was dangling from where it had snapped from its source, clinging and swinging by only a few remaining strands of bark and tree. My grandfather wanted us to cut the branch as high as we could and leave the remaining piece dangling above the sidewalk. Needless to say this was not satisfactory to my mother, the property owner and person who would have to deal with the chaos if that limb came down on a small child several months later; I believe this was her example all those years ago to try and guilt the empathy in the retired Buffalo Firefighter. Instead, my grandfather wouldn't have it and they kept arguing about it so she told him to go away and find a new job to do; she and I, instead, grabbed the branch and began to twist in the hopes that it would snap from where it was already starting to sever. Thankfully my Mom, who was taught these types of things from my grandfather in the first place, was correct and we were able to get the whole branch down, preventing any future issues from reoccurring including the making of widows. As the wood dried, we were slowly starting to stack it inside the garage where it would reside until being selected for burning - something that would become an even more essential part of our house than we knew before.

   While my grandfather and I were close and did many things together, there were only two times I ever slept in the same room as him: once when I was very young and he was very worried about me sleeping over at his house so he insisted on me sleeping on the floor of his bedroom, just in case; and the second was that first night he came over because we needed to sleep by the fire in order to keep warm. Upstairs, my Mom was pretending to sleep with every blanket we had on top of her, trying to insulate in anyway we could - when I say pretended to sleep, this is something I learned years later in hindsight, but my Mom told me that she got barely any sleep the first few nights, like many Western New Yorkers, especially because no matter how many blankets she had, it was still cold. While the weather was temperate while working, overnight and in bed was not as ideal. Gramps and I attempted to get some rest by the warm instead - he on the couch and I in one of our comfy chairs with an ottoman. This only lasted two nights, but is still a memory I hold onto for strange, sentimental reasons I can't quite explain - of all memories to share with someone who is no longer with us, this doesn't seem like it should be at the top of the list, but for whatever reason it has stayed with me. Perhaps it's because it's one of the few times I ever saw him seek out help from one of us, or accept it for that matter. Or maybe it's the first time I realized that my Gramps whom I idolized so much wasn't invincible, that it took a once in a lifetime snow storm to truly knock him off his perch - though, to be honest, if that's what it took, it's still a great feat.

It started to get dark - and cold - which was an unwelcome but inevitable development. Back to candles and flashlights, something we assumed would only last for the night, but would soon become fixtures in our home. Amy called her sister, Lisa, who lived in Webster, east of Rochester. Besides being incredulous at our situation - again, Rochester was not touched by this storm - she said our brother-in-law, Dave Beh, was going to bring us one of his family business's generators *that same night!*

Wow, would that be awesome. With that, we could fire up the sump pump to pull the still 18" of water through the system and out of the house.

Sure enough, Dave arrived at about 11:00 pm, but in pitch darkness with no street lights, his GPS and lack of familiarity with the neighborhood took him, mistakenly, to the house of neighbors, Pete and Marcia LaForce. Pete, after spending the entire previous night securing Buffalo State College Students, had crashed hard to sleep and Marcia, who had been one of the neighbors alongside Amy and I dragging trees off our street for several hours earlier that day, had also fallen asleep. Both were exhausted and more than a little concerned to hear what else could be awaiting them from a knock on the door at 11:00 pm, only to find Dave who explained he was looking for us. *No, Pete and Marcia, this was not the "Generator Fairy" delivering you an extra generator; it was meant for us.* After a good laugh, they sent him next door to the correct house.

Once he had made it to our house, Dave said that during most of his trip on I-90 West (of the New York State Thruway) he saw zero evidence that there had been any storm at all. At least until, in the blink of an eye, near the Williamsville toll, he was alarmed to notice how the landscape looked like a helicopter had swung low and chopped the tops off all of the trees off, a sight he said he'd never forget.

Dave fired up the generator in the driveway and fed an extension cord through the bilco doors down into the basement where I then plugged the extension cord into the sump pump. It made the most beautiful sucking sound imaginable - a sentence I never thought I would say let alone announce to the world. It's the noise I imagine was like the one Ross Perot described in a presidential debate about jobs being "sucked down" to Mexico, only this was a good thing. The knee-deep water we were standing in began swirling down the corner well, into the drainage system pipes, and, most importantly, *out of the house!* Having lived in this house barely a year without any previous water issues, Dave pointed out three floor drainage areas that were completely plugged. So, obviously knowing far more than we did, he used a long plumbing tool to loosen them up to the point of taking water, as they were designed to. This was another awesome sight, but I couldn't help not berating myself about the pain and suffering we could have avoided had we only known this earlier before lugging **hundreds** of water-filled buckets up the stairs. In an enormously lame attempt at spin, my only consolation was that I carried out our own version of a Rocky IV workout: *Suburban Style.*

West Seneca Chamber of Commerce Executive Director, Joe Kirchmyer, personally attests to the level of difficulty finding a generator during this sudden supply shortage.

There are moments from the surprise October Storm that I'll remember as long as I live, such as the cracking of limbs from the maple trees surrounding my backyard and the "whoosh" sound the big ones made as they fell into the fresh blanket of snow below. And then there were the loud "booms" and the sky lighting up bright colors in all directions as countless transformers blew up on utility poles.

As the storm occurred, we (me, my wife Maureen and our children Andrew and Lauren) knew that we were experiencing a once-in-a-lifetime event. At least that's what I kept telling the kids, and I still think I was right in saying that. I also knew that without electricity, my basement would likely flood in a matter of hours once the snow started melting. My sump pump always moved a lot of water due to our always damp yard, and I was fortunate to have a battery back-up system in place for such an event. Unfortunately, those batteries will typically get you through a day, and I was now pushing two full days without electricity and the battery was on its last legs.

When I woke up on Saturday, October 14th — my birthday — I told Maureen that I was going to drive until I found a portable generator that would power our sump pump (and as it later turned out, other important household items such as our refrigerator, television, and my wife's blow dryer and curling iron).

My plan was to head toward Pennsylvania. Along the way I stopped in Dunkirk, New York, but it was still too close to home and there were no generators to be found at their Home Depot store. It was also not an easy drive. The New York State Thruway was as slippery as an ice rink and there were vehicles off the road left and right. I kept a slow, steady pace, but it was definitely a white-knuckle ride. I told myself that if people from Western New York had taken this trip before me, they were likely to stay on the (Interstate Rt) 90, a more familiar route heading toward Cleveland.

Once I reached Pennsylvania, I decided to jump onto the (Interstate Rt) 79 and head toward Pittsburgh instead.

The first exit or two seemed very nondescript, and then I saw a sign for Edinboro University. Being a college town, I figured there had to be some larger stores in the vicinity. Sure enough there was a Walmart, but they did not carry generators. One of the employees suggested a hardware store in town, but I was unable to locate it based on his directions. Frustrated, I was going to head back to the Thruway again. In the meantime, I heard from my wife. The battery had completely died and the basement was starting to take on water.

Out of the corner of my eye I noticed a sign for a small auto supply store, Dobber Auto Supply. That name has always stayed with me. Once inside the mom-and-pop-style store I was greeted by the owner. I believe his name was Bob. Bob Dobber.

"Any chance you have any portable gas generators," I asked, expecting to hear the worst.

"I have a couple right here," Bob said as he brought me back toward the front of the store to point them out.

Bob and I had a nice conversation. I told him I made the drive from Buffalo in search of generators due to the storm. He said he had been getting details about it on TV, and ended up selling me both generators at a significant discount. I think they were just over $200 each. The few generators that were making their way to the Buffalo area were being scooped up way too fast, and with heavy price tags of $750 to $1,000 each! Before leaving I also purchased a large gas can to fill up on the way home because the gas pumps *were not working near home due to the power outage. And on my way out of Edinboro I did finally spot that hardware store, where I stopped and purchased a chainsaw to cut up all the branches that were still waiting for me in my yard, and in my mother's yard just six houses away.*

When I made it home, one of the generators quickly made it into the hands of one of my brothers, Jeff, who lived a few miles away at the time and was also without power. I kept the one that was on wheels, and that turned out to be a very wise decision.

After pumping out my basement and sump pump, I let my closest neighbors know that I had a generator and was willing to help them out as well. Several immediately took me up on my offer. Not that I wanted or asked for any payment, but everyone was very generous and offered some barter in return. One gave me steaks that I grilled for dinner later that evening. Another gave me a delicious box of candy. I imagine this is how people commonly did things years ago, and it was actually a lot of fun helping them.

An older gentleman living directly across the street heard of my traveling generator and stopped over to ask if I could pump out his sump pump. "Of course," I replied, and quickly gathered my now essential tools and headed over.

As I entered his house, the neighbor asked me if I smelled anything funny. I certainly did, but I was unsure what it was. "Let me look around," I said. Sure enough, the smell was gas escaping from his stovetop. One of the burners was turned on full blast, but there was no flame. When I turned around to tell him, I was shocked by what I saw, and it's no wonder I didn't smell natural gas. He had somewhere around twenty candles burning throughout the house! I quickly ran around carefully extinguishing the small flames while shouting for my neighbor to open all of his doors and windows as quickly as possible. I can't even imagine what would have happened if he had waited another twenty minutes or so before contacting me!

To this day I remember that story every time I look across the street at that house, and it still gives me goosebumps.

Now, thanks to Dave, we had a generator that helped us in *so* many ways, first and foremost being that he saved our appliances. The electricity distributed by the generator was just enough to power **one thing**. The first couple of days, with all the melting snow, it had to be on the sump pump to keep the basement from flooding (again). Once most of the snow melted, we could pick and choose other appliances to power, for example, we'd plug in the coffee maker – just to make a pot and then switch to one light, then to the refrigerator for the overnight hours. We had candles burning all over the house constantly; Amy dug up every candle she was ever given by her students as Christmas or end-of-year gifts. Despite this minor inconvenience, and more importantly, we no longer faced a second straight sleepless night of manually staying on top of the rising water; this modest sized generator was able to power up our most targeted electrical needs, and Dave even left us with a full tank of gas on the side and just asked us to return it next time we came his way. While Russ had been a hero of our street, Dave Beh was a hero of our home that night and to whom we'll always be grateful. He bailed us out - figuratively and literally. We owe Amy's sister, Lisa, much thanks as well for arranging this during a real time of need!

We were certainly not the only ones who had this issue as

generators sold out so quickly in WNY that my sister and brother-in-law, Tracy and Scott, who lived in Butler, PA just north of Pittsburgh, later told us that hardware stores, big and small, were selling out all the way down there because of the run in Buffalo, as Joe Kirchmyer attested to earlier. The ones that were available were selling for $1,500 - and more than likely someone paid that out of desperation to a price gouger's benefit. A few weeks later, after we returned Dave's generator to him, Scott gave us an extra one that they had, which we still have today.

To be clear, Billy and I have been sharing our own personal stories about the damages suffered to our homes and other associated challenges, but we're fully aware that we are merely a "sample of two" and that there were so many more basement-related stories, many probably worse than ours, that occurred as the result of this storm. To more fully comprehend the extent of the massive damage to the Western New York Region, one must multiply our own situations by hundreds of thousands of Buffalonians who were dealt similar, or much worse, personal and property damage – albeit with their own unique challenges and details.

But first, let's talk about exactly *how in the world* did this **freakish** "storm of the century" happen in the first place?

FIVE
WHAT (ACTUALLY) JUST HAPPENED, METEOROLOGICALLY SPEAKING

"SILENTLY and with a strength as cruel as it was wet and clammy, a snowstorm swept down upon Buffalo last evening and smothered the city in a blanket of slushy white.

Never in its history has a storm so secret, so vindictive attacked the city and today it looks as if it had been swept by a tornado. Branches and whole trees litter the streets, crushed with a weight of wet snow. In the parks, all is havoc and devastation. Big trees are wrenched out of shape, big limbs are scattered everywhere and beautiful shrubs are mangled and borne to the ground.

The crushing force of the falling sleet was hard to realize at first. This storm came slowly, changing from a deluge of rain to heavy wet snow, almost imperceptibly. Clinging to all it touched, it bore down in tons upon the boughs and tore them from their stems in thousands. Telegraph, telephone, electric light and power wires were borne down in all parts of the city and most of the street car lines on the East Side were *tied up for the greater portion of the night." - Buffalo Enquirer, "Lives and Property Destroyed!": **Oct 11ᵗʰ, 1906.***

MANY CONSIDER OCTOBER TO BE BUFFALO'S MOST BEAUTIFUL AND pleasant time of the year. This is debatable as Buffalo's summers are often near perfect with weather that almost makes the winters worthwhile, but having grown up as a skier in the Adirondack town of Speculator, NY, I have always had an appreciation for the winter months. December through February - that's it. As for March and April in Buffalo? Not so much. Having daughters that played "Spring" sports in High School and College, I know firsthand that rarely do those March and early April games *feel* like springtime, but they were still enjoyable - as long as you dressed for it. One notable exception was March of 2012 when the Bills were aggressively pursuing Free Agent star Defensive End, Mario Williams. The week he visited Buffalo featured a solid stretch of 80-degree days. Word spread amongst the organization, *"No one shall tell him that this isn't normal."*

The National Weather Service's (NWS) office in Buffalo described the October Surprise Storm that struck Western New York on October 12ᵗʰ and 13ᵗʰ, as a "dramatic, crippling out-of-season event" with "unprecedented meteorological parameters"[1] - far from the beautiful and pleasantly seasonal weather the region was used to. The severity of this storm was not lost on the NWS stating: "Words cannot do justice to the astounding event which opened the 2006-07 season"; even they described what happened to the Buffalo area as "historic" due to the devastation to the utility infrastructure.

---

[1] US Department of Commerce, NOAA. "Lake Effect Snow Event Archive: October 12, 2006 to October 13, 2006." *National Weather Service*, NOAA's National Weather Service, 11 Oct. 2016, www.weather.gov/buf/lesEventArchive2006-2007_a.

They also went on to state that "extreme parameters of this event" led to what some might call a "perfect storm."[1]

While we were pleased with the great contributors we'd brought on board so far from various industries like radio, clergy, insurance, and law enforcement, along with Bills and Sabres personnel, we felt a need for the perspective(s) of weather professionals to explain *how* this monstrous storm developed. So who better than the local meteorologists from Buffalo's three major public local news networks, Channels 2, 4, & 7 (WGRZ, WIVB, and WKBW, respectively) to talk about their own personal and professional experiences with the Storm. We were particularly interested in how they forecasted this most unusual weather event, and then how they personally reacted as it developed.

The consensus for the reason the October Storm was so devastating was the combination of heavy wet snow that came far too early in the season, when all of the leaves were still on the trees, which massive chaos and destruction lasted much longer than the Storm or even most of the snow did - so what *actually* happened to create this literal perfect storm?

Aaron Mentkowski and his team over at Channel 7 (WKBW, the local ABC affiliate) knew something unusual was on the horizon, but what *exactly* it was remained unclear right up until it started:

> *Several days before the storm hit Western New York, we knew something big was going to happen. The computer models were back and forth on what the temperature would be for this storm. In this case, a degree or two made a huge difference in what type of precipitation we would receive. Some computer models forecasted an all Lake Effect rain event, others were calling for snow. We know now that the band quickly changed to heavy, wet snow and crippled parts of Western New York.*

Being in the Red Zone is great in football,
but very bad in a storm.

Although **Patrick Hammer** was born and raised in California, he came to Buffalo to work for WGRZ - the local NBC affiliate and Channel 2 on the dial - in 2015, still prepared for the snow that comes every year. During 2006, Patrick was working in Minnesota - which is also famous for some good snow - and he remembers the impact the snowfall had on the WNY region, through whatever was being broadcasted nationally. Deeply fascinated, Patrick decided to dig into some archives from the National Weather Service (NWS) to really capture how rare this type of storm was. According to Patrick,

> *First of all, you had a very deep trough of low pressure*
> *with very cold air, for the time of year, set up over the*
> *Great Lakes. At the same time, the water temperature*
> *of Lake Erie on our end of the lake was (an unusually*
> *warm) 62°. Usually when Lake Effect snow processes*

set up later in the season, the water temperature is at least 10 to 15° cooler than that so it was very rare to have such cold air aloft and such warm water in Lake Erie, which set up extreme instability. The pattern was well recognized to bring Lake Effect precipitation to the Buffalo area.

There was no surprise that a Lake Effect event was to occur, however initially it was believed that it would be warm enough for an all rain event. Even as late as Wednesday afternoon [on] October 11, the National Weather Service was still calling for all rain and no snow, which was only about 18 hours before the event was to begin. The reason for the "all rain" forecast was that the critical temperature needed for Lake Effect snow is -7°C [19.4°F] at about 5,000 feet in the atmosphere, but at that point the forecast still called for temperatures to be in the -4 to -5°C [24.8 to 23°F] range. Beginning Wednesday evening, forecasters began to realize that the models [they were using] were too warm with the storm and the actual air temperature was a few degrees cooler at that altitude. Also, observations taken further to the west revealed the cold reality of the air at that level, so that evening the National Weather Service altered their forecast to a mix of rain and snow with 1 to 2 inches of snowfall on grassy surfaces by Thursday night.

According to Patrick and the NWS reports he pulled from the archives, the Lake Effect rain showers rapidly turned into wet, heavy snow and the "Lake Effect storm warnings were issued - for 1 to 4 inches of snow, *possibly* up to six inches." Long story short, from what we can tell, even the National Weather Service wasn't quite on the ball with this one, even as the event began!

"The snow piled up slowly and noiselessly upon the trees and bushes, and as the foliage was still on the boughs the weight was enormous. Slowly the trees bent their tops, their limbs slowly sagged toward the earth, and then, in despair of holding up the weight, broke and fell. No blizzard that ever swept through the city ever made one half the havoc among the trees and bushes.

*Delaware Park is a wreck. Trees strew the ground in all directions and others have fallen into each tours' arms and stand in clusters pinned against one another by the wet, sodden slush. The other parks present about the same appearance, and the branches continue to fall." - Buffalo Enquirer, "Lives and Property Destroyed!": Oct 11th, **1906.**

Aaron, who was living and teaching in Buffalo at that point, went about his life as it was supposed to be; much like the other local meteorologists, still trying to prepare for what the day (and night) would hold for those just east of Lake Erie:

I worked the morning and noon show that day and then went off to teach a meteorology course at one of our local colleges. The class spent most of the time watching the storm develop. I let class out early as the snow was piling up, trees were snapping, and travel was becoming very difficult. By the time I made it home we had lost power and were without power from Thursday through Sunday.

We fired up the generator and had four neighbors run extension cords from our generator so they could keep [their] sump pumps going. I remember my wife and I, and our two boys, sleeping in the basement and listening to the Sabres game on the radio. On Sunday

we hooked a tv up to the generator and the neighbors
came over to watch the Bills game in the garage. No
power, but we still followed our Buffalo teams.

The storm was incredible and goes to show you what
Mother Nature is capable of. Forecasting continues to
improve every year and as we saw with Snowvember
[in 2014] - the models and meteorologist[s] who
interpret them are [becoming more and more] capable
[to] accurately forecast such events.

Per his NWS research, Patrick stated that "as the Lake Effect
snow continued, it was expected to weaken and then re-intensify
Thursday night which clearly occurred. The heavy snow only picked
up in intensity and the National Weather Service noted in their
2:30 am briefing that **20 to 24 inches of snow had fallen.**" He
went on to detail that in the NWS briefings, referred to as Area
Forecast Discussions, "you could clearly sense the urgency in the
National Weather Service's verbiage that something truly historic
was happening. Obviously, the greatest fear was the impact the
heavy snow would have on all of the trees in Buffalo that still had
all of their leaves, and we [now] know the results[,] that up to 55,000
trees were lost."

Chesley McNeil, former Meteorologist at Channel 2 WGRZ
(NBC's local affiliate) which is stationed in the heart of downtown
Buffalo, agreed with Aaron and Patrick that this was an incredibly
challenging weather event to forecast because: "There was nothing
really to compare the event to. We have had cold air early in the
season move over the lake, but we would get lake effect rain," much
like Aaron and Patrick also expected. Part of the reason for the delay
in response was due to the rarity of what was happening - so rare

in fact, that some records suggest that Buffalo had *never* "received a snowfall of over 4 inches so early in the season in recorded history."[2]

While we connected with Aaron, Patrick, and Chesley through each of their station's general email, we were unsuccessful reaching anyone from Channel 4 via the same. In their defense, during the 2020 pandemic, business practices were severely disrupted as many Customer Relations folks were forced to work from home. Nevertheless, we felt it was important for multiple reasons to have <u>all three stations</u> on board, but then we had a lightbulb moment. Having worked with "The Radio Voice of the Bills," **John Murphy**, for several years, perhaps John could reach out to his former Channel 4 colleagues for us.

After explaining the book project, John responded with two things:

1. He personally, given that he lived outside that ten-mile zone, was thankfully barely affected by the Storm and was stunned to learn of the wreckage that occurred *inside* the zone.
2. John offered, "How about if I arrange a phone call with Don Paul for you?"

My answer was an emphatic, "Yes, thank you, John, and - I owe you one."

"No problem - but you'd better be a fast note-taker because once he gets going..."

Perhaps no voice (and face) is more synonymous with Buffalo Weather than **Don Paul**. Don has been a meteorologist for all three of the local public news networks and spent the bulk of his career as

---

[2] Paul, Don. "Don Paul remembers the October Storm ... because we forced him to." *Buffalo News, 11 October 2016, https://buffalonews.com/news/local/history/don-paul-remembers-the-october-storm-because-we-forced-him-to/article_a99e47b3-0740-5dbd-b0f4-f28a8835aabf.html. Accessed 22 October 2020.*

Chief Meteorologist for Channel 4's WIVB Weather Center, which was where he worked during the 2006 storm.

As John predicted, our call with Don Paul hit the ground running. After sharing a couple of classic, hilarious Van Miller stories, Don immediately called our attention to a 2016 Buffalo News article for the ten-year anniversary of the storm, for which he was a featured contributor. The article pointed out that there were "some very early season major lake snowfalls in our more distant past, including 1906 and 1930"[1], the former of which dropped up to a foot (12") of snow in the suburbs to the east and south of the City of Buffalo. Much like news reports in 2016, newspaper articles from 1906 "focused more on the damage to the new electrical grid and telegraph lines"[1] that had been installed starting around the beginning of the 20th Century following the invention of electricity. While in 2006, we were distressed at power outages that lasted a week (or more), in 1906, "the invention of electricity resulted in power lines being strung across all of Buffalo"[3] making it one of the first cities in the country to electrify their world leading to one of Buffalo's nicknames, "The City of Light." Buffalo's broad foresight made it a bright focus on a brilliant new future and thus making it the perfect place to host the Pan American Exposition in 1901, "during which time it showcased its modern electrically lit city."[2] The primary concern at the time of the 1906 Storm was the downed connection lines to "the outside"[2] that left the city "floundering"[4]- a great irony when we felt disconnected because we didn't have television! This would happen yet again in a storm in 1930, which begins to suggest a pattern that we should have better expected, however, because of the rarity of this type of situation, Don Paul

---

[3] Hamilton, R. S., D. Zaff, and T. Niziol (2007), A catastrophic lake effect snow storm over Buffalo, NY October 12–13, 2006, paper presented at 22nd Conference on Weather Analysis and Forecasting/18th Conference on Numerical Weather Prediction, Am. Meteorol. Soc., Park City, Utah, 25 – 29 June.

[4] Buffalo Enquirer, 1906: "Lives and Property Destroyed!" Oct 11 1906, Pg 1.

admitted that this would have been hard for any professional to expect because it was "unique in my lifetime and unique in the lives of meteorologists working then right up to this day."[2] In fact, when we talked to Don, aside from offering up his mea culpa right from the opening, he also shared that Buffalo had not seen temperatures that low and that early in the season since the 1906 storm that was, ironically, almost 100 years earlier to the day. The difference was that "our 2006 storm focused on the most densely populated part of upstate New York, including Buffalo, the northern and eastern suburbs, and to a lesser extent, the immediate southtowns. It was the most costly storm in the modern era, producing more than $160 million in damage."[2]

Don shared a similar story to that of Aaron's - one of shock and dismay as this chaos continued. Don was very blunt, both in our talking with him as well as publicly, about how much of a "surprise" this storm was - he admitted, even calling his post-assessment a "mea culpa" that despite having some evidence that there should be some snow expected, most did not forecast anything significant. Don said in his Buffalo News article that "more than a week out" there were predictions of "a deep storm system crossing the Great Lakes with unseasonably cold air"[2], which Don predicted would lead to some snow, especially in areas of higher elevations where it is usually cooler. (He would like to point out that he did, in fact predict snow would fall by October 12th so he was, in at least one way, correct!) Chesley also recalled talking about "the *possibility* for snow" in his broadcast on Tuesday the 10th.

However, by Tuesday the 10th, one NWS model forecasted exceptionally unseasonably cold air (thanks alot, Canada!) - temperatures that Don had never seen before in such a way and especially not so early. Much like the other area meteorologists, Don was skeptical about those numbers because, at least from his knowledge: "Air just doesn't get that cold a mile up over Buffalo that early. I was wrong, since I hadn't looked up the climatology earlier in the 20th century."[2]

He said, per his memory, that the temperature in the morning on the 12th started off around 61°F with an expectation for about 2 - 4 inches of rain, but by about 12:30 pm, after staring at his monitor analyzing the information in front of him and comparing it to what he was beginning to see out his window, he let out a… well let's just say a particular four-letter-word that he'd prefer wasn't in print. Knowing full well that a shift in wind direction by a meager five degrees could affect 100,000 people of the Greater Buffalo Area, Don raced to the station early only to have the power go out by 4:30 pm - the station is right in downtown Buffalo and thus was hit a bit harder and earlier than the suburbs. By later in the afternoon, the heavy, slushy snow began to weigh down tree limbs onto power lines and soon after that the outages began, many even before dark. They increased exponentially overnight. At the same time, forecasting, as Don put it, "became a game of catch up,"[2] working late into the night trying to get the latest information out to the public in need.

Don assumed the 22° difference between the lake temperature and the atmosphere around a mile up would allow for the warm air above the lake to better rise into the cold and moist air, held aloft in convective bubbles; he figured that if some snow did form, it would melt from the warmth of the lake and forecasted on the 11th "a possible 2 to 4 inches with isolated 3 to 5 inch amounts possible in northern Erie County (which includes Buffalo), with the changeover beginning later in the day on Oct. 12."[2] (Miss # 1, Don.) In Don's defense, Chesley predicted similarly:

> *We thought that the ground was too warm for any snow to stick, and that we would probably get a rain/snow mix which would also keep levels low. The event started out as rain Thursday, then began mixing with*

snow late afternoon. Snow started sticking Thursday evening and that's when the fun began.

I remember going to bed that night around 9:00 pm thinking I need to go in a little early Friday. I only got about two hours of sleep. I was awakened by the limbs cracking on my roof. I started to make my way into work around 1 am, only to find half of a tree blocking the driveway. I made it in around 3am.

Chesley went on to share that because of this tree at the end of his driveway, he had to call the station to have someone come and pick him up, however the street he lived on at the time was tree lined so they could not get down it: "So I had to meet them at the corner. The same car passed me five times… that's how bad the visibility was. Finally I got in the middle of the street to stop the car and see if it was my ride." (Thankfully, he said aside from the felled tree he only lost a gutter in the Storm and recognized how lucky he was compared to others!) Something not often talked about, but also relatable to the recent Covid-19 Pandemic of 2020, is the necessity of essential workers and the challenges and pressures related to bringing the weather and news to the public; Chesley shared, "There is no 'I can't make it in' in our business. Someone will come and get you." He also said that because of this some of the on-air talent stayed overnight at the studio, just in case.

"Every street car line in the city has been more or less delayed by the litter of broken limbs falling on the tracks, and during the day tons of fallen foliage was removed from the streets. The telegraph service of Western New York was practically at a standstill. Even the press wires were down and none of the afternoon papers had telegraph news for their first editions.

> *Trains on every road entering the the [sic] city were late from one to five hours. In fact the general inconvenience to traffic and communication of all kinds was never greater during one of the severest winter storms of wind and snow, nor has the danger to life and limb been greater.*
>
> *Falling trees and the weight of snow on the wires themselves bore many live wires to the ground and created a condition of grave danger. At Masten and Emerson streets a wire fell killing a team. The horses were owned by C. W. Miller, and were driven by Charles Kipphurt. He saw the wire as it started to fall and leaped from the back. The wire fell across the backs of the horses killing them instantly. " - Buffalo Enquirer, "Lives and Property Destroyed!": Oct 11ᵗʰ, 1906.*

Don Paul also admittedly underestimated the degree to which the snow threatened the trees and other greenery in his initial report… As he would detail in *hindsight*, the "incredibly heavy water laden slush"[2] was coming down on trees that still had most of their leaves, making perfect perches for this clingy snow to latch onto; the problem was that the ground was already well saturated from a wet period before this storm. This is why the heavy branches were so much better able to pull entire trees down by uprooting them, leading to the devastating damage to the electrical grid in the area. Chesley McNeil was also incorrect in believing that the snow would not stick: "Even though it started snowing early in the evening, it really didn't stick to the ground until the evening when the storm turned the most intense."

The electrical outages would prove to be prolific, for many lasting over a week - over 400,000 were without power at one point or another; 70% of Buffalonians and 90% of suburbanites in the

Northern and Eastern suburbs were impacted. Don claims in his Buffalo News article, "It is safe to say this was the biggest and most destructive lake snowstorm in October ever experienced in the metro area. In terms of physical damage, it was the most costly storm in any month - period."[2] Ironically, shortly after the Storm was over, the weather shifted returning the area to more mild temperatures, saving some from cold sleeps. This shift in warmth was both good and bad, as Chesley highlighted: "It was good for the cleaning up process, but also led to some minor flooding in some spots."

Chesley went on to share that this tree damage and the chaos that ensued from the power outages were a bigger part of what led to this storm being a surprise at all rather than the weather itself:

> *The news media referred to the storm as a "surprise." It wasn't really a surprise that we received snow that early in October, and we had snow in the forecast. I believe the "surprise" was the massive power outages and tree damage, but you can't predict that. The heavy, wet snow rested on the leaves still on the trees really weighing them down. In fact the snow was [mostly] gone by the next day, as temperature[s] heated into the 50s and 60s.*

When reflecting on other storms he's forecasted, Chesley said that the damage and impact of this storm compared to a few hurricanes he'd been through, particularly Hurricane Isabell that went through Richmond, VA "where we were without power for two weeks and suffered a good amount of damage. You would expect that with Hurricanes… typically not with Lake Effect snow." In fact, Chesley could not think of any other Lake Effect storms around the nation that could quite compare, though he did share that he felt that this storm paled in comparison to Buffalo's infamous Blizzard of '77, as the impact then was more directly related to the actual weather.

The irony of forecasting and staying on the air throughout the Storm was something that many non-professionals talked about shortly after - *why bother when the people who you're trying to reach can't turn their TVs on?* When we asked Chesley about this at the time, he seemed to have a good grasp on the rationale:

> *It may seem odd, but people who are not affected watch the most. You would be surprised how glued we all are to certain events that take place in other places, especially weather events like hurricanes, tornadoes, snow and ice, etc. People want to see it. And here [in Buffalo] the people are so giving, they like to know how they can help.*

One of the more memorable parts of the Storm was the Thunder Snow and Blue Lightning - which was detailed earlier as the antagonist keeping Western New York awake, but *what was that?* Chesley described thunder snow as "rare" and "intense" that starts from a "strong uplift [that] caused cloud tops to reach 25 to 28 thousand feet." (For perspective, the white fluffy cumulus clouds that we all visualize when counting sheep are usually at about 6,600 feet.) According to him, these are more common in the summer and during rainstorms, but every so often Lake Effect snow events with thunder and lightning occur; Chesley said, "It usually lasts for a short [time] when this one lasted for a few hours."

Don elaborated on this in his Buffalo News article very technically describing the ratio of water to snow and how it varies, which is also why some storms can be harder to predict than others. Per Don's article, "The ratio that afternoon and evening was one inch of liquid to six inches of snow. It had begun as rain, then rain and graupel pellets (which produce an electrical charge), converting to maximum intensity thundersnow. Hours of thundersnow. Generally, when there is lightning with snow, it's snowing close to as hard as it can snow."[2]

A common misconception about the weather is that the entire Buffalo region is always covered with snow, or at least in the winter months for those who are more realistic - though, in Buffalo the definition of winter months is arguably flexible. With the Buffalo Bills and their Orchard Park Stadium, which is usually in the Lake effect snow belt, being one of main national television exposures for the city, it's very easy for out-of-towners to assume that's what the entirety of the region looks like, however when you see a "blizzard" at the stadium, it very well might be sunny just two towns away.

The day after the Storm, once the roads were cleared enough for even non-locals to navigate, the Weather Channel came to Buffalo and interviewed Don Paul - it is here he would like us to note that while people thought he was crying for some reason, he was *not*. He did, however, talk at length about Buffalo weather and reiterated much of what has been told.

Later that year Don attended the Annual National Weather Convention in Denver, where meteorologists from all over the country assemble. (As a side note, I can't help but wonder - when Weather folks get together, what topics do *they* use to break the ice in conversations? Insurance? The Middle East?) So, the emcee that year began the conference by calling out, "Is Don Paul here? Is Don Paul from Buffalo here?" When Don raised his hand in acknowledgement, the emcee called him up to the podium to tell the audience "what exactly happened out in Buffalo in October." The common amazement was that all of this happened ten full weeks before the official start of winter!

With that, the audience leaned in intently to learn... what we just learned.

Huge thanks again to Chesley, Aaron, Patrick, and Don!

"At 9 o'clock last evening, the safest places to walk was the center of the streets, and even there lurked danger from falling limbs as slowly the insidious brutality of the storm made itself felt.

The snow piled up slowly and noiselessly upon the trees and bushes, and as the foliage was still on the boughs the weight was enormous. Slowly the trees bent their tops, their limbs slowly sagged toward the earth, and then, in despair of holding up the weight, broke and fell. No blizzard that ever swept through the city ever made one half the havoc among the trees and bushes." - Buffalo Enquirer, "Lives and Property Destroyed!": Oct 11th, 1906.

SIX

"HAVE YOU LOOKED OUT THE WINDOW, YOU DUMBASS?"

AFTER YEARS OF STABILITY IN THE 1990's, THE BUFFALO BILLS experienced numerous "turnings of the page" since their last playoff appearance in 1999 in the infamous, heartbreaking *Music City Miracle* playoff game in Tennessee. Just weeks later, for salary cap reasons, the Bills felt forced to release future Hall of Famers, Bruce Smith, Thurman Thomas, and Andre Reed - on the same day. Every Bills fan who watched those legends then suit up in different uniforms the next season agreed - *it just looked wrong*.

In 2006, with Marv Levy as the new General Manager, who hired Dick Jauron as the new Head Coach, the Buffalo Bills saw a high number of Rookie players (12) see game action - something that is fairly common in pro sports when new leadership aims to put their own stamp on the roster. These young men were not only new to the National Football League, but new also to their adopted hometown of Buffalo, New York.

Being a rookie in the NFL is a major life adjustment. It was a privilege to work with Player Engagement Directors and with the rookies themselves as it related to their pay and how to handle their injuries. It surprises most people to learn that every time a player is injured, whether during a game, a practice, or a workout, it generates a Workers' Compensation claim. As one can imagine, in the most physical game of football, there are a highly disproportionate number of claims as compared to most "normal" businesses. Luckily for me, my boss Jim Overdorf masterfully argued the grievances and negotiated injury settlements related to the players' contracts. However, the several hundred claims per year were handled by yours truly. On top of that, every business is required by the State of New York to fill out and submit an annual work-related injury OSHA (Occupational Safety and Health Administration) report. For us, that meant sitting down with Head Trainer Bud Carpenter and his staff to log not only every player who suffered any type of injury, but also how many days - either fully or partial - the player missed of "work." Talk about trying to fit a square peg into a round hole! The meeting took a full day, sometimes longer, and my subsequent report required another two days to complete. Despite our due diligence and compliance, somebody from the Labor Department in Albany would inevitably call to question our numbers to which I always replied, "Yes, we *really* did have that many injuries." Then I'd ask myself (rhetorically), *Don't they also get these reports from the Giants and Jets?* I realized that's a 'no' as the Bills are the only NFL team that *actually* plays in the State of New York. This is why NY Workers Comp Attorney Roger Edel, as mentioned earlier, was so important to us at the Bills. Roger helped facilitate a substantial financial reimbursement back to the team for this most laborious and expensive work. My responsibilities were mainly to pay the doctors and hospitals and produce the medical records, in a HIPAA compliant way (ie. encrypted, password protected, and as a PDF) for our insurance carrier, agents, attorneys, as well as the players themselves. This was a time-consuming, heavy administrative lift that spiked even higher after the NFL Concussion settlement in 2011. In case you couldn't tell, I do *not* miss this aspect of my former job.

During the latter part of my tenure, player's pay was also my responsibility which, during the seventeen-week schedule, was a weekly task. Most players calculated their estimated weekly gross salary by simply dividing by seventeen. Unfortunately for them, many never factored in Federal and State tax withholdings, so it was painful to watch a rookie open his first regular season paycheck envelope and gasp at how much less it was than expected. I always wondered why their agents didn't prepare them for this reality. In later years, I tried to make it known to them either on the record during a meeting or off the record in person to be aware that your check is taxed – and heavily!

(The purpose of explaining my role here is mainly to help frame the nature of my interaction with the players, which will soon come into play. And since this may be the only book I ever write, it also serves as an opportunity to answer a question often asked of me – "What exactly *did you do* at the Bills?")

Another question I was often asked is, "What do you do in the off-season?" My own mother asked me this every January for twenty-seven years. Fair question. The simple answer is: all the same things we do during the regular season, except travel. Then, we hone in on yearly budgets. That's overly simplistic and sounds even boring, perhaps, but it's true. Ultimately, despite professional teams being multimillion-dollar sports enterprises, at the end of the day, they're still a business.

When all that most people know about NFL teams is what they see during games on TV or from the stands, it's easy to form a singular perception. Late one weekday afternoon at the office, I stopped by the bathroom before going home. Underneath one of the stalls I could clearly see a guy with sweatpants and sneakers struggling to fit into giant, blue, fuzzy feet (and thankfully it was not a major Buffalo State College donor sleeping). Now, in any other business, this might be something strange to find in an office bathroom, however to those of us at the Bills it was known to be the unmistakable, size 34, trackmakers that belonged to "Billy Buffalo", the mascot that entertains fans on game day. Many of co-Author Billy Klun's friends and family are probably laughing as they assumed the size 34 feet belonged to *our* nearly seven-foot-tall Billy, but alas Billy *Klun* has never had the chance to fill those particular oversized shoes. In this case, "Billy Buffalo" was gearing up to entertain at a weekday charity event. While washing my hands at the sink, I turned to another co-worker who could see the fuzzy feet as well and said, "*That* is what people *think* happens here in the office every day." He laughed and noted that folks probably also think the Bills' "Shout" song plays continually on a loop as well.

A quick note to any young children reading this book: This was not the real "Billy Buffalo"; it was just one of his helpers.

A quick note to die-hard Bills Fans: The Shout song *does* play continuously on a loop.

Pardon my swaying off topic just a moment longer, but can't resist one more mascot story. One December day, on the Mile High Stadium field in Denver, Paul Lancaster and I had finished our pre-game ritual and began walking off the field toward the elevators to the Press Box. Just then, the Broncos mascot, a crazy horse dressed in a Santa suit, came flying by on some kind of motorized sled-like vehicle and yelled "Hey, Don Purdy!" I couldn't have been more confused or startled. *Was my name written somewhere? No. How in the heck, then, could the Broncos' mascot know **me**?* He stopped the vehicle, looking back at me, appearing to wonder why I didn't reply. He then came back toward me as I'm really beginning to freak out and, in a loud whisper so as not to let anyone overhear him, said, "It's *me*, Brad."

It was our former mascot, Brad Post, the original "Billy Buffalo", who I'd completely forgotten went to Denver. If you summoned a group of Bills folks who knew Brad, we could easily collaborate on a most entertaining collection of stories about this fellow. A super smart and athletic guy who once won a "Mr. Six" contest at Darien Lake Theme Park - the elderly, thick-glasses wearing advertising character for the Six Flags campaign who could dance like a madman.

Player Engagement and Security Directors hold frequent, mandatory seminars to teach rookies "the way of the League" and, equally important, "the way of the team." The topics range from financial management, dealing with law enforcement, social media, and yes – even how to drive in the snow! *Don't grip the wheel too tight – don't **over** drive.* Since this topic isn't usually addressed until December, the 2006 Rookie Class found themselves uninformed and a bit blindsided on October 12, 2006 – more than *two whole months* before the official start of winter.

Keith Ellison, a California native, was one of these oh-so-lucky rookies in 2006. Keith shared his memory of the Storm:

> *The morning of the storm I was awakened by a phone call from my position coach, Matt Sheldon, telling me that meetings had been pushed back because of the storm. I was thinking, "What storm?" Going to bed the night before, I remember[ed] seeing the stars out. So, I was kind of puzzled we had to postpone meetings because of a storm. After I hung up the phone, I looked out the window and couldn't believe how much snow had fallen. It was an amazing sight! To see snow piled up to the bumper of my car was quite a shock. I didn't know what to do. I've never driven in the snow, didn't have a snow shovel, and almost was completely helpless.*
>
> *Luckily my neighbors were very nice and helped dig my car out and gave me a few tips on driving in the snow so I could get to practice later. But before I*

left I took some pictures of the snow on my phone and sent them [to] my friends back home. They couldn't believe it any more than I could. This was my first year with the team and I had only been in Buffalo for a few months at this time. [I'd] heard that it snowed in Buffalo but I never expected it to snow that much in one night and in October nonetheless! I grew up in Los Angeles and the only time [I'd] seen snow [was] when I went snowboarding. I was fortunate that I had not lost power or had any problems at my apartment. The only problem I had was getting used to seeing all that snow. So it was quite a morning for me and one I will never forget.

Another rookie player, **Ryan Neill,** received a call from his Defensive Line Coach, **Bill Kollar**, that was far less diplomatic than the one Keith received from his more soft-spoken coach, Matt Sheldon. If you were ever walking toward a Bills practice without yet being able to see the field, you would likely hear one voice stand out over the rest - it would be that of Bill Kollar. He projected a baritone roar that left no doubt what he *really meant*. This is not to suggest that other coaches, with more low-key styles, were not as committed or knowledgeable at all. It's just that Kollar's signature style was **volume**. And he happened to be a heckuva good defensive line coach. When asked about that morning, Ryan remembered:

I usually get up at about 6:00 am to do some reading. That morning at about 6:30 or so, my phone rang and it was Coach [Bill] Kollar. Bill told me that practice was being moved to noon and I seriously didn't know why. Coach, in his typical boisterous style, barked, "Hey, have you looked out the window, you dumbass?"

So, sure enough, I tried to open my front door, but there was too much snow.

It should be noted that Ryan pulled a GPA in the high 3's at Rutgers and was also smart enough to learn and master another position, Long Snapper, to make himself even more valuable to the Bills and extend his NFL career. Once again, those who know Coach Bill Kollar know and appreciate his tongue-in-cheek *tough talk* that he applies to all his players.

Starting Guard **Brad Butler** was drafted in the 4ᵗʰ round of that 2006 season from the University of Virginia. He grew up in the Hill City of Virginia, Lynchburg, so aside from an occasional light snowfall, he'd had little exposure to what Northerners would call "real snow" prior to 2006. He reflected on this:

*Coming from the south, I had rarely seen snow, so for me to witness a snow storm of **that raw power** was very new to me. I was warned early and often in my career about the perilous storms that Western New Yorkers face. So, I was actually not that surprised that it happened, just **when** it happened.*

Nothing about **Fred Jackson's** NFL journey was traditional. Fred had just joined the team's practice squad after playing in NFL Europe earlier that year. His wife hadn't yet joined him in Buffalo until – you guessed it – *that* week. This rough beginning was a fitting foreshadowing of the obstacles Fred would come to face and overcome during his NFL career. He played Division III at little-known Coe College where the great Marv Levy also attended. When Marv returned to the Bills organization in 2006 to serve as General Manager, he was made aware of Fred playing overseas in NFL Europe. He asked John Guy to sign him to the 90-man roster, for a chance - albeit a long shot - to compete for a 53-man roster spot. Fred surprised and impressed decision-makers enough to earn his way onto the Practice Squad.

It's an understatement to say that Fred made the most of his opportunity. He would become the Bills 3rd All-time Rusher - second only to OJ Simpson and Thurman Thomas. His production made it possible to trade Marshawn Lynch to Seattle and not pay what would have been an enormous 2nd contract. When the Bills spent a first round pick on Clemson star CJ Spiller, Fred upped his game even more. Spiller was plenty productive himself, but Fred continued to lead the back field and, as I often witnessed in our One Bills Drive complex, Fred mentored CJ as a player and a pro. In the building, CJ hardly carried himself as one might expect a highly touted 1st Round draft pick to act. He was most respectful to everyone, ie. "Yes ma'am, yes sir." and didn't think he was above some "rookie stuff" like picking up pay stubs from my office for the other Running Backs. He'd say their names out loud as an oral checklist and when he got to Fred he'd say, "Gotta take care of Fred because Fred takes care of me." Had Fred not suffered a season-ending injury mid-way through the 2011 season, he may well have earned the NFL MVP award that year. Fred never forgot his humble beginnings, was tremendously active in the Buffalo community, and was, is, and always will be a fan favorite.

With all that said about him, it's no surprise that Fred was promoted to the active roster during the week of the October Storm so naturally *this* would be the week his wife gave birth to their first child.

Shane Costa is an NFL Player Agent and an attorney whose humble beginnings in pro sports trace back to the Bills Ticket Office – exactly like mine did:

> *My experience with the 2006 "October Storm" was quite a bit different, I'm sure, than many who live in the Buffalo area. At the time, I was attending SUNY*

Fredonia located in a small college town about 45 minutes southwest of Buffalo. On the morning of October 13ᵗʰ, 2006, I was scheduled to work at 9:00 am for the Buffalo Bills Ticket Office. My supervisor, Natasha Moody, called me at about 7:00 am to let me know that, in her words, "Work is obviously cancelled." With a somewhat incredulous voice, I asked "Why? Are the roads bad"? Natasha, sounding equally incredulous that I even asked such a question, replied back: "Shane, have you looked out your window yet this morning?" While still on the phone, I opened the curtains and saw nothing but green grass and a chilly but otherwise normal, October Friday morning. She then explained that Buffalo had been hit by a huge winter storm the night before, and that almost everyone was without power. I had recalled that Fredonia had a few flurries the night before, but obviously had nowhere near the same amount of snowfall. We had gotten pretty lucky, because the line where the snow hit was only about ten minutes or so north of Fredonia.

Since work was cancelled, I turned my phone on silent and decided to sleep in. I was to travel home to Allegany, NY, later in the afternoon to attend my older brother's wedding rehearsal, as he was getting married the following day. Later that afternoon, I looked at my phone and realized I missed a few calls from my Mom. I finally called her back, and she sounded nervous and worried, asking if I could get back in time for the wedding and if I needed any assistance getting home. I had to explain to her that Fredonia didn't get hit with any snow, and that I would be able to drive home and make everything on time.

At the rehearsal dinner that night, my brother laughingly told me that they were starting to plan to come get me in a 4x4 truck and snowmobile so that I was able to make the wedding on time, as travel had been an obvious disaster in Buffalo. I was pretty lucky to dodge the bullets from the storm, and we still laugh about [the] "missing groomsman" that almost was.

Let me brag about Shane right here; I first met Shane when he, as a Ticket Office intern, emailed me requesting an in-person meeting. He'd even obtained permission from his supervisor, Pat Mathews, to make the connection; he did the same for John Guy and Paul Lancaster. While these steps were not necessary, it showed a high level of respect that we appreciated. When he first came to my office, he appeared nervous but driven to ask if he could help with any salary cap related work. It just so happened that I kept a spreadsheet on league-wide rookie pay as a tool to help negotiate with agents. For example, if the 12th pick in the 4th round received a bonus of $X last year, then the player selected in the same pick/same round this year should be paid in the range of Y% more. Anything above or below market sets the tone, the standard for all the other picks. Not just by a team, but by all the teams in the league by staying within the limits of the League-allowed Rookie pool. These contract offers were not allowed to be "slotted" or it would have invited collusion charges by the Players Union, but rarely did a drafted player get paid less than the player selected after him. It's just the way it worked.

Jim Overdorf taught me how to use this tool, but we kept our own spreadsheets independently. After setting the formulas, it became mostly data entry. After meeting with John and Paul, we felt like we could trust Shane with this and perhaps some other tests. He nailed my project and everything else we threw at him and eventually he'd earned a two-year Graduate Assistantship with the

Bills. Before going any further, the lesson Shane's journey reinforced for me was: _it never hurts to ask._ Otherwise, once again from Pink Floyd's Dark Side of the Moon, to sit idle and wonder yields only, "All you touch and all you see - is all your life will ever be."

When Shane moved upstairs to work with us, he got initiated quickly. Every year, we played one regular season game in Toronto. For only a two-hour bus ride north of the border, it was a huge logistical and administrative lift - especially considering we would need five buses to do the job. We were far from exempt from the strict rules of border patrol. We tasked Shane with collecting all passports from the players and coaches to then bring them to my office where they were stored in my combination safe. The players were given a memo by Paul Lancaster on that Monday to bring them in by Wednesday so Shane collected about 80% by Wednesday, and another 15% or so by Thursday, but on Friday there were _still_ a few players who hadn't turned them in - and travel day was Saturday. Ryan Fitzpatrick, our starting Quarterback, was one of them. Problem was – Ryan _insisted_ that he'd given it to Shane. Shane was a hot mess. He turned his office upside down. We went through the collected passports multiple times, in case it was caught inside another. Nothing. All he could imagine was the Head Coach being told that our starting quarterback would be unable to cross the border – _because of him!_ Saturday, travel day, came. Shane sat with me at the check-in table, hoping and praying that Ryan had his passport with him. As Ryan approached, he casually tossed his passport on the table and winked. I thought Shane was going to pass out from relief.

I can totally relate to this paralyzing torment. When we played a regular season game in London in 2015, _I_ was assigned responsibility for the players' and coaches' passports. When we departed the plane in London after a red-eye Charter, one prominent defensive player _insisted_ that he'd given me his passport on the plane, only it was no joke: he _really did_ think he gave it to me. It was an actual nightmare

I'd had days before the trip that really came true. After nearly two hours that felt like two days of searching, including the airline disassembling every nut and bolt of the player's plane seat, team buses gone to the hotel, and being told by authorities that we had to pay £2,000 pounds just for the *opportunity* to make our case before Parliament, the player's passport spilled from an upper-zipped pocket of his suitcase onto the floor. I, like Shane, almost passed out from relief. As the player shrugged and chuckled, "How 'bout that? There it is."

Shane, not surprisingly, went on to become a fine lawyer that our current startup company, Avrij Analytics, has consulted with regarding contract language and other advice. As an NFL player agent, Shane was one of just six chosen by the NFL Players Union to complete a written exam that all agents would need to take every two years. Shane scored so highly that he tested out - for life!

The Bills selected Tight End **Kevin Everett** in the 3rd round of the 2005 NFL Draft out of the University of Miami. As an especially early riser, he didn't need the call from his position coach, Charlie Coiner, to be alerted to the conditions outside that morning on Friday the 13th. Kevin told us, "I like to rise a little early to get things going and my blood flowing, so I took it upon myself to peep outside and WHOA." He paused for a moment and went on to say, "What. Is. *This*? **What** *is going on here? I am barricaded in.*"

Moments after trying to make sense of the most unfamiliar landscape outside, Kevin's phone rang again. This time it was **Roscoe Parrish,** Bills receiver and Kevin's former teammate at the University of Miami, who lived a few miles away and was clearly panicked. Roscoe, who had gone to bed at 10:00 pm without a clue about the weather, awoke to a phone call from his Receivers Coach, Tyke Tolbert. Roscoe's first instinct was to call Kevin, who had an Escalade, making clear to Kevin that he wanted NO part of driving in those conditions.

Kevin had done *some* Buffalo winter driving the previous year

(2005) when, then Tight End Coach, Mike Miller gave him some most helpful pointers that Kevin remembers using successfully on the Route 5 Skyway one day: approaching a hairpin turn exit too fast as he was heading into Downtown Buffalo, Kevin could hear Mike's voice saying, "Pump the brakes. Pump the brakes." Employing this method helped Kevin avoid crashing into the concrete barriers "by centimeters" and provided a driving lesson he'd never forget. With this experience and having just put new tires on his Escalade, he agreed to pick up Roscoe, but told him, "Be fully dressed and ready to go because, dude, I'm just inching through this parking lot right now."

After the successful pickup, it was show-time. Kevin admits:

> *I was extremely paranoid during the drive, but somehow, I maintained my focus to get us to One Bills Drive safely. It was definitely a bizarre, new experience for me. I was blown away by Mother Nature that day. Roscoe cracked jokes (as he is prone to do) the whole way there about all the snow and ice, I think that took the edge off me while I was driving... I think. Hey, we got there safely.*

The South Floridians discussed when and where they'd ever seen snow before. Roscoe contended that it was from a bus while playing at Syracuse, but Kevin seemed a bit more sure that it was at Boston College in 2003 - either way, having safely pulled into One Bills Drive that afternoon, a relieved and impressed Roscoe gave major props to Kevin for his driving by noting, "It was a crazy ride, man!" and that despite being nervous to drive it on his own, Kevin drove like he "*owned* it."

Every Bills fan remembers the national story about Kevin Everett that occurred one year later on Opening Day of the 2007 season versus Denver; Kevin collided with a Broncos player in such a way that he lay paralyzed on the field for about thirty minutes. It was a freakish, life-threatening football accident that resulted in the Bills Team Doctors, Andrew Cappuccino and John Marzo, employing emergency treatment on the field and continuing as he was being taken out. Kevin was flown to Erie County Medical Center where Dr. Cappuccino, after consulting with another prominent doctor in the same field, who just happened to be his wife, employed a seldom-used procedure that lowered the patient's body temperature to a dangerously low level. This reduced Kevin's swelling long enough to stabilize the paralyzed area, thus enabling Dr. Cappuccino and surgeon, Dr. Kevin Gibbons, to perform a four-hour, life-saving surgery.

The next morning (Monday), Doctors Cappuccino, Marzo, and Gibbons held a much anticipated news conference to update the public on Kevin's status. As a staff, we hung on every word as we watched on our office televisions. The news was sobering. While the doctors had successfully reset the fractured spinal dislocations, Kevin was being kept in a drug-induced state to keep the swelling in check and a respirator was needed to help him breath. Dr. Cappuccino was bluntly honest to assess that even if Kevin progressed through this dangerous phase, his prognosis for ever walking again was bleak.

As the person who managed Worker's Compensation at the Bills, this case entered very unfamiliar territory for me. The expenses were unlike anything I'd ever seen for medical care, but our owner, Mr. Wilson, made clear through our treasurer, Jeff Littmann: "Do not hold back a dime on *anything* needed for Kevin's treatment." It's what we came to expect from Mr. Wilson as this was his general sentiment regarding the health of all our players and staff. For Kevin's situation, this included traveling back and forth from Buffalo to Houston for surgeries and even to and from different parts of Texas on an "Ambulance Plane." I got to know the folks at Houston's Memorial Hermann Hospital quite well as they called me for approval every time they entered a new phase of this most unusual treatment. As per Mr. Wilson's decree, my answer, after consultation with the trainers, was always the same: "Yes."

On December 23, 2007, less than four months after his death-defying injury, Kevin gingerly, but triumphantly, walked onto the Ralph Wilson Stadium field to thunderous applause from the crowd. I doubt there were many dry eyes in the stands of The Ralph that day. There was certainly not a dry eye amongst our staff.

Kevin and Dr. Cappuccino would later appear on the Oprah Winfrey Show to share the amazing details of their story. A lengthy Sports Illustrated article praised the efforts of Player Engagement Director Paul Lancaster and VP of Community Relations Gretchen Geitter, primarily for how they worked with the wonderful, but devastated Everett family, including his then-fiance, Wiande. Led by Head Trainer, Bud Carpenter, the Bills Training Staff of Greg McMillen, Shone Gipson, and Chris Fischetti, was also recognized nationally and by the NFL for their instinctively precise decision-making in stabilizing and safely transporting Kevin to the hospital. During a phone conversation with Dr. Cappuccino, he quipped, "The two most important decisions I've ever made in my life were how to deal in that moment with Kevin and... asking my wife to marry me. Both worked out as I'd hoped!"

Reaching out to Kevin privately, first through Facebook then by text, for his memories about the October Storm, he seemed very happy to not only re-connect, but also to talk about something regarding his Bills experience *other* than his injury. Sensing through the series of back and forth messages that he was interested in perhaps hearing more about his adopted hometown of Buffalo, I asked if he would have a Zoom meeting with us to which he quickly agreed.[13]

Billy and I, in an unspoken agreement, had no intentions of bringing up Kevin's life-altering accident. However, after simply asking about his family - specifically his wife, Wiande and his four daughters - Kevin opened up about everything, including his 2007 injury. He stated that 2020 was especially tough due to just having to stay inside and having some family affected by Covid-19, including losing his grandfather.

Regarding how he keeps busy, Kevin notes "I was thrust into that whole life of being a motivational speaker. I'm naturally a shy guy, [and] have always kept to myself, but God had a purpose for me to share that testimony with people."

He clearly did not view this as an unwelcome burden. His positivity, including his sense of humor was abundantly genuine. Affirming to him that he is consistently viewed by Buffalonians in that regard, I suggested that he would be an excellent guest on former Bills Center, Eric Wood's, podcast. Both he and Eric liked the idea and seemed determined to make it happen.

Billy asked him his route to the office that morning which took us down a rabbit hole, one that Kevin nostalgically enjoyed telling about the businesses he frequented during his Bills tenure, most notably savoring a milkshake at Taffy's in Orchard Park as Billy does the same thing when he comes back into town. Kevin nearly got choked up recalling how Buffalo embraced him and how, for at least one full season, he got to fulfill his dream of playing in the NFL:

> I was SO excited about being there, man. Preseason and Training Camp went so well. [Offensive Coordinator] Steve Fairchild had planned for me to be a big part of the offense that year. [...] But then it was like the rug was just snatched from under me.

Given his level of comfort discussing his injury and his natural sense of humor, I shared a story about that home opener game against Denver. I had given my two complimentary tickets to our young neighbor friend, Tom Cavanagh, Jr. and his father, Tom. Young Tom was a football-aholic. He loved watching, playing fantasy, and of course *playing* the game of football. His mom, Lisa, however, was not too keen on her son *playing* the sport. When Kevin sustained the injury in front of their eyes at that game, Tom and Tom, Jr. both agreed, *We shall not speak of this to your mother.*

When they came home from the game, Lisa asked them how everything went. Assuming (and hoping) that she was tending to her garden on that beautiful Sunday afternoon instead of watching the game, they each said something to the effect of, "Was a good game. Loved the start [as there's usually a goose-bump inducing flyover just before kick-off], but what a tough way to lose at the end."

Lisa asked, "But what about that young man that got hurt so badly?"

They looked at each other quizzically, "What do you mean? What injury?"

Lisa responded forcefully, "I'm not stupid! They stopped the game for a **half hour** with an ambulance in the middle of the field!!!"

… Oops. *Busted.*

Kevin got a kick out of that story. We wrapped up the conversation by talking about some miscellaneous fun points like Paul Lancaster's Super Bowl ring with the Eagles, of which I sent him pictures just before the call. Kevin, now sporting a beard of his own, acknowledged Paul's "playoff beard" during that Eagles' 2017 run, admitting that Paul's had him beat in length, but Paul's was also grayer - a trade he'd take on balance. All jokes aside, the one sentiment Kevin wanted to leave us with was his appreciation for his adopted hometown: *"I loved Buffalo. LOVED it. The energy, the people, great experience that I think about often still."*

A few other Bills' players also thought back on and shared brief, but noteworthy experiences with that memorable Friday the 13th:

Rookie Linebacker **John DiGiorgio** was a Michigan guy. Despite this, John said he'd never experienced any such weather like this in his entire life. John, like so many others, had no idea any storm was supposed to occur, so his first knowledge, like so many others, that something strange was happening was when his phone rang at 6:00 am Friday morning. On the other end of the line was Coach Chuck Lester who was asked by Head Coach Jauron to call all players to inform them that practice was being pushed back until noon. Finding out practice was delayed was about the closest thing that would ever resemble a "snow day" in the world of the NFL, however even rarer in that everyone knows weather very rarely has any effect on a game or practice. Looking out his window, John immediately understood why practice was delayed. Though he was from the northern part of Michigan in Macomb and played his college ball at Saginaw Valley State in Michigan, he had never seen storm damage like this before in his life. He carefully ventured a short distance to Target to buy candles and was without power in his apartment for four days.

Rookie Cornerback **Ashton Youboty** was born in the Republic of Liberia on the west coast of Africa, known for lush tropical rain forests and one of the hottest equatorial climates on the globe. He and his family moved to Houston, Texas, before playing his college football at Ohio State, but not even his four years in Columbus could help Ashton acclimate to what he experienced in October of 2006. Unaware that the loss of electricity disabled the sump pump, Ashton suffered major basement flooding in the West Seneca home that he'd purchased just one month earlier. While he was looking forward to soon coming off the Bills Injured Reserve list to play again, not traveling to Detroit that weekend provided an opportunity to address the issues with his new home which was at least *one* silver lining.

Wide Receiver **Josh Reed** lost power at his home as the storm blew in. Above and beyond the normal problems that causes, Josh's car was in his garage and the door was stuck shut. Once he remedied this situation with a generator, Josh hosted Bills players and staff to help get their minds off the chaos, including Paul Lancaster and his family, who lived just down the street.

Lee Evans, a starting Wide Receiver for the Bills, suffered damage to his chimney, but was fortunate to escape any more damage to his house from the trees that fell on his property.

For Defensive Tackle **John McCargo**, the storm made life especially miserable. Five days prior, John broke his leg playing against the Bears in Chicago. It required surgery and then, of course, the dreaded crutches. Nearly killing himself trying to get around on the crutches in the snow, he finally decided it was just easier to stay home.

Linebacker and Special Teams standout **Josh Stamer** reflected on the differences between the various places he's lived and played as compared to Buffalo, and well, there aren't a lot of comparisons according to him:

> *Growing up in Iowa, going to The University of South Dakota, I thought I knew about snow. Little did I know it would take moving to Buffalo to **really** know about snow. I've never seen that much snow fall in that short period of time, that early in the year. I remember driving around days or weeks later thinking, this is going to take many years to recover from. BUFFALO STRONG!!*

Bills Scout, **Matt Hand** (now with the Raiders), left town the day before the storm. Matt remembered

> *I had just flown down to New Orleans on Oct 11th to visit my college buddies and to scout my alma mater Southern Miss game vs Houston that coming weekend. It was a significant trip because most of my friends were still rebuilding their homes which got destroyed from Hurricane Katrina just little over a year prior to my trip. A few of my friends who stayed glued to The Weather Channel because of Katrina*

kept telling me "You need to see what's happening in Buffalo right now!" I immediately called my neighbor in Cheektowaga NY who rented out half the duplex I was renting out from someone on the Bills' staff. His roommate confirmed, "We have no power and the street is blocked with fallen trees." I ended up delaying my flight back to Buffalo a few days. When I got back home, I recall most the snow had melted but trees were down everywhere with massive damage. We did not have power back into my duplex until early November! I ate, showered, and, on real cold nights, slept at One Bills Drive until I got power back. It is a memory I won't ever forget.

So, as Coach Jauron and Security Director Chris Clark sent driver Bob Schultz out on the treacherous roads to safely bring back as many players and coaches as possible, the Bills Stadium Operations still had their hands full with an office building without power, impassable roads, and severe damage to the practice facility that posed problems never before experienced.

SEVEN
THE SHOW MUST GO ON

DEB DRISCOLL'S RISKY DRIVE OVER FLAMING LIVE ELECTRICAL wires and through two feet of unplowed snow over the infamous Skyway to (barely) get to One Bills Drive served to reinforce the NFL narrative, "The ball **will** be kicked off Sunday at One." As Marv noted in his foreword, hosting a home game was not the challenge this time, but rather dealing with a major disruption of operations, restoring a practice facility and work place, safe transport for the players, and most importantly, regrouping in one short day to travel to Detroit.

When our Punter, better known as Brian Moorman, received his phone call about delaying practice from Special Teams Coach Bobby April, he used the opportunity to shore up his home. Brian's memory of that day was crystal clear - as it was also filled with shock:

> *We knew we had the backup on the sump pump, but we had no idea how long the power would be out knowing that it was out in the entire area. With that in mind, we also had no idea how long the battery would last. That couple[d] with a freezer full of food, I figured I should get a generator first thing in the morning if I had time. I went to work as usual. It took me about 20 minutes to get there with the way the*

roads were, and it usually only takes about 7-10. As I was pulling into the stadium I was called and told we would be pushing practice back until noon to allow for guys to get in safely. This was perfect. It was about 6:45 am, so I figured I would run to Lowes really quick and get a generator. I had no idea that there would not be a single generator available in all of Western New York by the time I decided I wanted one. It blew my mind.

*I figured I would try Arthur's in Orchard Park, since it was on my way home. You never know right? Nothing. Except I was about to experience the reason why people love Western New York, and why people move back after they have been gone. Dave Archibald, who many know, works there at Arthur's, and walked over to me to explain that there was no chance of finding a generator anywhere nearby. He must have been able to tell I was a little concerned because then he said, "Why don't you use mine?" As I tried to decline, he insisted that he never lost power and that he probably won't so it's no big deal. I couldn't believe it. Here was a guy I didn't even know offering to let me use his generator even though there was surely someone he knew better that might need it. Not to mention, when I returned it to him it turned out he did lose power that day, and didn't even ask for it back. **That** is the kind of generosity we heard about all weekend, and I'll never forget being on the receiving end of it. More importantly, I will always go to Arthur's first before I go anywhere else, for anything.*

Coincidentally, the Buffalo Sabres NHL Hockey team arrived in Detroit for their game versus the Red Wings on Thursday night, *before the storm*. According to Sabres VP of Marketing **John Livsey**, while at their Detroit Hotel, news of the Storm back home, including the scarcity of generators, reached the team. This prompted Team President Larry Quinn to purchase generators for all the players so that their families would have power while the team was traveling. It's impossible to quantify how external, off-field factors affect how a team plays. Talent, coaching, and execution will always win the day while some luck, good or bad, can't be discounted; but one would like to think that this generous gesture by Larry Quinn had something to do with leading the Sabres to a win over Detroit on Friday the 13th in a shootout after a scoreless 3rd period.

Kevin Sylvester, who had just joined the season before to co-host the Sabres' Television broadcast, has vivid memories of managing the roles of father, husband, and broadcaster. We reached out to Kevin who graciously responded with his captivating story in a voice recording which we kept true to his radio personality and matching voice:

> *The first thing I remember is the transformer blowing in my neighborhood and that sound and then everything going completely dark on that Thursday night. And I remember going outside, just to take an assessment of things because everything was dark, and I remember standing in the sidewalk in front of my house and everything was pitch black. All you could hear was the hum of a few generators and the cracking of trees and to me, it felt like the bones of the trees were breaking, right? I mean everything was just cracking and [I] heard it repeatedly, one crack after another, one bone going after another. One tree being broken and broken. So that part was just eerie, I'll never forget that sound standing out there in that darkness and hearing that go.*

Then the next day came and, you know, working for the Sabres on the television broadcast and also having to produce the broadcast, the team was on the road, they were in Detroit and I figured, "Ok, well, they're in Detroit, no one has power, we're not doing this." And we were back and forth on the phone, whether or not we can do it - should we do it, can we do it - and our Managing Partner, Larry Quinn, I remember him calling me and said, "Hey, we're doing the show, I need you to get there." and [Kevin now laughing] I remember arguing with him, I think mostly because I looked over at my wife and my two young kids thinking, "Why are we doing this?" I had two kids under the age of five at home, my wife, no power - I didn't have a generator. He said, "No, we need to do this - our fans need us. We need to give people that distraction, the diversion" So that's what we did.

So I gave 'em a hug goodbye and told my wife it would be OK and I got in my car and was driving to our studio in North Buffalo, it's about a twenty-minute drive - everything in Buffalo is - so you know I took the 33 Expressway. Nobody was on it, I mean nobody. I think I was the only car going in, it was dark, 'cause it's the fall, and I remember getting off at Scajaquada and pulling up near Delaware Park and I said, "I'm gonna roll my windows down." Just the dead silence of everything and seeing all the tree limbs down, I mean all those great trees that line the Scajaquada like Delaware Park and just to see all these limbs down was sad. It was sad and apocalyptic - it looked like a ghost town. And then I got off, the Studios were on Elmwood Avenue, [...] again everything is dark and

pulled in station - we had power, obviously with a
generator, and I go in the studio and we pretty much
had a full crew, which was astonishing to me - that we
all found a way to get in and just sharing how things
were in our neighborhoods.

With the power outage being so wide spread, few in Buffalo would be able to watch their favorite hockey team play that night. Because it was his job, WGR 550's, Mike Schopp, found a way: "We were still using a generator to watch [the] Sabres-Red Wings [game]. The Sabres won in a shootout. Right before the winning goal my phone rang, which I predicted was my sister, Kim, calling to tell us they had won. I was right; her TV was a few seconds ahead for some reason, I guess."

That Saturday night, after winning the previous night in Detroit, the Sabres hosted the New York Rangers. The Rangers were scheduled to fly into Buffalo the day before, but were unable to because of the Storm. Instead, they flew in the morning of the game, then hurriedly suited up to play that evening. Sabres' Head Coach Lindy Ruff, understandably, did not expect many fans to show up, but to his surprise, it was nearly a sell-out crowd. Kevin wasn't sure the game against the Rangers would even happen, noting:

Watching the game [in Detroit], leaving [after the
broadcast] and saying, "Ok, we'll see if we play at home"
I mean, Detroit didn't have the issue, Buffalo did.
I remember the next day, [the day of the Rangers
game,] there was no morning skate, that the players,
you know, stayed home to take care of their families.
We went and did the game, it was kinda the same
thing: help hold down the fort at home and then leave
to go to work. And of course, people showed up to
the game! They made their way down there to watch

*the Sabres - I don't even remember who we played
on that Saturday night - I remember it was Detroit,
but I have no idea who we played on that Saturday.
Like, I remember we played San Jose the first game
after Flight 3407[5], now that brought the community
together, but I forget who we played on the October
Storm, and I could look it up, but it doesn't matter - I
just remember how good it was to see people and see
that we all made it through the storm, and I don't even
remember if we won or lost - either game, frankly, and
it still doesn't matter to me to this day - it's not what
I remember from it.*

*Then oddly enough, Sunday it was finally, I
looked at my wife like "OK - we somehow need to find
a generator." My father, who also lives in Lancaster,
procured one for me and I remember getting it hooked
up the next day afternoon, apologizing to my wife
and kids that Daddy had to work and then I get the
generator humming, we hook up the fridge, we get the
sump pump hooked up to it, and literally twenty-five
minutes later the power comes back on.*

At One Bills Drive, the logistical and communications issues
were still being dealt with, but unlike the Sabres' downtown Arena,
the Bills practice facility had sustained damage to the roof, which

---

[5] Colgan Air Flight 3407 was a connector flight from Newark, NJ to Buffalo,
NY which operated as a Continental Connection Flight for Continental
Airlines on February 12th, 2009 that subsequently crashed into a home in
Clarence Center, NY just 5 miles away from the end of the runway where the
plane was headed. It is believed that the cause of the crash was a result of the
pilot not responding properly to warnings that the plane was stalling, resulting
in the death of all 49 people on board, including all passengers and crew, as
well as one other person in the house when the plane crashed.

incidentally may have been the draft that John Guy felt overnight when he couldn't fall asleep in his office. Some of the heavy snow that crashed through the roof now lay at one end of the field. With Head Coach Dick Jauron expressing the need to hold some kind of practice, and with outdoors not being an option, it fell on VP & Manager of Operations, Joe Frandina and Perry Dix, to find a way.

EIGHT
GETTIN' 'ER DONE

ON A CRISP, SUNNY OCTOBER SUNDAY AFTERNOON IN 2007, THE
Bills hosted the San Diego Chargers at Ralph Wilson Stadium.
Just minutes before kickoff, electricity went out in the <u>entire</u>
<u>stadium</u>. All of it - the sound, the wiring, the lights, and most of the
communication. The cause could not have been more innocent. In
the parking lot, a fan in an open limo released their birthday balloon
which became entangled in electric wires, causing the entire stadium
to go dark. The ball being kicked off at 1:00 pm was in jeopardy.
Far more concerning was that 74,000 people were now trapped in
one building that had no power.

I didn't see him that day, but those who encountered Joe
Frandina, Bills VP of Stadium Operations, said he looked like he'd
seen the ghost of Michael Faraday (who invented the rubber balloon
and *yes*, I had to look that up). But Joe calmly directed his staff to
restore power, using whatever means and resources necessary, as
timely as possible. For 45 *long* minutes, including 16 minutes of
actual game time, the game proceeded most strangely in complete
silence, other than the mumbled rumblings of the crowd.

This occurred in 2007, just one year after the October Storm.
It's safe to suggest that the challenges Joe faced with the Storm a
year earlier helped prepare him for this pressure cooker situation; and
the irony of playing the "Chargers" that day was not lost on anyone.

Aside from the obstacles that faced all Western New Yorkers with the October Storm, the work that prepared Joe for that game against the Chargers was no small feat: Joe was being asked to artificially produce light and heat in an office building as well as a huge practice facility that currently had a hole in the roof and snow on the turf.

As he tried to sleep that Thursday night of 10/12/06 with heavy snow coming down, falling trees, and downed power lines in Tonawanda, Joe knew full well he'd better start preparing One Bills Drive for the same. Joe shared his memory of the morning after the Storm:

> *I called Perry [Dix] around 6:00 am to find out what conditions were like at the stadium. He reported that power was out in the region. Whenever we experience an outage, our first approach is to determine if it is site specific or regional. He also reported (by the way) about two feet of snow in some areas of the site.*

Perry was on it. He had already called in the snowplow crew, consisting of Bill Connell, Jim Willibey, Russ Zink, and Matt Gassman, earlier around 4:00 am. These Operations personnel each possessed their own unique skills and crafts (ie. architecture, electrical wiring, drywalling, carpentry, just to name a few). Joe and Perry were themselves engineers and heck, one former Stadium Operations official, George Koch, was actually a rocket scientist! But they stood on-call, ready to be called into plow duty to ensure safe ingress and egress (as long-time Bills VP Bill Munson would say) for players, coaches, and staff. While they were definitely caught off guard by this mid-October surprise, as Deb Driscoll could attest, they still found a way to break out the plows from summer storage and get it done in a timely way. Perry also reported to Joe that, with travel severely hampered, coaches and some staff were having trouble making it in.

What Joe had not counted on was his *own* commute being so difficult: "I started to make my way into Orchard Park from Tonawanda when I was turned around by police about miles from home. So, all direction and communication between me and Perry had to be done by phone." While this was not ideal, they'd make it work - as they had always done. Joe and Perry had a long history of working together, even prior to working at the Bills; in football terms, they had great chemistry.

Perry was hilarious, often in a self-deprecating way, about his very large frame and stature - we're talking "offensive lineman big." Once, after an extremely hot September game in Jacksonville, Perry, having worked the Coaches' sideline communications (headsets) system under no shade for the last four hours, walked back into our visiting locker-room, completely drenched in sweat, and declared, "There's a whole lotta Perry left out on that field." Another time, I sat directly in front of him at a company HR-sponsored Wellness seminar about nutrition and when the presenter showed the recommended portion of pasta to be about the size of a fist, Perry leaned forward and whispered, "No way. Not. Even. Close." Needless to say, it took deep restraint to control my laughter.

Joe recalled his conversations with Perry that morning, specifically what the plans were to address the main problems they were facing:

> *With our first priority being to open Bills Drive and [make] parking available to any coaches, players and staff that could make it in well under control, we turned our focus to restoring power to the facility. With the offices and player areas under emergency generator power, we needed to somehow provide lights in the*

fieldhouse so the team could continue with preparation for Sunday's game in Detroit. Our options included:

- *Find a generator large enough that could be mobilized quickly and wired up within about three hours – not likely!*
- *Hope that NYSEG has power restored in the next three hours – probably not going to happen!*
- *Provide temporary lighting – let's try it!*

We called Admar (a company we dealt with often) for any available portable lights that we could rent. Almost all of their inventory was being used on the NYS 90 paving project some twenty-five miles south of the stadium [most likely due to some of the work that Police Commander Mike Nigrelli was focusing on to get the NYS Thruways safe and functional]. Admar allowed us to borrow [what they had left] so Perry sent Jim Willoughby and Bill Connell to pick them up. At the same time, Russ Zink started to gather a handful of the portable lights we already had on site."

Leaving the longest-serving and versatile Stadium Operations staffer, Tom Christen, back to hold the fort, Bill and Jim ventured south to Springville with a truck to pick up diesel powered lights and heaters. Driving only a few miles south on Route 219, Bill remembers, "We soon found ourselves in a *completely* different climate: green grass, blue skies, and beautiful fall foliage. A different world." Driving back after successfully picking up the equipment, Bill and Jim found themselves back in that ten-mile wide zone of havoc and ready to fire up this equipment for the team. *Mission accomplished.* Joe said that within about three hours,

We had mobilized and set up at least twelve portable generated lights in the fieldhouse. Doors were opened to alleviate the exhaust smell from the gasoline generators. This, with the lack of heat due to the power being out resulted in the team practicing in cold, dim conditions. Nevertheless, Coach Jauron commented that the players actually enjoyed the practice as it reminded them of their high school days playing night games under dim lights.

Brad Butler, then Guard for the Bills, remembered the same, saying:

"They worked great. I will always remember the smell of diesel as we practiced in the field house. Since the stadium facility had no electricity, the team had to use gas powered lights to illuminate the field house for practice. There is something very humorous about fighting for breath as you go through a tough NFL practice only to breathe in toxic fumes of diesel! But we had a job to do – to play the Detroit Lions that weekend and I had my complete focus on defeating them."

While Safety **George Wilson** was frustrated by not being able to watch (game preparation) film at his home, he too was most impressed with how the Stadium Operations department "rigged up the 'big lights' that lit up the Fieldhouse so we could practice. That's called ***Gettin' 'er done!***"

If you'd expect any member of the Bills organization during that era to be a "cheerleader" that lifted everyone else around him up, it would be George Wilson. He was signed by Buffalo after being released by the Lions. George faced tough odds to make the team as a Wide Receiver given the team's strength and depth at that position, but John Guy and Defensive Backs Coach George Catavalos asked him to try converting to Safety. George immediately accepted the challenge since the alternative was to be cut. Changing positions, particularly from Offense to Defense (or vice versa) is extremely rare in the NFL as positions are so specialized, but George, given his athleticism and determination, pulled it off. In his very first start at Safety, George returned an interception for a Touchdown – a Pick Six – on a Monday Night game versus Tony Romo, Terrell Owens, and the Dallas Cowboys on National TV! I can personally recall getting choked up after that play.

George was always conscious of the needs of others. Every season, after the roster was cut down from ninety players to the league-allowed fifty-three players, the Head Coach would grant Liz Malstrom, our HR Director at the time, and me fifteen minutes (not sixteen) to address the team. Deb Driscoll always kept us in the schedule from year to year to lock in this time for us. The Head Coach would open the meeting, followed by brief comments by Paul Lancaster who then turned it over to me and Liz. We had it scripted down to the minute. I explained to players how to get paid, which always kept their attention, and how to handle their football-related injuries as Workers Comp cases. Liz would then enroll them, their families, and dependents in the personal health insurance program. Again, this happened all in fifteen minutes as the Special Teams Coach (Danny Smith, Bobby April, Bruce DeHaven, or Stan Kwan) would stand in the corner chomping at the bit to jump into their 8:15 am meeting. Time was of the essence. Every second counted.

One year, at the start of the meeting as we were passing out important printed handouts. George instinctively grabbed a stack of papers and started handing them out to players. This is not to say the other players were not polite or attentive, they most certainly were, but George always went the extra step. At the conclusion of the meeting, it was typical to hear George yell, "Thanks, Don. Thanks Liz."

As stated earlier, players picked up their paychecks in my office every Wednesday morning. Sometimes, if running close to a meeting, they'd hastily forget to take their personal items. One day, a devotional book was left behind. I opened the front page and the inscription read "George Wilson." The next day I told George in the cafeteria that he'd left it in my office. He said, "Thanks. But keep it. I must have left it there for a reason." For the record, I did read it and was positively influenced by many of the lessons.

Kicker **Rian Lindell** also remembers that day of practice in the dark: "It was something different – it kind of broke up the monotony of how a regular practice usually goes for a kicker. With the darkness, I had no idea whether some of my kicks were landing on unexpecting players. I don't think it happened, but if it did, I was just doing my job." (I would become the direct recipient of this myself two days later, but that will be shared soon enough…)

So Joe, Perry, Bill Connell, and the Operations Staff had done it. It wasn't pretty, but they restored just enough functionality at the facility to give Dick Jauron's team one valuable, productive practice before a road game. Driver Bob Schultz had delivered several players from their homes in terrible driving conditions. Only one player, Long Snapper **Mike Schneck**, could not be "rescued", mostly because he lived in Snyder, not a short jaunt in good conditions from the Stadium in Orchard Park, that was only worsened by the Storm; he said,

> *Trees were crashing on our house all night, no power.*
> *My son at the time was six months old with a bad*
> *cold. I was the only one that didn't make it to practice*
> *because I wouldn't leave my wife and son. At 6:00 pm,*

we were able to get on the Highway and they drove to
Pittsburgh and I stayed in a hotel west of the city for
ten days.

For the record, Mike *was* able to travel to Detroit to play the Lions before rejoining his family in Pittsburgh.

That evening, from his makeshift home in his One Bills Drive office, John Guy called his neighbor at the complex where he lived. More bad news. He was informed that there was *still* no one in or out; everyone was still stuck. So, John would spend his second night in a row in the office building.

Seeking the perspective from the Insurance side of the equation, we had the pleasure to sit down with **Mike Sirianni** who, much like Joe and Perry, spent the morning after the Storm navigating similar operational problems, except he was trying to suddenly figure out how to process thousands of claims from his home that had no power. Mike, now a Property Claims Supervisor for Erie Insurance, was a fairly green Property Claims Adjuster at the time of the Storm. When we sat down with Mike, he shared that while he had been hired at Erie in February of 2006, he was not "solo" until, you guessed it, October 1ˢᵗ - <u>less than two weeks before impact</u>; there would be no training wheels for Mike Sirianni.

Mike's memory of the Storm starts a little differently as his goal the morning of the Storm was not to focus on his *own* property damage but instead to find a way to start working. Mike worked primarily from home and without any power, those claims were not gonna process themselves! Mike said his boss was already on top of it and a "mobile response unit" aka "an RV parked in the middle of town" was already set up for them. Mike's Chevy Impala at the time was "not getting me anywhere" so his boss who had a 4x4 "got as close as he could, but I still had to hike down the street, carrying my tower - because, at least at the time, that was where everything was still." We immediately began laughing at this image of Mike walking down his street, climbing over trees and limbs, carrying a bulky computer tower, something we all agreed was about as "2006" as one could imagine, however Mike's imagery did not stop there.

We naturally asked Mike about the *types* of claims he had been working on and how he prioritized them. He noted that the properties with the most extensive damage, a process albeit somewhat subjective, had to be dealt with first, "the ones with house damage, trees on property, that sort of thing." He was clear to say that despite this triaging, the majority of the damage was basement flooding from foundations being overwhelmed by a lack of power to sump pumps as well as the incredible amount of water entering the water table as the heavy, wet snow was melting rapidly. Mike also admitted that the repetition of seeing such similar claims became a depressing blend after a while.

One memory that clearly stood out, however, was a home with basement flooding - while he said it was not unheard of to have water crawling up to the the top step, if not into the house itself, the painful part - much like Don's worries earlier on - was that *everything* in the basement was lost or destroyed beyond repair. In this one particular home, as they were surveying the water reaching the upper steps of the basement, the family's washer *floated* by. That's right - ***floated***.

We asked Mike what the worst part of dealing with these claims was and, without hesitation, he unequivocally said "the kids." He went on to share that meeting with families who had just suffered severe damage to their homes - sometimes trees knocking an entire addition right off the foundation or a large tree crashing through someone's house - but the kids, he said, "They don't understand - they don't know what's happening. All they know is that their toys and playrooms - that were often in the basements - are all gone." Mike said that Erie Insurance instructs all their claims adjusters and supervisors to carry teddy bears in their cars to give out to kids in these such occasions, with the parents' permission; he acknowledged that it's just one small thing they can do for these families in need and that the kids really appreciated it. Mike said it was very difficult talking to people who just lost everything, but they tried to focus on a person-centered approach, spending extra time on the client and their needs, making time to listen and to make sure that they felt supported. Mike said that clients, as grateful as they are, would often say to him - and still do, which he never takes the wrong way, "I hope I *never* see you again."

Naturally, as Mike has worked for Erie Insurance in the same region since he started, we began discussing the differences in the October Surprise as compared to others, especially the Snowvember Storm of 2014. He said that these were "two completely different beasts" as the 2006 Storm was more widespread and the trees were "nothing but weight." Mike kept referring to the "sheer volume of claims more than the severity" of the October Storm. He did admit that Erie Insurance customers had one advantage that also set Erie up for a disadvantage; at the time, they had *unlimited* coverage for issues like basement flooding which meant that people would often be reimbursed much more than other companies that had caps of $5,000 or $10,000, but that also meant that each of those properties needed to be inspected which led to more time delays in people getting the money they needed whereas companies with caps "they could just know how much was lost, know it exceeded the cap, and just cut a check - we had to do our best to make sure our customers were getting covered for **all** of their losses." Mike said that this has since changed and that caps are much more common, although he could not confirm nor deny that the costs to Erie Insurance were part of their motivation to implement this cap ASAP!

With the Bills Stadium Operations team having patched some form of work day together, it was now up to the travel team to ensure that players and coaches could safely navigate their way to the airport for the road game at Detroit the next day. The roadways to the airport hangar in Cheektowaga went right through the jaws of the Storm damage, much of which still hadn't yet been dealt with.

Arriving home after her soccer game,
reluctantly but graciously, Anna posed for an
innocent "snow pic" before it got real.

*The large Oak tree that fell on Don's house in
the Storm - at this point still unaware that it
was *in* his house and not just on it.*

The zombies emerge to start the "Hi view haul."

*Billy's Mom, Kate's Storm Log and Diary from her annual
scrapbook - naturally it was destined to become a book.*

*Damage around WNY captured by Buffalo News
photographers, Derek Gee and Robert Kirkham -
generously provided by Paul Maurer.*

NINE
MISSION TO MOTOR CITY

THE MORNING THAT I'D BEEN SO CONCERNED ABOUT FOR THE LAST thirty-nine hours had arrived. Having to leave my family in such a mess, with no signs that either electricity or heat would return any time soon, was tough. And oh, by the way, there was still half a tree **in our attic**!

But this was my professional duty - never had it been lost on me the awesome responsibility and trust granted to a kid who grew up in the small Adirondack town of Speculator, New York, to lead an NFL team's travel logistics. And it stands to reason that such responsibility comes with sacrifice, as does any job, but it's especially prevalent in pro sports. I missed my cousin Johnny's wedding, my grandfather's 90th birthday party, and plenty of other family events due to my job obligations.

On the flipside, some away games offered an opportunity to connect, at least briefly for an hour or two for dinner with family and friends who live near NFL cities: my sister and brother-in-law, Tracy and Scott in Pittsburgh; with my niece and nephew, Jordan and Tory, and Tory's wife Marissa in Seattle; my cousin Johnny and his wife Mel in Indianapolis; cousin Bob in Washington, my Aunt Carolyn, Uncle Doug, and Cousin Carolee in Green Bay, Tom and Laurie Orser in Denver; Uncle Johnny and Cousin John, Jr. in New England; and Cousin Leanne in Philadelphia. This does not include when my nephew Tory, this time in Arizona worked our sideline during that huge overtime win over the Cardinals after we'd moved our offices there for a week or when our neighbor Haley Bajdas in Cincinnati worked picture duty on our sidelines; as Larry did in Atlanta. I always enjoyed getting together for dinners with my October Weekend friend Anthony in Tampa and Miami. There were also ample opportunities to meet up with former Bills colleagues who'd moved on to work with other teams.

But this day's mission to Detroit was no such trip.

Incidentally, as for this trip and all the others, Amy, Anna, and Claire could not have been more supportive during this situation. Before going to our airport hangar, I made a *very necessary* detour to the stadium, with its generator-powered electricity, to shower, change into dress clothes, and charge my cell phone. While there, I sent a group email to my Weekend friends explaining what happened with the storm and regretfully informed them that we'd likely have to cancel this year's October Weekend that was now just six days away.

While we were preparing the Bills to travel to Detroit, others like Billy were just seeking some sense of normalcy without going crazy: "We spent the bulk of that first Saturday continuing to clean up whatever we could and helping neighbors as they needed it; we kept going back-and-forth, cutting between yards and carefully making large, cartoon-like steps over downed lines, but ultimately we were able to help people out and not go too, too stir crazy."

As an organization, we were very concerned about all the players making it to the airport on time. Making it back and forth to practice on Friday was one thing, but, as evidenced by Deb Driscoll's adventure, Kevin and Roscoe's wild ride, Bob Schultz's trials, and numerous other untold scary driving experiences, players now needed to travel from Orchard Park to Cheektowaga – right through the heart of the damage. Unfortunately, some of our fears would be validated.

Building in extra time, I arrived at the airport first, as was my responsibility, along with Security Director Chris Clark, Security Manager Marty McLaughlin, VP Media Relations Scott Berchtold, and VP of Business Dave Wheat – the regular early crew as per their roles. So far, so good.

Chris immediately told us about the destruction at his home and worse – the destruction at his elderly mother's home. Dave's home was also pounded and he did not foresee power being restored any time soon. Scott was leaving his wife, Pam, and young boys, Sam and Jack (then 4 and 2, respectively) in a difficult situation at their house in Hamburg. Unable to celebrate Pam's birthday that Saturday, Scott and Pam went out to dinner at David's Grille in Orchard Park two days earlier on that Thursday, the start of the Storm. They noticed the sky looked "ominous" and decided to leave the restaurant early, but, like everyone else, grossly underestimated what was to come. Shortly after getting home, the power went out so the whole family slept together in their fireplace room, with Scott waking up hourly to feed the fire. When Scott had to leave on this Saturday for Detroit, Pam said, "OK, I've got this, but do me a favor - you don't have to tell me how nice the hotel room is, or even how good your dinner was, but make sure to tell me what the hot shower feels like!" He did just that and incidentally, when they purchased their new home a few years later, they made sure to have an automatic backup generator and gas appliances, especially a hot water heater.

In a strange way it almost escaped me until that point that others had endured their own set of problems with the Storm. For the past day and a half, our family and neighbors had been, for the most part, isolated from the rest of the region as we were solely immersed in damage control. We had the battery-powered, replica mini-Coca Cola machine transistor radio on 930 WBEN constantly, but it didn't equate to talking with people *personally*.

It was a bittersweet moment. I felt particularly bad for Chris's situation, but also felt reminded that most everyone else traveling had experienced, to varying degrees, the wrath of the Storm. They, too, were leaving their homes and families behind to go on this trip. Great news came from Amy that her parents, Joy and Tony, planned to come from east of Rochester on Sunday morning to remove the tree from our roof. It was a huge relief not only because they would help take care of the worst unsolved problem left at on our home, but also because they'd provide great company to Amy and the girls while I was away. Anyone who can fulfill that for your family on your behalf is a welcomed guest.

I keep calling this travel event a "trip" for lack of a better term; it's not wrong, but a trip is often synonymous with a vacation or a getaway. In the case of an NFL road game, the "trip" boils down to a necessary, logistical function to transport an NFL team from their home city to go play another NFL team in their city – *and beat them*! It's business and the business is to go win the game. *That's it.*

Every aspect of the trip is far more comfortable and convenient than most commercial travel, and this is by design. Surely it has escaped few that most NFL players are *very* large men. The charter plane offers every passenger an open seat next to them and teams go to great lengths to make sure their players are comfortable and well-fed. During Rex Ryan's tenure, he charged me with assigning the eight players with most NFL seniority to sit in First Class. LeSean McCoy was always on the bubble, that eighth or ninth guy. But then, because of injuries or signing free agents with more seniority, I'd have to bump him back to Coach. Fully aware of the hierarchy, LeSean caught me one day in the cafeteria and asked, "Hey Purdy, where am I sitting this week?"

"Same seat. You're up (in first class) again."

"But what about when we bring Felton back?" he asked. (Jerome Felton had been with the team before and had one more year of NFL seniority).

"We haven't brought Felton back." I said.

"Yeah, but he's coming back. I'm telling ya'. So then what?" asked LeSean.

"Well, then, *he'd* be up there. If that happens. You know I will always let you guys know in advance." I said.

The next day, our Personnel Department did indeed bring back Fullback Jerome Felton. *How the heck did a player know this before me? Oh well.*

It's always funny to watch a staff member travel for the first time: they simply cannot fathom the continuous parade of food that comes by their seats. The Strength Coaches strategically arrange for this early "stockpiling" of a caloric intake necessary to prepare the players for the next day's on field battle, but the food is offered to all with no distinction made between player and staff, so staff must quickly learn to be disciplined and not accept everything that comes by. New travelers always look puzzled like, "Am I supposed to be eating all this?" It's quite amusing.

The road game, again, has one purpose - to deliver the team efficiently to the NFL city to win the game. There's a bit of an "us against the world" feeling as the visiting team certainly faces a hostile environment. When our buses pull into the visiting stadium parking lots, the gestures directed at us are often vile and/or funny. Odds are you'll see at least one guy mooning the bus every trip. Once, in Miami, a traditional looking family (Mom, Dad, and a couple of young kids) saw us coming, jumped up from their tailgate chairs, ran toward our bus, and ALL gave us the middle finger. As if that wasn't enough, all four were wearing T-shirts depicting a dolphin performing a sexual act on a buffalo. *Lovely.*

This heckling continues behind our team bench before, during, and after the game as well - and no, I'm under no illusion that Bills fans don't do the exact same.

One week very early in my career, my Ticket Office boss, Jerry Foran, asked my office mate, Paul McDonnell, and me to travel with the team that upcoming weekend to Indianapolis for the game at the Colts. We were definitely excited about the opportunity, but there was a catch, and a big one: being "new guys" there'd be an initiation of sorts in that we'd be required to sing the Bills Shout Song *on the plane. Yikes.* During the week leading up to the trip, Scott Berchtold, VP of Media Relations, stopped by our office to deliver printed lyrics of the song. Oh man, this was getting real. Marv Levy even mentioned in passing, "Hey, I heard you're traveling with us to Indy this weekend. Bring us luck." Then deviously grinned and I think even winked.

"Oh boy, even *Marv* is in on this?" I wondered.

When Paul and I got to the airport hangar, dressed in our best suits that cost $200 as opposed to the $2,000 suits the players were wearing, we braced ourselves for more ribbing about our singing assignment. Strangely, nobody mentioned it or even winked or grinned. The atmosphere was very business-like, but the butterflies in my stomach were flapping wildly. We made our way up the plane steps and into our assigned seats. Still, nobody said a word. Maybe they forgot. Maybe it was all just to scare us, which was certainly working. Feeling somewhat relieved as it appeared most had boarded, Darryl Talley walked past, leaned down, and whispered, "Make sure we can hear you in the back."

Ugh. Back to sweating it out. The flight to Indy was just over an hour, but felt like twelve hours. We were never asked to sing, but the whole joke "worked" nevertheless.

In the mid-late 1990's, even General Manager John Butler, an intimidating man of large stature, would participate in a classic gag that tormented interns on their inaugural trip: upon arriving at the private hangar, a security guard would ask the intern if they had their boarding pass. Mind you, it was a charter plane - there was no boarding pass, but interns didn't know this. They'd very nervously respond, "Um, no sir, I never received one."

Security would respond, "It was left on your desk yesterday afternoon." He'd then bring the first-timer over to GM John Butler to alert him about the problem. John would say "Son, this is the NFL. You must *always* be prepared."

John would then sigh, and instruct, "Just follow closely behind this Security Guard up the plane stairs. Do NOT make eye contact with anyone until you reach your seat. And you *should* be ok… this time."

Oh my, it was cold. Like the Burl Ives Narrator Snowman in Rudolph when he saw the Abominable Snowman, I'd shudder and turn away as it was so difficult to watch sometimes. It was pure empathy for the young person as he wondered whether he had just ruined his future in the NFL for a simple misstep – a misstep that wasn't even real. *Ouch.*

When our intern, Shane Costa, first traveled the screeners wanded over him repeatedly – each time asking him to remove a piece of clothing until he was down to his boxers and a t-shirt.

There was a "boy cried wolf" situation that once backfired on poor Kenne Pitts. Kenne was a second-year, full-time trainer who, one year earlier, had been on the receiving end of this "initiation." Having boarded the plane, he was told by a couple of colleagues who came on board after him that there was smoke emanating from the hood of his car. Kenne figured they were just pulling his leg. "C'mon guys. I'm not a rookie any more. Nice try." The problem was – his car *really was* on fire. He rushed off the plane, still skeptical, until he saw smoke and sprinted toward his car. With the help of some operations guys on the ground, they extinguished the fire. Upon return to Buffalo the next day, Marshawn Lynch gave him one of his cars to use until he purchased a new one.

In 2009, I caught a verbal lashing from starting Quarterback Ryan Fitzpatrick for being an accomplice in a prank involving per diem. By league rules, as negotiated with the Players' Union, players were required to be paid a meal allowance during necessary travel for a road game. On a typical Saturday travel day, players were fed breakfast at the stadium before their light, walk-through practice. Lunch was served on the plane, so it was then my responsibility to provide each player with the league-mandated amount which, in 2009, was $45. We paid this amount in cash for two reasons. The first reason is, the players, despite what they earned in salary, *loved* the cash. Marshawn Lynch used to kiss the envelope. TE Jonathan Stupar used to ask if it was a million dollars. Behemoth and Berkeley-educated Offensive Tackle, Langston Walker, cleverly dubbed me Don "Per Diem" to the point where he'd announce it in a rising, Michael Buffer "*Let's get ready to Rumble!*" voice whenever I walked into the locker room (unless we just lost a game); the nickname actually stuck amongst his Offensive Line mates.

(The second reason in a moment.)

One day, during the 2009 season, Center Geoff Hangartner, pulled me aside in the cafeteria. He asked if I could issue him certain bills in which the serial numbers contained multiple numbers of the same digit. On the upper right side of every bill, there is a unique eight-digit serial number, bookended by letters on each side. Needless to say, I was puzzled why that would matter. He further explained that in the back of the plane, a group of guys would play a friendly game of "liar's poker" with the bills. He pleaded for me to "set him up" to increase his chances of winning, albeit illegitimately. Geoff also promised he would pay back *EVERY* dollar to the guys at the end of the season.

I kind of laughed and said, "I don't know, Geoff," as I wasn't that comfortable being complicit in rigging the game. And frankly, I really didn't have time to scan the bills that closely. He begged me to consider it and once again, promising yet again he'd pay it all back to the "victims."

While packaging the money that week in my office, I contemplated his request. While glancing at one twenty-dollar bill, I happened to see a "stacked" one like Geoff was talking about. I thought, "Oh, what the heck." And placed it in his envelope. I did not do the same for the other twenty or the other five that made up his $45, but at least there was likely to be one winner. Besides, if every bill was a winner, guys would get suspicious pretty quickly.

When Geoff came through the airport hangar that week, I could see him trying to make eye contact with me. As I handed him the envelope, I winked. And he whispered, "Nice." I did this for the rest of the season. Just one of the three bills. It didn't take much time and I hadn't heard of any conspiracy blowback. So far, so good. until...

After one game as we departed the plane after a win at Carolina, Guard Seth McKinney asked, "Hey, Purdy, Hangartner seems to be winning our little cash game a lot. You wouldn't know anything about that, would you?"

With a "seriously?"-type head pull back and somewhat incredulous look, I shook my head, no, and mumbled something incoherent, but generally negative. It pained me not to level with him, but as long as I trusted that Geoff would pay them back, and I still did, I'd continue my part of his little scam. Over the coming weeks, others like Eric Wood, Andy Levitre, and Garrison Sanborn would ask me the same question, prompting my same, lame but apparently acceptable reaction.

Then came our final road game in Atlanta. As I walked into the full meal room at the hotel, a booming voice penetrated from the back of the room over the collective murmur.

"PURDY! PURDY!" I heard, as did everyone else, as Ryan Fitzpatrick rose from his chair and started marching toward me. With his eyes slanted and lips pressed together, he soon began pounding my chest with his index finger while growling, "I'm on to you. And. I'm so mad. *So* mad that… **that *I* didn't think of this first!**"

(For the record, and this was verified by the numerous victims of the scam, Geoff did pay them all back over the course of dinners and otherwise.)

The next season, a player naturally asked if the bills were legit; I assured him that the "funny money" was a thing of the past and that I assigned an intern, Mitch Reynolds (who later earned a Super Bowl ring as Andy Reid's closest assistant with the Chiefs in 2019), to now fill the envelopes instead of me. I also told him that, for good measure, I placed the final labels on the stuffed and <u>sealed</u> envelopes so there was zero manipulation. Clean as a whistle and even the player seemed satisfied!

These little pranks were thankfully not a regular occurrence and they happened just a few times per season. We *mostly* stuck to our routines. On these trips, Paul Lancaster and I would typically go out for dinner and a couple of drinks at a place showing College Football on TV and were always back to the hotel by about 10:00 pm. We were often joined by others who knew our moderately-priced and low-key routine. The extent of the variance was to partake in some local flavor (i.e. fish in Seattle, Cajun in New Orleans, Mexican or Southwest cuisine in Los Angeles, steak in Houston, Tex-Mex in Arizona, Cheesesteaks in Philly, Sandwiches with Fries and Coleslaw on them in Pittsburgh, and of course, barbeque in Kansas City). Walking back to the hotel after those KC barbeque indulgences, we always commented that we felt the "Kansas City meat sweats" coming on. Too much of a good thing for sure.

We'd also take in a few liquid refreshments to wash the cuisine down with. If Kevin Meganck was with us, the servers were always thoroughly tested about how and when the beer was brewed, often even scoring some taste testing. Lest they thought the quiz was over after the drinks, another round of polite interrogation awaited them about the food.

After a meal like that we'd sometimes try to walk it off so one night after a dinner in Green Bay - though I don't recall it featuring cheese - we began walking up the city street when a man in a wheelchair asked for a push. I asked, "To where?"

He replied, "Just up a few blocks." We had some time to kill and were walking anyway, so we agreed. Shortly into the walk, he mumbled something about "rolling."

I commented, "Yeah, we're rolling," not really sure why the man was stating the obvious.

Almost instantaneously, Paul shot back, "Uh, no man."

A few minutes later, the guy asked again, "Are you sure you can't roll one for me?"

Paul immediately responded again, "Uh, no bro, and this is where we part ways." At that point, it finally occurred to me what the man was asking for. Clearly Paul's "street smarts" kicked in before mine did. We always get a laugh, at my expense, about that one. I deserved it for sure.

Paul was a great friend outside the office as well. His wife, Janine, and sons came over to our house in the summer to swim, cook on the grill, and enjoy a summer cocktail. When he signed with the Eagles after being released from the Bills just three months before me, he made a point of coming to visit our house that next summer to show Amy, Anna, and Claire his spectacular Super Bowl ring and share the cool story about how Eagles ownership made the presentation. He, along with former Bills colleague, Casey Weidl, invited me to their Novacare Center facility in Philadelphia to ultimately engage the Eagles in some business with my new company, Avrij Analytics, who developed an amazing hiring and scouting AI platform.

At the Bills offices, Paul and I often found a way to inject an appropriate, private level of humor into our professional communication; one day, his office being on the other side of the building, he called my extension and said, "Tommy Boy coming at you." and quickly hung up. I was a bit thrown off, but at least knew some new player was likely coming to my office. While Paul, as Player Engagement Director, was one of the first to officially greet new Free Agents, followed by the HR Director Liz Malstrom and in later years Barb Evans, they'd then come to my office to sign up for Direct Deposit. So on this day in 2009, sure enough a large figure darkened my door and entered my office with a haircut and baby face similar to that of the late Chris Farley, only this guy was a serious-looking, chiseled mass of muscle; it was Richie Incognito. *Thanks alot, Paul for putting me at a "composure disadvantage" during my first meeting with Richie.*

Richie was not very well-known in 2009, but had achieved some notoriety, fairly or unfairly, during his time with the Dolphins. When the Pegulas took a chance on signing him back in 2015, they, Richie, and the team were well-rewarded. Teaming with the consummate professional, Eric Wood, who I've been privileged to work with in our post-Bills careers, the Bills offensive line became one of the league's best and Richie, seemingly appreciative of his second chance in the NFL, was truly a pleasure to have in the building.

After these stories of frivolity, you may be questioning the tone of the road trip. Do not. Road games were serious to the point of being militaristic in terms of planning, timing, and execution, but at this point in the week, the game planning is done so the only thing left is to transport the team from Buffalo to the opponent's city. Even with that, we grouped coaches together on the plane according to positions, so the Offensive Coordinator sat near the QB, Receivers, and Offensive Line Coach - so on and so forth.

Back to the per diem – the second benefit of the "cash in envelope" distribution was that the labels on the envelope - thanks to Celinda Santiago-Mathews for running them all those years! - were printed from the most recent flight manifest so they served as a backup method to account for everyone. If the report time was 1:30pm, at 1:20pm Chris Clark, our Security Director, would ask who we were still waiting for. I'd relay those names on the six or so envelopes remaining and verify with the airline representative that those were the same names they showed as outstanding. We'd then text Paul Lancaster and Head Trainer Bud Carpenter those names so they could call each individual. There were always some, who shall remain nameless, who pushed the envelope every trip. Some were staff who had good reasons because they were wrapping up their duties at the stadium. Some were players who, quite frankly, didn't have a good reason as ample time was scheduled for their commute from the stadium. Every Head Coach we ever had made clear to us: the doors close at 1:30 pm – or whenever that deadline was. If someone came at 1:31, they were responsible to find their own way to the NFL city. They'd be fined for missing the plane and fined again for missing the team meetings at the host city. This happened *very* rarely, but it did happen a couple times during my tenure. Once again, I will spare those guilty parties as they shall remain nameless.

A strict dress code was also in place. No media was allowed at our mostly private, very secure hangar. Perhaps the iciest stare I ever witnessed was one that Head Coach, Doug Marrone, on his first road game, leveled toward the players who were not dressed perfectly to his standards. Paul Lancaster, being in the size range of the taller players, would even bring extra ties and coats for the first regular season road game. Despite drilling the dress code rule into their heads during the week, there were always a few who didn't quite get it. Some rookies, in their defense, were so immersed in their play books that other details like this got overlooked. The dress code only came into play for those few minutes, upon arrival at the team hotel, where there was always local media present. Often, on the return trip, especially after a win, the Head Coach would allow more comfortable clothes to be worn. Part of this decision was predicated on the fact that it was dark and there was no media allowed at our airport hangar in Buffalo.

As for this most difficult travel Saturday to Detroit, by far the main concern was players driving safely and on time to the airport. If we'd had another day or two to prepare, we probably would have arranged for buses to bring players from the stadium, but the timing of the Storm didn't allow for that. We used buses in the preseason as there were ninety players on the roster, many of them rookies who didn't even have cars yet. But this was Week Six of the regular season and the 53-Man Roster had been long established. New players, knowing they made the roster, had purchased cars or bought their own from their hometowns. They also had their own homes or apartments and were at least somewhat familiar with the area, including the route to the airport, but again, on this post-storm October day, many of these roads were still not passable and many may not have had "back up" routes.

Many players, including **Jabari Greer,** were forced to take alternate roads because of the downed trees and powerlines. At the 1:30 pm deadline, there were still five or six players missing. All but Jabari came peeling into the parking lot within a few minutes of the deadline. Upon being told that Jabari was the only player not yet to arrive, Paul called him regarding his whereabouts. Jabari was panicked as his normal route was blocked, but assured Paul that he was within minutes of arriving.

Jabari was always on edge. Having to earn his way onto the roster as an undrafted rookie – long odds indeed – he never took *anything* for granted. He was a lightning fast player from a big-time College program at University of Tennessee, so it was curious as to why he wasn't drafted. He, like John DiGorgio, used this "underdog" label as a driving and motivating force to over-achieve. One time, in March, when most players are away from the facility, it was my responsibility to call those who'd earned incentive bonuses, including Performance Based Pay checks. Again, at the time, these were still hard checks, not direct deposit, so we needed proper mailing addresses to send them along with tracking (Fedex or UPS). When I called Jabari in March of 2007, I obviously first asked how his off-season was going, then informed him that "the Performance Based Pay checks were cut and ready to be sent."

In a panicked voice, he asked, "Cut? Did you say I'm being cut?"

I said, "No, Jabari, the CHECK was 'cut.' Not *you*. So sorry it came out that way."

He let out a giant, "Phew," then laughed and verified his address.

As Jabari sought out alternative routes to the airport, Paul told him to relax, concentrate, and stayed with him on the phone. He ended up pulling in twelve minutes late that Saturday. Jabari rushed out of his car, sweating, while straightening up his tie and tucking his shirt into his dress pants. He sprinted into the hangar. We told him he was fine as we all walked briskly to the plane and locked up the hangar behind him.

It felt victorious to close the plane doors with everyone safely on board only twelve minutes behind schedule. But there was still a game to play.

TEN
MISSION AT MOTOR CITY

HAVING SUCCESSFULLY "HERDED" EVERY PLAYER, COACH, AND STAFF member required to travel to Detroit, we could finally exhale and re-charge for Sunday's game. It was always paramount to ensure that all the team's needs would be met at the hotel, but given the huge hurdles of the past two days, it was even more important during this unprecedented time. It didn't take long to be tested.

Our hotel in Detroit was one of the finest we would stay in all season: 5 stars, *The Ritz Carlton*. We always stay in very nice hotels that were determined by, among other things, the amount of meeting space and privacy, but this hotel was a cut above the rest. It felt almost museum-like where you were afraid to touch anything.

At every hotel the team had a separate entrance; sometimes it was the main lobby that was roped off while other times it was a back door or even a service entrance. Players then pick up their keys in an envelope on a table near the elevators prepared by the team's advance person who arrived two days earlier, who I believe was Media Relations Director Chris Jenkins that particular day. Gail Zielinski, Jim Overdorf's most able Administrative Assistant, assigned the rooming list and always arranged for players' rooms to be on two consecutive floors. Just outside the elevators on those floors sat a security guard, usually a current or former police officer - including Police Commander Mike Nigrelli who, for this trip was still busy closing down the Interstate, but often served as one of our regular security detail. (Thankfully this was not one of his trips!) These security details were equipped with a table, chair, newspaper (a laptop in later years), and *always* coffee. It was their responsibility to ensure that **nobody** outside of the team came on or off the floor. They'd remain there until about 5:00 am, catch a couple hours sleep, eat breakfast, then jump on a bus to the stadium for their gameday duties on the team sidelines. After completing this mostly sleepless tour, it was common to see these security professionals sleeping on the returning plane trip. And they usually had their regular police duty to follow just a few hours later.

To get away from the awful mess at home was nice. To finally relax on a bed in a room with electricity was even nicer, but, as many of us would attest, there was a low-level, prevailing guilt factor. Not that there should have been – it was our livelihoods; we had a special job to do. In the NFL, there are only eight regular season road games a year. They're all <u>so</u> important. It was a challenge to compartmentalize the fact that our families were still dealing with big problems at home, but it was necessary and I'm thankful that Amy was as understanding as always about this.

On this night, there was not even a thought about leaving the hotel. Instead of going out to a restaurant, I sat with Paul, the team's lead reporter Chris Brown, and Web Site Manager Gregg Pastore in the team meal room where a snack was served. As with "trip", the term "snack" is also misleading. Lest one imagine a couple of card tables with Rice Cakes and Toaster Strudels, do not. The team snack was a full buffett of meats, pastas, cheeses, salads, soups, sometimes pizza and always ice cream. For those not wanting to leave the hotel for whatever reason, the snack more than ensured they wouldn't starve. And the Team Snack is offered above and beyond the issued per diem.

The prevalent conversation at our table and at most other tables that evening was, you guessed it, the Storm. Walking back to my room after dinner, I wandered through the lobby where a large gathering of other hotel guests (we don't actually *own* the whole hotel for the evening) mingled at some type of a black-tie affair, perhaps a wedding or a charity fundraiser. These people were living it up large. Ladies in gowns, men in tuxedos, sipping champagne, laughing, and – if that wasn't enough – they were even keeping an eye on the lobby televisions showing their beloved Detroit Tigers in the World Series. I looked around and thought, *None of these people have the slightest clue what we have been dealing with the past few days and must still face when we go home tomorrow night.* It wasn't their fault, just an observation.

Upon returning to my room and doing a face-plop on the giant bed, I received a call from Defensive Coordinator **Perry Fewell**. His wife called in a panic that their basement had flooded back in Orchard Park. He asked if I could possibly arrange a hotel room for their family. Since I had handled all the Coaches' relocations just eight months earlier, Perry felt comfortable asking me for this help during this extraordinary time. He insisted that he'd pay for the room, but I told him, "Coach, consider it done. Tell your wife there's a room in her name at the Millennium Hotel. Get some rest." I called up our very reliable contact back in Buffalo, Linda at the Millennium, who immediately got it done. Had it been a player, he'd have to pay for the room or I'd be committing a salary cap violation, but as our Defensive Coordinator - a coach, not a player, I just wanted him knowing his family was taken care of so he could focus on the game.

Shortly after dealing with Perry's request, my cell phone rang again. This time it was my friend, Anthony, from Tampa and one of my "Weekenders." It was good to hear his voice. He had received my email earlier that morning from my office after showering, changing, and charging my phone, that this year's "October Weekend" was very much in doubt. Being only six days away, with no return of electricity in sight, the timing was terrible. Yes, we could make due with all the guys at the hotel, but our home is "home base." I couldn't have guys over, for Amy's sake, without electricity and with still so much to clean up inside and outside. Given the hardships so many Buffalonians were enduring, worrying about my friends coming seemed trivial, but real nonetheless.

Anthony said, "Hey, got your email. I know I speak for everyone in saying we totally understand the situation. Don't worry at all about us. We can reschedule."

His concession was a relief to hear, but also no surprise. Then Anthony followed up by saying, "But, Don, just consider this – I know I also speak for the guys in saying that we would help you move those trees. We could knock it out in one day. And when it's done, we'll clean ourselves up and feast on those wings like nobody's business. Just think about it."

After thanking him and hanging up, I called Amy which I'd planned to do anyway. It was important she knew that my default position about "The Weekend," was to postpone. But the idea of having eight able-bodied guys spend a few hours attacking our massive downed-tree problem was intriguing enough to run by Amy. Her reaction, somewhat surprisingly, was very receptive. I had figured that she wouldn't even consider this scenario without any power. When I convinced her that we'd shift our "home base" from our house to the hotel, she said, "Let's do it."

Back in Buffalo, much was happening on this Saturday night. On a small scale, John Guy, who hadn't slept at home since Wednesday, finally left the office. Surely by now it would be smooth sailing, right? Nope, not yet. John was *still* unable to pull into his driveway. Turning his front bumper into a battering ram, John finally knocked through the snow wall on his tenth charge. *Home, sweet home.*

On a large scale, the Eastern Hills Mall parking lot had been designated by the State and County as Command Central for over

500 trucks that had come from out of town to help Buffalo's own crews restore the region's electricity. According to the State's Official Report:

> *Using draft procedures developed from an alliance with Florida Power and Light, the mall supported 500 crews during the restoration. Crews that were assigned long distance lodging early in the restoration were bussed to the staging areas. Crew assigned lodging accommodations were as far away [as] Rochester and Erie, Pennsylvania, and then moved closer to the restoration when lodging became available. Crews were fed breakfast at the mall staging area and provided box lunches to aid in productivity. Line trucks were fueled and restocked with material supplies in the evening when the crews were resting.*[6]

In the words of 1970's musician, C.W. McCall, *"Mercy sakes alive, looks like we've got us a convoy..."* and for the record, these crews never *crashed the gate doin' 98.*

Learning about this gathering, it was here that WGRF 96.9 FM (97 Rock)'s DJ **Dave Jickster** and a gentleman named **Paul Maurer** (take note of this name) formed their own crews to show these hard working truckers gratitude and Buffalo hospitality with coffee and donuts - their 2nd choice after beer and wings, which they correctly assumed would have been frowned upon during this non-party time. To say that Paul was moved by these truckers coming to Buffalo's aid was an understatement, though Paul would respond by taking action of his own later that is both commendable in its own right as much as these crews. While Paul was there supporting the many

---

[6] New York State, Department of Public Service. October 2006 Western New York Major Snowstorm: A Report On Utility Performance. May 2007. p. 11

who came to remove the destruction, he would soon become part of the solution to reintroduce the beauty that was lost.

Later that evening in my Ritz Carlton Hotel room in Detroit, my phone rang again. It was Chris Bergstrom, another "Weekender" friend, who suggested exactly what Anthony had earlier. Chris, who lived in Niagara-Wheatfield, had served almost as a co-host the previous year in terms of housing guys and driving them around. He even offered to hold it at his house since they'd only received about five inches of snow and expected to get his power back the next day. It was an option to which I gave serious consideration. He assured me that he'd do all the chauffeuring, etc. again and was thrilled to hear that Amy signed off on the idea.

Feeling some sense of relief, I fell asleep. And hard.

The next morning came - game day was upon us which felt like reaching a huge operational milestone. The butterflies in my stomach were about one thing – winning the game, which is how game day mornings usually feel, but this game was especially important; we knew what winning could and would mean - we all knew it and we all felt it.

The team meal room at breakfast was typically quiet with an incredible amount of nervous energy as kickoff loomed just hours away. Many players sit alone, getting themselves mentally ready; some gather together, but conversations are low-level. There are TVs around the room tuned into ESPN that show highlights from College football the previous night. It serves as an acceptable level of background noise.

Perhaps most encouraging was what players and coaches were *not* talking about this Sunday morning. The previous night during dinner, conversations were almost exclusively about the Storm. Every time I walked by a table, it was almost a certainty to overhear at least one of the words: generator, sump pump, electricity, basement, trees, power, and/or insurance; it felt like a "Word Bingo" that no one was winning.

Thankfully, this was not happening during this game day Sunday morning - everyone was rightly focused on the game. Perry Fewell did stop by my table to briefly thank me again for setting up his family, but he was otherwise locked in.

For a 1:00 pm kickoff, the buses typically take the team from the hotel to the stadium, with a police escort, at 9:30, 10, and 10:30 am. The staff usually boards that last (10:30) bus, which takes us directly into the tunnel of the stadium and drops us off by the locker rooms and the field.

My normal pre-game routine is to briefly check into the locker room, then Paul Lancaster and I would make our way to the field to watch warmups until about 11:45 am. Paul often connected with the other team's Player Engagement Director as they usually knew each other from League Meetings. Not having duties during the game itself, we'd then make our way up to the Press Box from where we'd watch the game. Following the game, I was responsible to work with our screeners and the TSA to ensure that authorized people - and *only* authorized people - boarded our five buses to the Charter plane. Regarding the pregame, Marv Levy, upon returning in 2006 to serve as General Manager, commented to Paul and me before one early season game, "These are the longest two hours of the week." He was *so* right, as usual.

There was, however, a two year stretch where I was called into serious game day duty. When Buddy Nix was hired as GM, he re-evaluated *everything* on the football side, including the size of the traveling party, seeking to ensure that all traveling staff had a purpose for being there. My situation was interesting since my purpose for being on the trip was the trip itself - overseeing the screening at the beginning and the end, without an actual duty *during* the game. So, per the advice of the Video Department, Buddy assigned Paul Lancaster and me to take the pictures in the Coaches' Booth. Sounds easy, right? Not quite.

Seated at a computer with a control screen that showed the live plays on a black and white monitor in a booth high above the field, we were required to snap four pictures of every play - offense, defense, and special teams at precise moments dictated by Defensive Coordinator, Dave Wannstedt, who was also in the booth. We then had to quickly enter the *result* of the play including the yardage (gain or loss), including any penalty. Finally, after each series, we quickly printed and distributed the hard copies to the respective coaches before dashing back to the desk for the next series. The coaches studied these photos hard, looking for any edge, any advantage, any mismatch, anything at all they could correct or use later in the game - all from an aerial view.

So, during the first preseason game in 2012 versus the Washington Redskins, Paul and I took our initial turns in the hot seat. To say it didn't go well would be an understatement. There's no way to sugar coat it - we sucked. After the first penalty, we fell behind the pace of play. The buttons on the screen looked like the cockpit of a 747. I began sweating like Ted Striker in Airplane! SO many buttons and knobs. We were giving coaches Down and Distance reports that read "2nd and 65 (yards to go)." We had the game going in the wrong direction, wrong teams on offense. Missing a single play is unacceptable - we were missing the entire <u>series</u>. Coaches were furious. They were yelling, which just made matters worse. Paul and Assistant Coach Adrian White nearly got into a fistfight.

After the game, Dave Wannstedt, who I'd personally gotten along with very well, demanded a change telling Head Coach Chan Gailey, "This is how we'll lose games." But Video Director Greg Estes assured Chan and Buddy that we could do it, not just by the regular season but *by the very next Preseason game at Minnesota,* with

<u>one</u> training session during the week. Buddy agreed and after Video Crew members Dexter Carlo, Wes Burnard, and Casey Weidl spent an hour with us that following Wednesday afternoon, Paul and I got it. It clicked. We made some key fundamental corrections that made us confident and calm - but we still had to prove it in live action.

In the Minnesota hotel the night before the game, Dave Wannstedt told us to meet him in the conference room where he showed us on the big screen exactly when the pictures should be taken, ie. when the quarterback pulls his arm back to throw or as he hands the ball off. That *too* was helpful. The night of that 2nd preseason game in Minnesota, with Buddy Nix standing and observing directly behind us so closely we could feel his breath, we nailed it. At half-time, Dave Wannstedt slapped us on the back and even gave us a "Nice job." *Phew.*

During the season, Paul and I got so good that Coaches trusted us to handle more nuanced instructions such as, when we saw extra pressure (a blitz) happen on third (down) and long, *then* update the picture. The following year, Paul and I were asked to spend the season training a full-time (gameday) picture-taker, Joe Loecher, who did great, earning the nickname, "Joe Kid" and secured the job going forward so Paul and I could fully attend to our primary assigned duties. Once he was comfortable, we messed with Joe by relaying that one notoriously high-maintenance coach in the booth, whose stature didn't come close to meriting such authoritative behavior, was making special demands. It began as a true request to have the papers stapled a certain way, which solicited an eye roll, but Joe complied. So Paul and I fed off that by telling Joe that this coach was now demanding water with lemon and a foot rub.

We still laugh to this day about our baptism by fire that first preseason game. As one who hated preseason because of the spike in injury claims, I'd never been so thankful to have three more games to be ready for the regular season. Turned out, we only needed one, along with much appreciated support and trust of the Video team,

Chan Gailey, and Buddy Nix. Incidentally, it should be noted that our messing around with Joe about the absurd, fabricated coach's demands occurred during breaks in the game - NOT during actual play!

On this day in Detroit, I basically followed the same pregame routine - with one exception. Up until this point, during events of the last few days, I believed I'd kept proper focus on most every task, both at home and with my professional Bills duties.

… until now.

While on our sideline in Ford Field, where I was properly credentialed and it was a normal place for me to spend some time during pregame warmups, I decided to make an important phone call to our insurance company. While Amy and her parents, Joy and Tony, were trying to surgically remove a tree out of our roof and attic, I could contribute *something* to our overall recovery by at least starting the insurance claim for our roof, fences, and flooded basement.

During this pre-game time, I found a way to make use of "the longest two hours of the week" when my duties wouldn't resume for another five hours at post-game. However, I admittedly suffered a momentary lapse of reason for a few unfortunate minutes. For a bit more privacy, I purposefully migrated away from my colleagues on the sidelines toward the back of the end zone where there was no one but a yellow-jacketed security guard. I dialed MetLife's main 800-number and was pleasantly surprised to reach an attendant on a Sunday morning after only about five minutes of waiting. The representative was a pleasant lady who, upon hearing my (716) area code, knew instantly why I was calling, saying, "Buffalo, NY – October 13th, right?"

I said, "That's right. Sounds like you're all too familiar with this one."

She responded, "Yes, we've received thousands of calls from Buffalo and expect thousands more. Let's get your info." Then she said, "What's all that music in the background?" Her tone, understandably, sounded annoyed as she likely pictured me in my car, maybe rudely choosing to not turn down the volume on the radio.

I tried to explain that the pounding music was the stadium sound system. Pacing back and forth in the end zone – sort of in my own type of zone - I tried to focus and relay all the proper information. All the while there was something very distracting (above and beyond the stadium noise) happening around me. I finally realized that the "annoyance" was a steady stream of footballs, every thirty seconds or so, courtesy of our kicker, Rian Lindell, who had the *audacity* to begin his Pre-game Field Goal warmups. Even worse, for a split second, being so deeply engaged in my conversation, I actually glanced at his direction and thought, *"Must you do this now?"*

Oh man. What an embarrassing lack of awareness. I'd always prided myself on "knowing my place" during my tenure with the Bills. As a kid, my Mom shared a paraphrased proverb from the Gospel of Luke that always stuck with me: *"When you are invited to a wedding feast, don't sit in the seat of honor. What if someone who is more distinguished than you has also been invited?"* (KJV, Luke 14:8). My personal interpretation of this being that it's better to first go to the back and be invited forward than go to the front and be told to get back. For example, at the buffet line at the team hotel I always yielded to players, coaches, and essential staff like trainers who faced a very physically challenging day. As a staff it was imperative and, quite frankly, our jobs to pave the way for those performing on the field in every manner possible. Most staff were also very aware of this mind set.

On the Sunday morning that we were checking out of our hotel in London in 2015, about to play the Jaguars, EJ Manuel stood behind three staff members in line at the desk to square up his incidentals from our week-long stay; the second-to-last bus waiting just outside the door, scheduled to leave in about four minutes, I immediately thought, *Wait. EJ is our starting quarterback today. This isn't right.* We, the staff, had thirty-four minutes until our bus, the last bus, departed. Since I, along with Gail Zielinski, approved the hotel bill, I quickly told EJ to just leave, get on the bus, and I'd payroll deduct his charges from his paycheck when we got back in the states, to which he quickly thanked me and took that advice. Perhaps waiting in that line was a case of EJ being *too* polite, which is not unsurprising for him. On that day EJ had a terrible first half, but brought the team all the way back into the lead which should have held up for the win if not for a ridiculous pass interference call on Jacksonville's final drive by Nickell Robey Coleman - yes, the same Nickell Robey Coleman who famously, and even admittedly, obliterated Saints receiver Tommylee Lewis in the NFC Championship game that did *not* get called and sent the Rams to the Super Bowl. *Oh, the irony.*

"Knowing your place" is a practice that, I think, served me well during my pro sports career, although it's good to recognize rare times when it's proper to promote yourself. I'll save the "psych" talk for Billy... I digress... Again...

(I later told Rian Lindell the story about his footballs raining on me in the end zone. He laughed and said, "Yeah, I saw you. And, *of course*, I was gunning for you. You were right between the pipes!")

Rian was a bit of a prankster, too. One Monday morning, as per my daily routine, I walked into the cafeteria to grab my normal two water bottles where Offensive Lineman Kirk Chambers motioned me over to his table while eating breakfast with Rian. Bottled water, Gatorade, juice, and other healthy drinks were positioned everywhere and promoted heavily with signs practically screaming *Hydrate!!* throughout the building, directed at the players for obvious reasons; a player coming out of a game for a dehydration cramp was harshly frowned upon as a self-inflicted and easily avoidable "injury."

The staff fully enjoyed the privilege of this convenient (and free) perk as well. Kirk asked me if he could change the W-4 tax withholdings on his pay to which I responded, "You bet. Either stop by my office or I can leave one in your locker."

Kirk told me he'd stop by my office later. Before leaving the table, I joked with Rian, "Sorry you got robbed of those three points yesterday." I was referring to the great trick play the day before where Rian was lined up for a short Field Goal, but as the ball was snapped, holder Brian Moorman quickly stood up and fired a pass toward the sideline to a wide open Ryan Denney, who was left totally uncovered, for a Touchdown. So, the Bills put seven points on the scoreboard instead of the three points had the Field Goal been kicked. The stadium went wild and it was, by far, the most played highlight on the sports news.

But rather than laughing at my joke like I'd expected, as naturally Rian wouldn't care about being "robbed" of the three points for his own personal statistics since the touchdown was obviously better and we won the game big, he instead gave me the oddest look. His eyes opened wide and he shook his head sideways, practically vibrating it, and pressed his lips together as if to say, "Get off this topic *now*." I was baffled by his reaction.

Finally, Rian said, "Geez, Don, the guy is sitting *right there*," referring to Kirk.

Kirk then piled on, "Thanks a lot, Don. I was feeling real good about holding Patrick Kearney to no sacks, then you had to go *there*."

"What? Go where? What am I missing?" I wondered, not knowing what to say next.

Rian then whispered, "Kirk was just telling me *he* was the one who missed the block."

Kirk then said, "I get it. I missed the assignment. So, it got blocked. Can we let it go?"

It finally hit me they were referring to a Field Goal attempt that was blocked the day before which nobody cared about since we still won the game by 24 points. I began damage control by pleading that, of course, I was referring to the trick play, but they continued to shake their heads in disappointment. Kirk even put his hand up and said, "Too late. Damage done."

Realizing they had "gotten" me, they both started laughing hysterically as I then smiled, nodded, and conceded, "Well played, gentlemen."

At the Ford Field end zone, upon my sudden and embarrassing realization about serving as Rian's target practice, I quickly bolted toward the corner of the field to continue my conversation with MetLife, which ended up going very well. They accepted the claim without hesitation and scheduled an insurance adjuster to witness the damage within a few days.

I then immediately called Amy back home, excited to pass along some good news while she was still deep in the midst of the mess. Her news back to me was even better: Amy's parents, Joy and Tony, had driven from their home east of Rochester to help the cleanup effort. While Joy was clearing brush, Tony climbed on our roof to remove the huge tree. It was *only then* he discovered that the tree had penetrated **through** the roof and into our attic. The actual removal just became much more complicated. Fortunately, Tony was able to masterfully use his chainsaw to surgically cut and remove each section without further tearing open the hole in the roof. He patched the hole with some scrap wood from our garage to prevent rain penetration for a few weeks until our insurance claim came through. It was a huge relief to have such a major problem resolved. I probably haven't told Joy and Tony enough how much I truly appreciate what they did that day while I was away. What they did for us was not at all surprising as they had always helped us since we were married. They will surely at least receive a complimentary copy of this book to tell them - ha!

It's worth noting that Amy and I are blessed with such giving parents. To this day, my Mom still wants to pay for dinner when they come to Buffalo and, more importantly, nobody is a better listener. And before coming out, my Dad always asks what tools he should bring on the assumption that we'll work on fixing. maintaining, or building something together.

At Ford Field in Detroit, following our pre-game ritual, Paul and I made our way toward the elevators to the Press Box to watch the game. Walking up this inclined tunnel ramp instantly inflamed the deep soreness in my legs from bailing buckets of water up our stairs two days ago. *Was that just two days ago? It felt like two weeks ago!*

Kickoff did happen in Detroit that day, as it always does, at 1:00 pm. Paul and I joked, "Let's not let *that guy* sing too much today." As Bills fans sing along to the Shout Song at home games after touchdowns, the Lions have a guy dubbed "Theo Gridiron" positioned on the sidelines who runs to a microphone after scores and belts out the Lions' own victory song, "Gridiron Heroes." It's super annoying to us only because of the association of having been scored against, but Lions fans love it and I've gotta say, the dude has an *incredible* baritone voice.

As NFL games go, this one was not especially memorable. No Bills fans outside of Mike Schopp are likely to recall details from a 3-point loss to an NFC team in a non-playoff year. In fact, the entire 2006 football season was representative of seasons that "shoulda, woulda, coulda", with a game here or game there - even a play here or play there - that could have produced a different result. Two more wins could have put us in the playoffs as a 6-seed, where teams in that position have gone on a "hot and healthy" run to win the Super Bowl. On opening day versus New England, a pick-six by Donte Whitner that could have sealed the win was called back by a phantom block-in-the-back penalty by Nate Clements where replays showed no contact at all. And on Christmas Eve, the Bills allowed Titans QB Vince Young to escape multiple tackles to scramble thirty-six yards for a go-ahead Touchdown with ONE SECOND left in the first half en route to just a 30-29 win. *Ugh.* Surely the Bills closed the deal on close wins that season, too, where opponents also dwell on a blown call or play that shouldn't have happened.

On this day in Detroit, Roscoe Parrish did haul in a 44-yard bomb for a touchdown, so clearly he wasn't too psychologically damaged from his scary ride with Kevin Everett. The game also included Rian Lindell booming an impressively long 53-yard field goal so apparently I hadn't messed up his pre-game warmups after all. *Uh oh, maybe he'd want me to serve as target practice again for future games... Nah.*

For players, coaches, and staff, all losses hurt. Marv cited this for retiring as a Head Coach in 1997 – that the losses hurt worse than the wins felt good. Plane rides home after winning or losing are vastly different in terms of mood and atmosphere, as one can imagine. Personally, this loss hurt a little more than usual given the extraordinary efforts of my work colleagues. Our record now stood at 2-4 with the Patriots coming to town next week. (*Would my friends be too?*) There's no time for pity in the NFL as preparation for that big game happened immediately. I could at least take some comfort that we did not sustain any serious injuries. After the previous week's road game at Chicago, I had helped John McCargo with his personal belongings down the plane stairs to a vehicle where the trainers would take him for surgery on his broken leg. Selfishly for me, there was no spike in medical claims, but, oh how a win would have been nice that day in Detroit.

Flying home on the silent plane, I saw something out my window seat I'll never forget.

THERE IT IS.

From about 30,000 feet, as we began the descent into Buffalo, the setting sun behind us from the west provided just enough light to see the exact path of the Storm. It was as if God had painted a solid, ten-mile wide stroke of snow through the region with a heavenly-sized paint brush. There were lights to the north and south, but complete darkness throughout the glacier-like path. This visual evidence explained how my friend, Chris Edwards, was so incredulous that Buffalo got pounded while looking at his green grass in Ellicottville, how Bills' Stadium Operations staffer Bill Connell found himself in a different climate after driving just a few miles to pick up the lights for practice, and how callers into Mike Schopp's WGR Sports Radio program reported a man grilling in Orchard Park while a lady was electrocuted in downtown Buffalo. Being "in the zone" versus "out of the zone" - *what a striking difference.*

It was also a stark visual reminder of what still awaited us back home.

ELEVEN
IS THAT ALL YOU GOT?!

Act of God; noun, Law: a direct, sudden, and irresistible action of natural forces such as could not reasonably have been foreseen or prevented, as a flood, hurricane, earthquake, or other natural catastrophe.[7]

ACT OF GOD IS A PHRASE MOST COMMONLY USED IN THE INSURANCE industry to describe an event that may or may not get covered, depending on the policy; sometimes it comes down to whether the buyer pays a premium to protect against such possible occurrences. So, what exactly are these occurrences that merit such a powerful association?

Insurance companies define an Act of God as:

1. a natural occurrence and
2. not preventable.

It is clear that our October Surprise Storm squarely fits each of these criteria.

In the movie Forrest Gump, Lieutenant Dan, after having lost his legs followed by his will to live after the Vietnam War, joined

---

[7] "Act of god." *Dictionary.com*. Dictionary.com, (n.d.). Accessed 6 Nov 2020.

Forrest on his shrimping boat in Louisiana because, well, he had nothing else to do. When a hurricane rocked their boat (literally), Forrest hunkered down, but Lieutenant Dan angrily and defiantly climbed up the mainmast, shook his fist, and screamed toward the heavens, "*Is that all you got?!*" Actor Gary Sinise who portrayed Lieutenant Dan has since claimed that acting out this scene was actually life-changing regarding his own personal faith journey. We all know that Forrest Gump was just a movie in which Lieutenant Dan's fortunes turned out OK, which viewers learned when he showed up for Forrest's wedding with a cane and wearing a clean white suit at the end. (Again, Forrest Gump was released in 1994; we shouldn't need to do a spoiler alert - but if you haven't watched, watch that one after you finish the book - you already walked away for *Shawshank Redemption*. It's our turn now.)

As Marv noted in his foreword, during his Bills head coaching days, the team *embraced* that type of ***bring it on*** mentality and 'psych ops' regarding the harsh weather conditions as they watched their less acclimated opponents struggle with it. Marv also noted that this was applicable to winning a football game and that this extraordinary weather event presented challenges that extended far beyond the football field.

In real life, the launch and subsequent, spectacular failure of the Titanic offers an example of how challenging God did not go well - *how's that for an understatement?* Historians differ about who actually uttered the foolish words, "God himself couldn't sink this ship", but few deny the announcement was made and heard by many. And who knows if this would be considered an Act of God. While the ship did strike an iceberg, it was the Captain at the helm of the ship – people, not weather – that caused the crash. Insurance companies today would likely label the Titanic a "Man Caused" disaster. The late comedian George Carlin, known for his edgy critiquing of language, would have had a field day dissecting this term.

For me to tackle "Why God lets bad things happen" here is

beyond my spiritual scope. While I have my own personal views, I'd fear misplacing biblical words, albeit unintentionally. One TV series that Amy found during the 2020 pandemic on Amazon Prime was Goliath. Billy Bob Thornton plays Billy McBride, a former partner in a huge international law firm that cast him out in disgrace. While still exceptionally skilled, his work has now been reduced to low-level ambulance chasing, that is until a case presents itself against his old firm. Knowing full well Billy McBride's dangerous abilities, the firm uses its deep and secret resources to make his life miserable. In one episode (*spoiler alert*) this includes having a truck run over and kill his new girlfriend who's also an integral part of the case. In the morgue, standing over her body, heartbroken, and with a shaky voice Billy McBride begins reciting, " *And David put his hand in the bag and took out a stone and slung it. And it struck the Philistine on the head and he fell to the ground.*" Billy then pauses, then closes with "*Hoosiers. 1986. Amen.*" So much for the deep spiritual insight. It felt weird to laugh at a scene so tragic, you'd at least like to believe that Billy knew that his favorite movie was quoting the bible. (For the record, this is not an endorsement of the series as Amy and I were quite selective in who we recommended it to; while the drama, especially the court scenes, were incredible, it was no Disney Film but did lend some context here.)

One of, if not the most famous and notorious events that has challenged the faith of many was, of course, the September 11th terrorist attacks in 2001. As with millions of other Americans, we at One Bills Drive had our worlds rocked that Tuesday morning. Amy called me just before 9:00 am about the first plane. I immediately turned on my rarely-watched office TV to see the second plane hit the second tower live. Moments later, knowing that Beverly Angelo across the hall was from Pennsylvania, I asked her where Shanksville was. She was shaken to the core as she responded, "What? Why? My mom lives there!" Bev panicked further when she couldn't initially reach her Mom by phone. Once she finally did, she hugged me hard as she broke down in tears of relief.

Within the hour, I had a similar experience while on the phone with my cousin, Bob Van Wicklin, at the Capitol Building in DC who served as a Legislative Director for Congressman Amo Houghton. Half way through the conversation, the phone line cut out just as news broke on television that the Pentagon was struck. Once back to his Bethesda, Maryland home, he emailed me that he and his wife Melanie, who also worked in DC (at the Discovery Channel), were safe and that one desert region of the world was about to "turn to glass."

Like most every American alive at the time, Billy and I could write several chapters about our 9/11 experiences. The last applicable point to share regarding 9/11 was that at One Bills Drive, with the League cancelling games for the first time since World War II, team President Tom Donohoe and Head Coach Gregg Williams felt the need to mourn and reflect on the tragedy as a full organization – players, coaches, and staff – with a proper ceremony. I don't recall whether it was voluntary or mandatory, but I believe everyone attended. Tom Donohoe's memo asked attendees to dress as they would for church and invited the Director of Buffalo's Athletes in Action, **Fred Raines**, to deliver some healing words.

Fred was a terrific choice. While he was a practicing Christian leader, Fred was also aware that other faiths were represented amongst this group of over 200 people. He chose to share bible passages that addressed how God *does* allow bad things to happen, but that good ultimately comes from them; how while we live in a fallen world, God will never leave us and is always in control; and how we should love each other and lift each other up. The message was very well-received throughout the building as it struck a tone of hope much needed during those dark days.

Fred and I became close friends after my release from the Bills in 2017. He arranged for us to read some faith-based books that

he'd always wanted to try, then meet every couple of weeks at
Leo's Pizzeria in Orchard Park to discuss. My book-reading history
included all of Neal Peart's (the former Rush drummer who also
wrote their philosophical lyrics) epic, thought-provoking books and
some other sports biographies, which naturally included Marv's! But
Fred turned me onto some by Max Lucado and one called "Facing
the Blitz" by Jeff Kemp, former NFL quarterback and son of the
great Jack Kemp. One day in 2020 during the pandemic, Fred texted
me, "What's up next for our books?" To which I snarkily responded,
"I'm actually *writing* one." Fred laughed and it was during that
exchange where my "overhead lightbulb" lit up and my recollection
of his role and words after 9/11 prompted me to ask him for his most
insightful perspective here.

Amy and I moved to Buffalo in 1989 when she took a long-term
substitute teaching job in West Seneca and I accepted a part-time job
at the Bills Ticket Office. We didn't know anything about Buffalo
area churches, but a family friend at Camp-of-the-Woods and former
Buffalonian, Norm Sonju, recommended we check out The Chapel
(then on North Forest) as he'd attended there during his time as
General Manager of the Buffalo Braves NBA team[8]. So we found it,
attended, and Norm was right. We really liked it for many reasons:
Pastor Andrews delivered messages that were challenging, funny,
easy to follow, and most importantly, biblical; Anna enjoyed their
"super cool" youth program so much that she often brought along
a school friend; The congregation was quite racially diverse which
was important to us in raising our family; and, perhaps the least of
the reasons but nonetheless a real one, being a large church helped

---

[8] The Buffalo Braves were a professional basketball franchise of the National
Basketball Association (NBA) based in Buffalo from 1970 until 1978. In
1978, Braves owner John Y. Brown Jr. swapped franchises with Irv Levin who
owned the Boston Celtics; Levin then moved the team and renamed them
the San Diego Clippers until the franchise moved again in 1984 and became
how it is now known: the Los Angeles Clippers.

us avoid the "Hey, we noticed that you weren't here last Sunday", which was so often the case during the Autumn Sunday's because of my Bills schedule.

Beyond the two morning Sunday services, which were the same, offering attendees a choice between 9:00 am or 11:00 am, The Chapel produced a magnificent, multi-night Christmas program that drew tens of thousands of people from all over Western New York. One year my parents, as well as my sister and brother-in-law Scott and Tracy brought our nephew and niece, Tory and Jordan, to the event. While the first part of the program features a fun, light sing-along with Jingle Bells, Santa Claus, and the like, the story naturally moves into a breath-takingly beautiful portrayal of Christ's birth in Bethlehem - similar to that of The Rockettes at NYC's *Radio City Music Hall*. The Three Wise Men follow the star to Bethlehem and present their gifts, but in The Chapel's version, Santa Claus then approaches the Manger, kneels, and bows his head. I remember looking down at Tory seeing his eyes tear up as he was just old enough to grasp this deeply symbolic imagery. He shared with us later that The Chapel's Christmas program was a pivotal moment as a young Christian and he remains today a rock solid man of faith running his farrier business in Washington State.

Incidentally, in December of 1999, Claire, as a two month-old infant, portrayed baby Jesus for a few of the shows (something many family members still rib her about) while Amy served as a baby-sitter for staff behind the stage. Pastor Andrews had fallen ill with pancreatic cancer earlier that year. We had hoped he'd be well enough to dedicate Claire as he had done with Anna five years earlier, but it wasn't to be. Upon revealing his terminal condition for the first time to the congregation months earlier, leading to not a dry eye in the building, he appealed for prayers not only for his family, but for the church. No one had ever known The Chapel without its founder, James Andrews, but his simple, passionate appeal to the congregation was to forge ahead, without him, remembering

The Chapel must be "about Jesus, not Jim." He repeated this verbally multiple times. During his messages for months after, it was easy to forget he was suffering from this illness or feeling lousy from treatments. He'd miss a Sunday here or there, but remained remarkably strong and upbeat. Late that fall, it became too much. We never saw him at church again. While I didn't know him well enough to visit him at home or in the hospital, according to those who did he never complained or asked, "Why me?" What he said in public, he also said in private which shows so much about the character of a man. He passed away on December 10th of that year, 1999, and to this day, I've *never* seen anyone die with such dignity.

But, as Pastor Andrews himself had promised, the church he had built, while never forgetting him, needed to move on. A guest pastor, Al Cockrell, was chosen to succeed Pastor Andrews. He shared a similar style as Pastor Andrews minus the familiarity with the Chapel "family." His messages and communication style were well-received, but while he felt the calling to this position, Pastor Cockrell made it very clear it was an interim period to bridge the gap for someone younger. Despite knowing the church yearned for stability, he continually, Sunday after Sunday reminded the congregation, "Please trust me when I tell you, God is grooming your next pastor. When the time is right, I will step aside to fully endorse this young man from Georgia. You will love him and he will love you. I promise." *Hmm. OK.* As much as everyone wanted to believe him, they also were "used to" and felt comfortable having a true Buffalonian like Dr. Andrews at the pulpit.

Amy and I were in attendance for Pastor Jerry Gillis's first official service at The Chapel when he stepped into this role. He had actually been a guest speaker before and we remember his energetic and even humorous messages, but being "The Every Sunday (and more) Pastor" was now the real deal. It turns out that God, in a continuance of His perfect record and calendar, knew what He was doing. The packed house left The Chapel that day, and to a person, there was no doubt that this young man from the south had just consummated the mutual adoption. *And it was good.*

Pastor Gillis brought a fresh perspective and style, with targeted and effective humor, to the pulpit while staying true to the word of God. This extended to the Christmas programs where, like Pastor Andrews, Cockrell, and Fred Raines - he knew his audience, particularly that this program might be their only visit to church all year. At the conclusion of every program, he and the wonderful Chapel staff ensured that the audience left The Chapel entertained, but more importantly fulfilled and reminded that God loves them.

Speaking of The Chapel staff, one personal story that is indicative and representative of the staff as a whole occurred during our youngest daughter, Claire's, lacrosse game at Williamsville South High School one year (2015 or 2016, I think); a gentleman set up his lawn chair directly next to me on the sidelines and when I looked over at him, he looked so familiar, but I couldn't connect the dots. Truth be told, I privately sighed at the prospect of a fan (most often a relative) of the other team sitting right next to us. Historically, it just doesn't go well. At the very least, it's uncomfortable; at worst, unpleasant words are either indirectly or directly shared about the game. The refs usually take the brunt of the verbal banter, but messages, verbal, implied, or otherwise, are sent about "dirty play" and the like. This phenomenon is all too prevalent in high school or travel sports and quite frankly, more difficult to manage than it should be - myself included!

But there was something very different about this man - he immediately started commenting on the good plays by *both* teams. He asked me what jersey number my daughter was to which I asked the same about his granddaughter. Before we knew it, we were engaged in a most pleasant small talk while still following the exciting and competitive game. Finally, I connected the dots and realized that it was Associate Pastor Richard George from The Chapel! As mentioned previously, not attending that regularly more than likely is what hindered me from recognizing him faster, but it's something I'll never forget.

With that bit of history from my perspective, perhaps no Buffalonian could frame how the Storm brought out this "love thy neighbor" narrative for the City of Good Neighbors better than **Pastor Jerry Gillis** of The Chapel Crosspoint. It is truly a privilege to have Pastor Jerry accept my invitation to share his experience about the October Storm:

> *Growing up in Georgia, and then serving on a church staff for eight years in Southwest Florida, did not prepare me for the weather in Western New York. Truthfully, prior to moving to Buffalo, the only thing I knew about it was the Buffalo Bills and snow. After my arrival to the Buffalo region in 2002, I was able to work through a few winters that were both cold and snowy. But October of 2006 was altogether different. I had heard from native Western New Yorkers about the blizzard of 1977, but at least that occurred in late January when people expected it. But October? This was not something any of us were prepared for, and that Friday and Saturday – October 13 and 14 – felt out of place.*
>
> *As a pastor of a church called The Chapel, we made the decision to go ahead with our worship services that Sunday as planned. Did we have power at the building? No, we only had generators. Was there a travel ban? Likely, but because of power outages virtually everywhere not everyone had been alerted to that. We were concerned that many in our congregation had needs but didn't have any way to get help, so they would likely drive to the church on Sunday morning. We didn't know how many people would come, but we opened the doors. Shockingly,*

we had over 1,100 people come to one of two worship gatherings we held that day. We sat in the cold under emergency lighting in our worship center, were led in singing through a microphone powered by a generator, and then I taught a lesson from Matthew's gospel about how Jesus cares for His own. When we finished, we asked for people that had needs or a problem to make themselves known so that we could see how we might help them. As each person called out their issue ("My basement is flooded", "I have a tree on my roof"), people in our church stepped up to meet that need. The generosity and kindness was extraordinary.

In one case, a widow had a flooded basement. A number of men in our church went right over there to get it cleaned up and taken care of. Many people were without generators, and one of the men in our church went to Home Depot and bought six new generators to give to people. Some of our folks lived in neighborhoods that were devastated by fallen trees and debris, so dozens of men from our church showed up to the neighborhoods with chainsaws and not only helped to make the roads passable but also helped to safely remove dangerous fallen trees near houses and power lines. As well, members of our church were hosting other members in their house to sleep, shower, wash clothes, and stay warm.

This was an extraordinary introduction to Western New York for me. Not only was I able to see firsthand that this truly is the "City of Good Neighbors", but, more importantly, I saw people of faith living out the teaching of Jesus to "love your neighbor as yourself." I hope that it doesn't take another storm for all of us to continue to live in the light of that eternal truth.

Perhaps most admirable here was that Jerry and The Chapel's congregation responded not just to what they *happened to hear*, but rather that they *sought out* those who needed help; they operated under the premise that some folks surely needed help and put the word out, "Who are you? Where are you? And what do you need?" They then backed it up by responding in force with their time, effort, and money. When Pastor Jerry pondered what that October Sunday might look like - especially at a church with no power, no heat, and still treacherous roads - he saw 1,100 people pour out of their houses to gather together at The Chapel Crosspoint, then seek to lovingly and *practically* embrace the neediest among them.

For the Buffalo community following the October Storm, **THE QUESTION** *"Is that all you got?!"* surely captured one collective sentiment. The National Weather Service stated there were fifteen deaths, both directly and indirectly, related to the Storm.[1] Property damage was suffered like nothing the region had ever seen. The Toronto Sun called it "one of the most devastating snow storms in US history"[9] yet it still couldn't break the will of the region.

THE ANSWER came in the form of Russ providing a tractor, Dave delivering a generator, Joy and Tony removing the tree, young Tom, Derek, and Haley helping us bail out our basement, and now, the Chapel's congregation helping the widow and others, not to mention the countless other examples that we experienced first hand in addition to those that were happening all over the region. These are just a few examples Billy and I, as merely a sample of two, either witnessed in our own circles or learned through the course of diving deep into the October Storm and the lives it touched. Certainly, there are thousands of other selfless acts replicated around Western New York that also answered the call.

[9] Henry, Michelle. "30,000 homes still without power." *Toronto Star,* 21 October 2006.

"Joliet Jake" Blues (John Belushi): "We're putting the band back together."

Mr. Fabulous (Alan Rubin): "Forget it. No way."

Elwood Blues (Dan Aykroyd): "We're on a mission from God." - The Blues Brothers, 1980

TWELVE
LET THERE BE LIGHT

WHILE IN DETROIT, TENS OF THOUSANDS OF PEOPLE WERE STILL coping at home in Buffalo - something that none of us could forget, but something we kept trying to keep in the back of our minds while we focused on the work. For Billy and his family, Sunday was the start of the wreckage of the Storm turning back in their favor:

> *On Sunday the 15th, as we had been doing all along, we called one of my grandfather's neighbors and a close family friend, Mrs. Cusick, to check on the house as well as progress on the street. As there were a lot of older adults in that neighborhood as well as on that street, that section of South Buffalo had become somewhat of a priority for locals to get this section turned back on. Thankfully for both my grandfather, his neighbors, as well as my Mom's sanity, he was able to return home that Sunday night and sleep in his own bed. I however would continue to sleep by the fire for a few more nights. Later that night, still having no power and trying to find things to do, my Aunt Nancy and my cousin Pattie who lived nearby trudged through the remaining snow to come join us for an evening. We enjoyed half of a frosted cake and a few other bare*

*essentials, as our cabinets were still lacking, but the
four of us still had a nice time celebrating my Uncle
Tim's birthday despite the fact that he couldn't be there
to join us.*

*A few days after this, we would see my grandfather
again, against his will as at that point as he only
wanted to stay home, because my Aunt Marlene and
Uncle Tim invited us all over for a "Recharge Party" -
an opportunity to bring cell phones, GameBoys, and
whatever other device that needed some juice to come
over and plug in. While they lived in the same town as
us, they lived in a newer development where all of their
power lines were buried underground so they never lost
power. In fact, it wasn't until that Saturday or Sunday
that they were told that their power would have to be
turned off in order to do some of the major repairs to
the transformer(s) for the other neighborhoods. Their
experience was very different from ours, however they,
like many who were in a similar situation to them,
opened up their home to friends and family to have
a bit of a party, just because. Conveniently enough
though, this was also my Uncle Tim whose birthday
had just passed so he ended up getting his birthday
party after all - even if it wasn't with the **entire** cake
we had intended him to have.*

Having returned from our game in Detroit, it was back to the
reality on the ground. Back to dealing with the aftermath. Back to
a whole neighborhood *still* without power for who knows how much
longer.

The front lawns of many houses on our street were littered with
huge piles of tree branches, whole trees in some cases, that had been

dragged out by the homeowners and whomever else nearby was willing and able to assist. It's worth noting here that the Town of West Seneca's Sanitation Department did an incredible job picking up the unprecedented amount of debris in people's front yards over just the course of a few weeks. We had hundreds of branches downed mostly in our backyard, but were scheduled to have some manpower on the way: The Weekend was about five days away and, since Tony and Joy removed the tree from our attic the day before while I was away, huge progress had already been made, with plenty more to go.

Pro Bowl Defensive End **Aaron Schobel** recalls how, in just a couple of days since returning from Detroit, the weather conditions improved so dramatically - granted, the bar had been taken down *very* low: "The day after we got back from Detroit, I went over to [Chris] Kelsay's place and we sat outside and had a cold one. The snow and ice were melting behind his house forming like a river, creating a new ditch. Couldn't believe how things changed in just a couple of days." The improving landscape was a testament to the extraordinary cleanup effort as well as Nature offering gifts of warmth and new temporary waterways, like the one Aaron described, to help the remaining snow evacuate back to the water tables.

As Aaron noted, there were some noticeable improvements, but still a long, *long* way to go. Schools and most businesses remained closed, for better or worse as it left both parents and kids safer, but also forced them to face the wrath and ruin of the Storm with little to do. FEMA had sent its resources to help remove the collapsed trees alongside electric companies as well as volunteers from Rochester, Syracuse, and all over the Northeast and Midwest to assist in the efforts.

Our offices were fortunate to have been restored to full power. We were preparing to play the New England Patriots that coming Sunday, October 22nd - thankfully this game was at home so there was at least *one* less stressor. Senior Vice President of Business Operations Dave Wheat and I had a daily running joke: our offices were just around the corner from each other, so every morning we'd look at each other and say, "Nope, not yet" – referring to whether power had been restored at our homes yet. It was a contest reminiscent of the *Cheers* episode when Sam was trying to fit in with some wealthy, new investor friends and they invited Sam to play a game where every year they'd all pick a stock to invest an amount equivalent to "throw away money" for them, but was uncomfortably substantial for Sam. Whoever lost the most money "won." The "winner" of our depressing game ended up being our Web Site Manager, Gregg Pastore.

At home that Tuesday night, Day Five without electricity, we had done a decent job of using up the food in the refrigerator before it spoiled and were making due with canned and boxed food, but finally our cupboards were essentially bare. I don't throw around the word "*deserve*" too often as it suggests blind entitlement, (especially when the word gets abused by sales campaigns as "You deserve this product!" *Really? How do they know what every person on the receiving end of the ad deserves?*) but on that night, we felt like we deserved some pizza. After the last five days of our world being turned upside down, was that asking too much? Unlike an average "pizza night", we had to go on a mission to find pizza - somewhere, somehow, whoever was able to sell it. We called every pizza place, parlor, factory, and stand we knew within a 10-mile radius and *none* had opened back up yet. Until, finally, a place called Perfect Pizza in Wimbledon Plaza in West Seneca answered their phone and said "We're open!" *Perfect.* We gleefully placed the order, which they said would take an hour. *No problem.* When I arrived, they had dim lighting run by a generator with apparently *just* enough power to operate, but most importantly, the ovens were powered by gas and the pizza was, as advertised, perfect; *It tasted like* **heaven**.

Having such trouble finding an open Pizza place sparked the realization that it wasn't only home-owners suffering such damage, so were businesses. Police Captain friend Mike Nigrelli called a few months after we first spoke (about this book) to pass along an experience he'd just had with his barber, Tony Scaccia, owner of Tony's Hairstyling on Seneca Street in West Seneca. Once firmly planted in his regular chair, Mike asked Tony how he and his business were holding up during the pandemic. Tony responded, "We're hanging in there. It's tough, but it's *nothing* like 2006."

Mike chimed in, "I assume you're talking about the October Storm?"

"Heck yeah," said Tony. "*That* was a beast to deal with."

Mike quickly said he wanted to hear the story, but then followed up by asking if he could share Tony's phone number so I could talk to him about it, to which Tony graciously agreed! So two days later, I gladly gave Tony a call. He immediately took me back to those few days in 2006:

> *It was snowing so heavily in South Buffalo (where their shop was in 2006) which made it so hard to get around. Power went out, but not for everyone. Some lost it, some didn't. In some cases, it even mattered what side of the street you were on. Or how old the houses were. We lost power, but were determined to find a way to stay open. I was going stir crazy in the house. I even had to tell a little white lie to secure a generator that someone wanted to borrow saying "my sister needed it."*
>
> *By word of mouth, since our shop phone was down and there was no social media at the time, regulars found out we were open. So too did some folks just walk*

in. With a six-foot tall standing light, the generator by my side, and strategically positioned space heaters, we did some crazy business, even having beers and drinks. My Dad happened to be here from Italy and couldn't believe the whole scene.

When the sun went down, we said, "That's a wrap." We took some damage to roof shingles and the gutter from falling branches, but fortunately no flooding. It felt good to use some ingenuity to serve our customers. And makes for a heckuva story!

As if we weren't pampering ourselves enough on that Pizza Tuesday night, the appliance we chose to power that night was the DVD player to watch the movie, Tommy Boy. This was possible only because it wasn't raining out, so we didn't need to run the sump pump. Although we'd seen the movie before, the novelty of the situation made it seem like the first time. Pizza and a movie? We were truly spoiled that night.

Many, like Tony, found creative ways to turn elements of the Storm to their advantage; after Kevin Sylvester shared his Storm memories with the Sabres via voice memo, he sent a follow-up text about something he'd forgotten to include: "I also remember grabbing stuff from our freezer and burying it in the ice and snow on our patio on the second day. I don't think that's recommended, but it work[ed]. I grilled the frozen waffles for the kids for breakfast [and] we used the grill for most hot meals that weekend!" Kevin was lucky, as this was something that Billy and his family had to address much earlier than five days in:

The next morning, now Saturday the 14th and about thirty-six hours after the storm started, we faced a new and unique challenge, especially for my grandfather: there was no way to make coffee. We had an electric stove top, and electric coffee maker, but no way to make coffee over the coveted gas fireplace. Well, in true Buffalo fashion and the brilliance of desperation and ingenuity, we grabbed out an old pot and an old baking sheet, turned on the gas grill that we had outside on the patio, and made a lovely breakfast for ourselves to both re-nourish after the day before as well as feast in preparation for the day ahead. It was at that point, as we were pulling out breakfast foods from both the fridge and what used to be the freezer, we realized that we were going to have to find an alternative way to start storing some of our cold food. Ice was not in large demand in Buffalo in October, and certainly was not something I had managed to bring back from Wilson Farms the day before, however there was still quite a bit of the natural stuff outside… So that's exactly what we did. We grabbed a cooler and started to dig a hole in the snow that was left in our backyard. We had a shady section of our yard that didn't get a lot of sun so it hadn't melted yet and would be the best spot to stash our goods; we grabbed as much snow as we could and relocated it to this shady corner, put the cooler in the snow, filled the cooler with the essentials, put snow inside the cooler in lieu of ice, and then buried the entire cooler in the snow mound. We agreed we only go in for absolute necessities, which did not happen often. That lasted us for a lot longer than any of us thought it would - a couple days, at least!

On Wednesday, October 19th, six days into the aftermath of the Storm, Claire broke down crying. She wouldn't say why at first, but she finally revealed that she missed school. In essence, what she really missed was not celebrating her 7th birthday with her classmates. *Oh man.* With the Storm having turned our lives upside down for a week, we'd forgotten. Not that we forgot her birthday, but we did forget that you're supposed to *celebrate* your 7-year old's birthday. We had tried to eat out the night before at the Montana's restaurant at Amelia Place in Orchard Park, but no sooner than we sat down, the power went out. While we were disappointed in not being able to stay, I think we were all mostly upset because we were looking forward to seeing Claire wear that moose hat!

We figured Claire knew that we'd have a delayed party for her once things got back to normal, starting with electricity coming back. But apparently we didn't convey that very well. Fortunately, our very thoughtful neighbors up the street, Chris and Kristine Bajdas - Derek and Haley's parents - did not forget. With a generator system that drew (knowingly, not pirated) from their neighbor's Cadillac system, their whole house was basically powered up. Anna had told Haley that it was Claire's birthday, so the Bajdas family spontaneously and graciously threw her a birthday party with Anna, Derek, Haley, as well as co-author, Billy. It was a nice escape for the girls from the dreary life of storm cleanup, not to mention for us, too! We will always remember and appreciate their thoughtfulness - just one more reason I will be eternally grateful to live in the "City of Good Neighbors."

Finally on Thursday, one week since the Storm hit, the utility trucks for New York State Gas and Electric (NYSEG) came down Hi View Terrace - *at last*. House doors burst open as practically every person on the street flocked to the trucks like ten-year-olds to an ice cream truck in July. It had been seven days without power that felt like seven weeks and it only seemed longer as we stared at the technicians and waited for the lights to pop on - following what I can only picture as a cartoonishly large and red-handled lever in a box hidden on our street that magically would turn all the houses back on.

The anticipation was unbelievable. We were pacing around, high-fiving with such joy as we watched them reconnect the downed power lines. Perfect timing too as my "Weekend" friends would be arriving the next day. Finally, after about twenty minutes, it happened: accompanied by a loud hum, there was **light**.

Except…. not at our house.

Or about six houses on either side of us. Or across the street. One pocket of about twenty of our homes remained dark. Treehaven Road, Billy's street directly behind ours, lit up like a Christmas tree, except mostly orange with Halloween decorations and lighting, as did the rest of our street to either side of the "Unfortunate Twenty." While no one on our street heard it, Billy insists that he heard several people from Hi View yelling expletives towards his street when the lights kicked on - interestingly he said the voices sounded like mine and my neighbors, too! Jokes aside - what we didn't know was that Treehaven wasn't as lit up as it looked. According to Billy,

*Much to the chagrin of some of our neighbors, one week after we lost power, it kicked back on - well, sort of. Only half of our neighborhood came back on, and we, being in the middle of our street, somehow got caught in the middle of these two lines, unbeknownst to us until that point. (But I will tell you half of a house lit up is better than none!) The fridge suddenly sprung to life, our bedrooms suddenly lit up just before another dusk, and nothing else seemed to matter. It was the first time in a week that our lives seemed somewhat normal again. To this day, even though I have left Buffalo, whenever the power goes out I still take a moment and wonder to myself, **How long will it be out for this time?** My Mom, on the other hand,*

> *takes the opportunity to try and find a shopping mall*
> *or a movie theatre to get away from the reminder of*
> *the cold, dark silence that we experienced for so many*
> *days and nights.*

The great anticipation we and our neighbors shared, only to be followed by such a tremendous let-down, reminded me immediately of the feeling of attending Super Bowl XXV at Tampa Stadium in 1991. It was the first Super Bowl ever for the Bills who battled the New York Giants that famously came down to Scott Norwood's Field Goal attempt in the final seconds - something that all Buffalonians, regardless of age, not only know of, but know to *not* talk about in certain company.

Our vantage point for the kick was from about the 30-yard line. I told Amy, as well as my Dad and Anthony who had attended the game with us, that if the kick was long enough, it would be good since Norwood's accuracy was a given. As soon as the ball came off his foot, it was clear that it would be long enough, so Amy stood up, arms in the air to celebrate. I couldn't yet tell if it went through the uprights since it was happening from our left to right, so I looked down at the referees waving the "no good" signal followed by the thunderous roar (as well as the dramatic shift in the air) from the Giants players and fans celebrating. Amy still didn't see this and I, still seated with my Dad and Anthony, had to tug on her shirt sleeve to let her know the kick was <u>no good</u>. *Utterly devastating.* (And for those of you who don't know who Scott Norwood is, a simple search for "Wide Right" and "Tears of Buffalo Fans" should give you all the answers you need.)

The NYSEG repairmen appeared puzzled - so we were flat out horrified. One of the technicians peered upward to see that the transformer above us had blown – the same transformer that Jason watched explode from across the street one week earlier at 3:00 am and turned the night skies blueish green. Even as non-electrical workers, it was clear there would be no power for us until this transformer was replaced.

Amy quickly volunteered, "Where can we get one? We have a Subaru! I'll drive there **right now** to pick one up!"

They politely replied, with a bit of a smirk, "Ma'am, the transformer weighs about 600 pounds. But we have them in stock in Tonawanda and we can have one in place by tomorrow."

Besides the landscape suddenly awakening with the sight of lights, the sounds changed as well, in the form of... silence. It was weird to notice the ambient noise decline as folks were now shutting down their generators one by one and that concert of rattled humming which had run continually for a week and blended into the background was no longer there. Silence never sounded so sweet and so unfamiliar as many of us had acclimated to the continual buzzing.

It was bittersweet as we watched Treehaven (which would fully come on an hour or so after the first half of Billy's house came on) as well as the rest of Hi view, outside of the pocket of "Unfortunate Twenty", seemingly turn on every light they owned just because they could; we felt like we were being taunted, but, as promised, the NYSEG truck came back the next day and replaced the transformer delivering us some of that sweet, sweet electricity!

This was just *one day* before "The Weekend." *Yikes.*

Guys were going to start pulling into town the next day, but this was no ordinary gathering we were trying to prepare for - we're talking about ten guys, away from their spouses and partners - one can only imagine! We only had room for three to stay in the house so the others had hotel rooms nearby, but during certain times of The Weekend, all of them would be in our house – starting early the next evening. I also knew that Amy, while appreciative of their willingness to help clean up the mess, was worried that the house was still not ready.

I also knew they'd be shocked by what they were about to see.

"And God said, Let there be light: and there was light. And God saw the light, that it was good: and God divided the light from the darkness.
And God called the light Day, and the darkness he called Night. And the evening and the morning were the first day." - Genesis 1:3 - 5[10]

---

[10] *The Bible.* Authorized King James Version, Oxford UP, 1998.

THIRTEEN
THE WEEKEND, THE CLEANUP

In April of 2005, our family ventured south to Indialantic, Florida, near Melbourne Beach, for our annual Easter break vacation at the ocean-view condo that my parents rented every year for the whole month of April. Besides being Amy, Anna, and Claire's school spring breaks, it was a good time to venture south as Buffalonians will universally concede that Spring in Western New York usually *just doesn't happen* with a flip of a switch on the Spring Solstice date on March 21st. In Buffalo, Summer, Fall, and Winter are mostly in full-swing on their official "start days" of 6/21, 9/21, and 12/21, respectively, but not Spring; Spring is too often a bit of a process, Spring is playing catchup, but much like a freight train, once it gets rolling, it gets you where you want to go.

In Indialantic, our days were spent at the pool, on the beach, and in the ocean. At night, after the early bird specials had wrapped up and cleared out, we'd enjoy our favorite restaurants on that Route A1A corridor like Dos Amigos, Long Doggers, Bizarro's Pizza, Squid Lips, and we'd also designate one day to hit up one of the Disney Parks. In 2005, we added a new tradition: my Dad and I arranged to meet two of my cousins, Doug Schoen from Apopka and Johnny Van Wicklin in Bradenton, along with two friends, Anthony Staiano in Tampa and Mike Mezzano in Apopka, for dinner at the ESPN Zone at Disney's Boardwalk. Amy, Anna, Claire, and my Mom enjoyed their own girls' night out shopping, followed by dinner and a movie.

It was awesome seeing these guys again. Some of them hadn't seen each other in over a decade. Shortly into the conversation, the topic turned to football. Doug mentioned, in jest, "I'd love to go to a Bills game, but I've never been invited to one."

I said, "OK, no more excuses. You're coming – all of you - *this* fall. We'll make a weekend out of it." And thus, "The Weekend" was born.

Upon returning home to West Seneca from vacation, I emailed the Disney Dinner guys to verify they were really in for a weekend Bills game and that it wasn't just the beer talking. They each confirmed they were fully committed so we now just needed a date. We settled on the October 9th game versus the Miami Dolphins - always a love-to-hate rival for Bills fans. As great as these plans already were, from there it still grew: I reached out to my brother-in-law, Scott Olsen (then of Butler, PA, now Seattle), cousin Bob Van Wicklin (then living in Washington D.C, now in Ellicottville, NY), close friend Larry Page (Gainesville, GA), old Houghton college roommate Frank Garrigues (Canisteo, NY), college friend Chris Bergstrom (local in Tonawanda, NY), as well as high school friends Ron Kuiken and Chris Edwards (of Albany and Ellicottville, respectively); They were all in, *too*! I cut it off there lest Amy thought it was Woodstock at Hi View Terrace.

Simply citing current locales next to their names falls woefully short of detailing my personal histories with this group: we played high school sports, roomed in college, spent summers, took road trips, attended Major League Baseball, NBA, and SU College Basketball games, and concerts - *so* many concerts. It seemed every time an artist died in recent years, like Eddie Van Halen or Neal Peart of *Rush*, my mind instantly remembered seeing them in concert with some combination of this group. We shared personal losses together.

But then we stood up in each other's weddings and several of the guys attended Super Bowls with Amy and me:

- Super Bowl XXV in Tampa vs. the Giants: Amy, my Dad, and **Anthony**
- Super Bowl XXVI in Minneapolis vs. the Redskins: my Dad, Mom, and **Scott**; Amy couldn't make that one because of work, but the rest of us met up with **Chris Edwards** and **Frank** there.
- Super Bowl XXVII in Pasadena vs. the Cowboys: Amy, my sister Tracy, **Scott**, and **Bob**
- and Super Bowl XXVIII in Atlanta vs. the Cowboys: Amy, **Bob**, and **Mike**; it's worth noting that **Johnny** sat with Amy at the home playoff game versus the Oilers that year that still stands as the greatest comeback in NFL history - and yes, they stayed until the end!

They all know each other from either growing up in Speculator, NY, and attending Wells High School, serving on staff at Camp-of-the-Woods (also in Speculator), or attending Houghton College. Several chapters worth of stories could be written about each and every one, but I won't take us down that rabbit hole here - which I'm sure they would also agree is a much better idea, too.

But being all together, in Buffalo, for a Bills game weekend, was a new frontier we couldn't wait to explore! In later years, we would be joined by Jay Briggs (Washington, D.C.), Earl Johnson (Almond, NY), and Tom Orser (Denver, CO). And, of course, it's always great to have my Dad there, who knows them all to some degree. While he doesn't partake in the Saturday afternoon recreational activities, he always ensures that we have a roaring backyard fire on Saturday night. As Director of Camp-of-the-Woods in the Adirondacks for thirty-seven years, where many of them had served on staff as teens, he would close his eyes, shake his head, and smile upon hearing the misdeeds that ~~they~~, ok *we*, have admitted to decades later.

For accommodations, I reached out to my great contact Linda Shultz, at the Millennium Hotel by the Galleria, who managed the Bills' Saturday night stays there nights before home games that season. Linda generously carved out a few rooms at a very favorable rate for us.

All of the guys, including the five who fly up from the south and were originally from the north, enjoyed living in the south. But they all agree - there's something special about that crisp autumn air up north. Not everyone is able to come back every year, life has a way of getting in the way, but some combination of them, and always a majority, are able to return to keep it going. Thankfully, and most importantly, Amy and the girls have always been so receptive to this gathering and the guys are always smart enough to thank Amy before me for making The Weekend happen.

The Inaugural Weekend of October 2005 went off without a hitch. It was a blast catching up and sharing memories of *the glory days* as many hadn't seen each other in fifteen years! Although not everybody knew everybody at first - there was probably 80% or so overlap - the chemistry was instant like lightning in a bottle - though this lightning was not as blue as the Storm's. Even Chris Bergstrom, years later, would share how much he appreciated the friendships that developed and grew from the foundations they had that have been fertilized with the memories of these Weekends.

The blueprint established this weekend would stand true for future Weekends, starting with a backyard fire on Friday night, many of which Billy can actually remember hearing from his house on the street behind us in hindsight, always happy to hear the wonderful friendships reconnecting year after year. On Saturday afternoon, we played flag football – where we, eventually and wisely, put my nephew, Tory Olsen, on one team and Frank's son, Joe Garrigues, on the other – young guns who could run all day long.

We injected more youthful legs from Anna, as well our neighbor friends, Derek, Haley, and Tom who would be the ones bailing us out - literally and metaphorically - only a year later. Thankfully, other than Doug wrecking his ankle one year, there have been no other injuries, other than all of us being sore for days after... Not that any of us would admit this when The Weekend was over.

We graduated to the Ellicottville Ropes Course (after which we challenged each other with 'grossest bruise pictures'), bowling, which naturally morphed into low risk, but still competitive golf at Silver Lakes in Perry. No matter how we spend Saturday afternoons, an evening of wings, cigars, and liquid refreshments awaits us at home for "recovery." In our 2005 inaugural Weekend, our limo of hungry savages invaded the Anchor Bar where, at least to the best of our memories, it seemed as though bottles somehow grew straight up through the floor under our table... Anthony and Chris Bergstrom have always been charged with ordering wings with a Copernicus-like calculation that sometimes exceeded 250. They would be deeply offended if even a single wing went uneaten. In the rare cases when that happened, they even took a photo of that shameful wing (which was our fault). Any healthy eating habits go on hiatus for forty-eight hours; not just off the wagon, we knock the wagon over and then push it off the cliff. Once, when picking up the order at Duff's in Orchard Park, we asked what their largest takeout order ever was to which they responded, "The Green Bay Packers [the night before their game against the Bills just around the corner in Orchard Park] once ordered 2,000."

The Weekend schedule concludes on Sunday afternoon at the Bills game where Chris Edwards hosts an awesome pre-game tailgate cookout in the stadium parking lot that I actually got to enjoy for an hour before changing into dress clothes for the game, a rare treat for those of us who have to *work* at the game. If the Weekend happened to take place during Ellicottville's Oktoberfest, Chris would host other friends for the game as well from the Speculator/

Piseco area including his brother Bill, Jon Swift, and Dave Blessing. Much of what I learned about organizing our "Weekend" I learned from Chris. He had organized his own great Winter Weekends in Speculator and Piseco where we'd ski at Oak Mountain or Gore, then meet for dinner at Melody Lodge or the Oxbow Inn. There, Rick Swift and Anthony Alfieri, who had tended to their businesses during the day (winter was very busy with tourists), were able to join us.

After the Bills game, we come back to the house where Amy had cooked up a crockpot of chili or a giant pot of spaghetti, after which most guys hit the road, often helping with airport drop-offs on the way. A few guys with early Monday morning flights stay over Sunday night, dubbed "The Winddown," when we watch the Sunday night NFL game or World Series. By this time, I am usually so deeply satisfied by the successful conclusion of The Weekend that I often express my satisfaction by falling to sleep, hard, almost always before the conclusion of those games.

Anna and Claire loved the infusion of a houseful of crazy, loving uncles, especially when their *actual* Uncle Scott was there. And Amy, who knew them all well, traded 'grievance stories' with the teachers in the bunch who more than validated her maternal style approach versus their more raw "Mr. Woodcock" ways.

On Friday, October 20, 2006, despite major doubt just a few days earlier, the 2nd annual "October Weekend" was underway. Chris Bergstrom, who lived closest in Tonawanda, was once again hugely helpful with airport pickups so I could tend to home base. Amy pulled into the driveway after her first time venturing away from the house in over eight days. *From where?* From the McKinley Mall, with a huge box labeled "Surround Sound." Nothing like *easing* back into normalcy. Her strategic purchase was inspired by another "we deserved it" moment as well as knowing amongst these friends there would surely be some skilled self-proclaimed electricians able enough to install the SIX speakers and box into our existing set up. Amy was right: Chris and Doug were all over it. Once set up however, a battle over TV rights between the Sabres and West Virginia College Football games ensued. Thankfully, it was a great night of laughs and catching up, mostly inside because of rain, before the busy day that lay ahead.

On Saturday morning, as Ron walked into our back room (which faced the backyard) he nearly spit out his coffee when he caught his first glimpse of the sea of downed trees. The guys had mostly come in the night before, in the dark, so this was their first glimpse of the carnage in the daylight. "Who agreed to sign us up for this? Is it in writing?" Mike jokingly asked.

Those who soon came over from the hotel had the same reaction. Even Chris Bergstrom, coming from North Tonawanda, couldn't believe how West Seneca still, one week later, looked like "Ground Zero" for something he had not experienced firsthand until that point.

"We're gonna need a bigger chainsaw," Frank said. The 2006 Weekend's Saturday afternoon "activity" this year was hauling logs, hopefully one activity that would never be repeated.

But before we took on the lawn monster, I had arranged to spend the morning doing something pretty cool. Dick Jauron was big on having the families of players, coaches, and staff feel a part of the organization and one way of showing this was to open up the Saturday morning walk through practice. With game planning already finished, the practice was very light: no real contact, no pads, just one last sharpening up. Those who took Dick up on this reciprocated with total respect for the practice by having family members watch safely from the sidelines so as not to interfere with any play.

Not wanting to abuse the privilege, but hoping to give my friends the opportunity to watch a live NFL practice, I asked Dick during the week if bringing twelve would be too many. My comfort level in asking was high since I'd worked closely with him and his staff, starting with their relocations from their very first days with the team. In full disclosure, I explained that while three were family, (cousins Bob, Johnny, and Doug), the others were close friends. Dick was also impressed to hear that they were helping clear trees and enthusiastically said "Yes." He went a step further, mentioning to grab him after practice so he could meet them.

And he did just that: at the conclusion of practice, he came over and cracked, "Don, you really admit to knowing *these* guys?" He then suggested a group picture, which he joined, and said to the group, "Good luck with those trees. Thanks for your support and hope you have a great time at the game tomorrow."

They were thoroughly impressed and returned the thanks. When the players cleared the field, we tossed a football around and kicked some field goals. Being a former soccer player, Frank was still able to hit from about thirty yards which was pretty impressive. In fact, I gotta say – they all still showed a good share of athleticism there as well as in the flag football we'd play in later years. Playing sports was a common bond we had since childhood, so I shouldn't have been surprised. The guys really appreciated the opportunity to watch practice, meet Coach Jauron, see the facility, and mess around on the practice field. This was only a warmup, however, as it was time to transition into lumberjack mode.

While we'd all worked our fair share of manual labor together, this would be our first group tree haul - although I do recall, during one preseason at Camp-of-the-Woods feeding downed trees into a wood chipper, including staff friend Jimmy Olsen quipping, "I've stood in line for many things, but never a wood chipper."

Before we even got started, Larry saw the equally nasty mess in our neighbor's huge yard and asked who lived there. I explained that it was an elderly widow and that after they all helped me today, I intended to spend the remaining fall weekends (aka the Saturdays before home games) working on hers. They all agreed, *Heck with that, let's knock them both out today!* Frank brought a few chainsaws, but Doug opted for tree-dragging duty since he had once taken over forty stitches to his thigh courtesy of a chainsaw leaving a scar that would make Quint and Hooper from *Jaws* proud.

We changed into our work clothes and immediately got into a good groove pulling trees. Being a Physical Education teacher, Frank called out the plan, fired up the chainsaws, and got things going. Amy, Anna, and Claire joined the tree dragging party too - though we did have to clarify a few times that it was a drag*ging* party, the second syllable really making sure to define the goals of the day. In the meantime, the daughter, who had come the day after the storm to bring her mother (the homeowner) back to her home so she wouldn't have to live without heat and electricity, had come to check on the house and was thrilled to tears to see us clearing the backyard. Seeing our numbers, she asked if we could help her with something inside their basement. Doug, Ron, and I were the closest, so we followed her inside the house and downstairs. *Oh boy, her problems were much bigger than needing a few things removed.*

As our basement had flooded over a week ago, so did hers, but while we were able to stay on top of the bailing and, more importantly, got the sump pump working, her water had sat there for **nine days**, ruining chairs and carpets. She conceded that the carpets were goners and asked us to pull them up and bring them to the curb to be thrown away. There were about ten sections of super heavy, wet carpet - and they smelled like… like carpet that had been sitting for nine days under stagnant water. Worse, a combination of liquids composed of the melting contents of the fridge and freezer seeped down into the fabric. Brian Fantana's "Sex Panther" cologne from *Anchorman*, with bits of real panther, had *nothing* on this carpet - though this too "stings the nostrils." I'd suggest that Law Enforcement consider this concocted potion for riot enforcement, except it would be considered too extreme. As Doug, Ron, and I brought the first section up the stairs and out the side door, Mike and Anthony crossed paths with us coming back from the street.

Catching one whiff of the carpet, they carefully avoided eye contact, picked up their pace, and briskly whistled their way to the backyard wanting *no* part of that project; Doug suddenly wished he'd hedged his bets and chosen chainsaw duty. *What's another forty stitches?* Chris Bergstrom recalls, "Seeing your guys' faces coming out of the house, I took advantage of all the other activity to choose another path and skillfully and shrewdly avoid *carpet patrol.*"

In about three hours, the eleven of us had cleared both our AND our neighbor's yards - it was a great feeling. We think Anthony even ripped a tree from its roots that was not remotely affected by the Storm. As we were wrapping up, Rich Costanza, our neighbor directly behind us and next door to Billy and his Mom, saw our gang and asked if we could remove a large branch that was hanging on the power lines over his house. I was going to respectfully decline, simply for safety reasons and knowing that either the Town of West Seneca or New York State Gas & Electric would take care of it for him. Seeing the potentially perilous situation develop, Chris was poised to say, "Run. Run away." But it was too late. Frank, perhaps still feeling the momentum, climbed the forty-foot ladder, with a chainsaw, and successfully dislodged the log as we all could barely watch. (Rich, who has since passed, was also the father of Anne Marie who joined Billy on his adventure to Wilson Farms the morning after the Storm!) Moments later, the daughter of our neighbor whose yard and basement we cleared, motioned me over in order to hand me an envelope. I tried to decline it, but she wouldn't take no for an answer; the contents of the envelope paid for the wings we were poised to devour that night.

After getting cleaned up and changed, the fourteen-passenger limo pulled up to the house to take us to the Anchor Bar, as we had done in our Inaugural year. Upon arrival, due to the hundreds of Patriots fans "owning the joint" (don't worry, Bills Mafia, we know you do the same and more at road game cities), we were told there'd be a two hour wait. *Hmm.* We all agreed that was too long, so we called Duff's in Orchard Park who said our wait would be less than half of that. *Sold.* That's where we ended up and it did <u>not</u> disappoint - not that it ever does. (Billy is on record as "Duff's of Orchard Park" winning the Best Wings of Buffalo argument - thanks to Phil Kinecki for making and keeping it great!) The Weekend guys were blown away by the variety of wing flavors and we left more than satisfied, but also very, very tired. That didn't stop Frank from arranging a 4:00 am wakeup call for Chris at the hotel though just to keep things lively. Problem was - when Frank told Bob (who'd joined us just earlier that day because of a business meeting) about the prank, Bob replied sarcastically, "That's just awesome because I'm his roommate tonight."

While Sunday saw the Bills fall to the New England Patriots, it was another fun tailgate and everyone made their ways safely home that evening or the next morning. The remaining weekends in the Fall would return Saturday afternoons to a sense of normalcy in that they, hopefully, would not require chainsaws, although I think Jay Briggs said he could still juggle them if given the opportunity. I couldn't have been more grateful for their willingness, starting with Anthony and Chris Bergstrom calling me a week earlier, while still in Detroit, insisting that they *wanted* to help Amy and me out. All the guys came through and even made it somehow a fun experience, mostly because they emulated the response demonstrated by Pastor Gillis's Chapel congregation and so many others across the Buffalo region.

"The Weekenders" on their visit to The Practice Field House at One Bills Drive; Left to Right: Anthony Staiano, Ron Kuiken, Frank Garrigues, Doug Schoen, Chris Bergstrom, Bills Head Coach Dick Jauron, Mike Mezzano, Larry Page, Tom Cavanagh, Amy, Claire, and Anna Purdy

Amongst nervous on-lookers, Frank climbs the ladder to wrestle the tree off the wires while Claire observes through one of the broken fence sections.

Weekenders after the "The Big (tree) Drag"
at Don's House; Ready for some wings!....
after cleaning up ourselves, of course.

There's something very therapeutic about being amongst friends. Not being permitted to fully engage with friends is a significant part of what has made isolating events like snowstorms, other natural disasters, and viral and safety epidemics like the Covid-19 Pandemic of 2020 such a difficult time for so many, myself and Billy included. And it doesn't need to be ten or even two people, just getting together or having a random phone conversation with **one** friend is a lift. Perhaps the only regret I ever have following The Weekend gatherings is thinking to myself, *I wish I could have spent more time with so-and-so.* We've both learned that so often the most important things in life are the people you fill it with. Chris Bergstrom noted retrospectively, "I think I speak for all the guys that our motivation to continue with "The Weekend" that year was multifold; while we certainly wanted to help Don and Amy, we also recognized it as our yearly opportunity to see each other again." *Well said, Berg.*

"Leaves are falling all around
It's time I was on my way
Thanks to you I'm much obliged
For such a pleasant stay
But now it's time for me to go
The autumn moon lights my way"
- "Ramble On", Led Zeppelin, 1969

FOURTEEN
WHERE ELSE WOULD YOU RATHER BE?:
A TRIBUTE TO MARV LEVY

"I will never forget that first time I walked into the Buffalo Bills' team meeting room in early November of 1986 upon being appointed in midseason to take over as head coach. [...]

What an odyssey I lived with those men, with their teammates and coaches, with all the wonderful people in the Bills organization, and with those incomparable Buffalo Bills fans. For six consecutive years they led the NFL in attendance. Who cared if it was bitter cold or if an angry snowstorm was raging? Their spirits were as tough as linebackers; their hearts were as warm as the thermal underwear I wore during those January playoff games in Orchard Park. And what about those great players and coaches against whom we competed so fiercely?" - Marv Levy Football Hall of Fame Enshrinement Speech, August 4th, 2001[11]

---

[11] Levy, Marv. "Marv Levy Enshrinement speech." Pro Football Hall of Fame Induction Ceremony, 4 August 2001, Pro Football Hall of Fame, Canton, OH.

It's hard to properly express the depth of my admiration for the man who graciously lent his words to this book as the foreword, Marv Levy. This chapter is dedicated to giving it my best shot.

It's no exaggeration to suggest that Marv is as recognizable and beloved as any Buffalo sports personality ever. Bills fans and NFL fans in general are familiar with his unique communication style that combines an ability to brilliantly and simply break down the game of football along with an English History background that resorted to quoting Winston Churchill during team meetings. His game day Jekyll and Hyde transformation saw him curse out referees in his unique style, including calling one referee an "over officious jerk" which helped launch NFL Films' sideline sounds feature into what football fans today enjoy as "Mic'd up."

> *of·fi·cious| ə'fiSHəs | (adj.) assertive of authority in an annoyingly domineering way, especially with regard to petty or trivial matters; intrusively enthusiastic in offering help or advice; interfering;*[12] *meddlesome, overbearing, or self-important.*

The NFL Network recently ranked Marv in the Top 100 NFL Characters of all-time, and if you've never watched the ESPN 30 for 30 documentary *Four Falls of Buffalo*, what are you waiting for? Steve Tasker, Thurman Thomas, and others perfectly describe the players' love and respect for Marv.

Beyond these public recognitions, he is even far more impressive as a *person*.

By total coincidence, as a Houghton College student in 1986, I actually attended Marv's first game as Head Coach of the Buffalo Bills. From high in the upper deck, I cheered on the visiting Pittsburgh Steelers - as my childhood friends and family will attest, this Gold and Black fanship was actually part of my identity; my Lynn Swann

---

[12] "officious." *Oxford Dictionary*. Lexico.com, (n.d.). Web. 4 Nov 2020.

and Jack Lambert jerseys are seen in more than half of any family photos up until that point. The Steelers lost that November Sunday on the windiest game I'd ever attended; at some point, my Steelers hat blew off my head most likely landing in Canada. I also took a face plant in the parking lot as my crutches, needed for a dislocated hip sustained two months earlier in a pickup football game, got tangled in the "people river" of exiting fans after the game, so that day could have gone better. But in just two short years I would find myself working for the Bills under the same roof as Marv Levy who was about to take the franchise to unprecedented heights – and *I* would be along for the ride. (Big thanks to Professor Dick Halberg at Houghton College for pursuing that internship for me!)

Incidentally, nobody was more surprised than me how quickly my allegiance flipped. In 1988, the Steelers played at the Bills again - this time I was watching from the Press Box as a proud Bills intern. Early in the game, a Steelers Defensive back intercepted a Jim Kelly pass in the flat and, with "plenty of green" ahead, had an easy Pick Six Touchdown except he pulled his hamstring and ran out of bounds. *I celebrated* (just in my head as that's the only celebration allowed in the Press Box). That play was my litmus test of sorts. Yes, I began hating the Steelers - although I will always cherish the Steelers dynasty of pre-1988. (Nothing against the Steelers specifically as I began hating *every* other NFL team that stood in our way of winning titles.) Despite my affinity for the Gold and Black, I was welcomed into the Bills family with open arms - quite a phenomenon. So much so that sometimes I still can't believe how blessed an opportunity that was.

In my early Ticket Office years, every Friday afternoon our Controller June Foran - wife of my boss at the time Jerry Foran, gave me three crisp $100 bills to take upstairs to Marv's office. Both Jerry and June Foran had a great personal relationship with Marv and Bill Polian from having worked with both of them at the USFL's Chicago Blitz before all joining the Bills. Friday afternoons were unofficially considered a wrap for the coaches in terms of game preparation for that coming Sunday. Sure, there would be a light walkthrough on Saturday, but that was mainly for fine tuning the game plans that were already scripted. This left late Friday afternoons as a chance for coaches, who had worked well into the evening all week, to actually dine with their wives in a restaurant, watch their sons play high school football, enjoy seeing their daughters play soccer, go to the movies, or just hang out at home – *something,* **anything** other than professional football to provide some small measure of balance. So, when I brought that money to Marv's corner office, a part of the building that I would NEVER go near without being assigned such a task, he would be standing by the window or at his desk, smoking a huge cigar (back when this was allowed indoors), and had a check already written payable to the Buffalo Bills. I had no idea what the cash was for. Doesn't matter. I presume he just wasn't a fan of credit cards as many during that time still weren't. Also, no coach would ever have an opportunity to leave the office to visit a bank during the regular season. At least players had Tuesdays off. Not coaches and definitely not the Head Coach.

Marv would always thank me, then before letting me leave, he'd ask how I was doing, how Amy was doing, and even how I thought we would do on Sunday. I'd always say win, of course, and we usually did. To say this meant a lot is an understatement. And I wasn't getting special treatment - other than being assigned this task for some reason; he treated *everyone* with dignity and respect!

In the 1990's, when the organization was much smaller than it is today, I served as Business Manager, which included handling Accounts Payables and managing the Bills merchandise sales under the long-distance direction of Christy Wilson Hofmann, daughter to team owner Ralph Wilson, who worked primarily from South Florida. Christy flew up for every home game and several times in the Spring to buy the merchandise in person. While unorthodox, it was an arrangement that we made work quite well.

When we won the AFC Championship for the fourth straight year by beating Joe Montana, Marcus Allen, and the Kansas City Chiefs, it meant we were headed to our fourth straight Super Bowl after having lost the previous three. The sentiment around the country at that point was, "The Bills? Again?" But the team, organization, and fan base truly didn't care about the rest of the league and country: we were thrilled to have another opportunity to win one – this time in Atlanta versus the Dallas Cowboys who'd beaten us the previous year.

Since there were two weeks between the AFC Championship game and the Super Bowl, some key front office members were sent to Atlanta several days in advance to prepare the hotel, practice facility, and other important advance work – an enormous logistical lift. I was assigned to stay back and work from Buffalo, still remaining in daily contact with those folks, and then travel with the team to Atlanta a few days later.

The day before we traveled to Atlanta, General Manager John Butler came storming into my office and growled, "Guys are wondering where they leave their luggage. Who's going to tell them?" (By guys, he naturally meant the players.)

Stumbling a bit, I said, "Bill Munson and Jim Overdorf have usually…"

John stopped me mid-sentence, "Well they're not here so who's going to do it? Is Schatzy (Bob Schatz) here?"

"Uh, no sir, Bob is also in Atlanta."

"Well, *guess* who's doing it then," he said, rhetorically. "The team meeting ends in fifteen minutes. Get down there *now* and make sure they all know what they need to know before they walk out that door."

"Yes, sir. I'm on it," I responded in a tone far more confident than I actually was.

Pure panic came over me. I'd been in my new position of Business Manager less than a year and my previous Super Bowl preparation had been in the Ticket Office, not in operations. I had **no clue** where the players were supposed to leave their luggage. Thankfully, from the adjacent office my colleague Mary Piwowarczyk overheard the conversation and, since she had actually been the one who made these arrangements, gave me the quick scoop. I think I hugged her before making my way down to the locker room where she was not permitted to go, but would have delivered the message herself if she could.

Mary was so trusted and loved by Mr. Wilson that once, during an office celebration of his birthday when he was unaware that a flame from his birthday cake caught on his sweater as he leaned over to blow out the candles, with a packed room paralyzed by indecision Mary began smacking his chest to relinquish the flames. While initially stunned, Mr. Wilson quickly realized why she'd done it and boldly, in his classic humorous style, proclaimed, "***That*** is a perfect example of why Mary will *always* work for me!"

As I approached the closed team meeting room door, I could hear Marv passionately telling the team, "They're going to say you don't belong. They're going to say you can't win. They're going to try getting under your skin. But we know who we are."

Just hearing the speech made me feel like running through a wall for Marv. The team echoed "Yeah!" after each of Marv's refrains. *What energy. What excitement. What power. And now, I was supposed to open the door and talk about luggage? What a letdown. And when exactly? What if it sounds like Marv is done, but he's really just preparing a dramatic pause and then I bust in too early?*

My heart was pounding through my chest. Finally, when I heard guys getting up from their chairs, I busted through the door and yelled, "Wait, guys – you are to leave your luggage in the tunnel next to the visitor locker-room in front of the equipment truck!" I did it.

They appeared to all hear me OK. Mission accomplished. I could now tell John Butler they knew.

Although the Super Bowl went smoothly with operations and logistics, we lost the game to the Cowboys in Atlanta. Despite the Bills building a touchdown lead at half-time, injuries and turnovers proved too costly in the second half versus the ultra talented Dallas team.

In retrospect, I believe that technically, I was the last person to address the full team, in person back in Buffalo, before Super Bowl XXVIII. One would rightfully conclude that the team would have been left in a better state of mind having last heard the amazing words of Marv Levy, one of the great Orators of our time, rather than my seemingly trivial, 17-second "luggage speech." This is something I've been meaning to get off my chest for a couple of decades now. To all of Buffalo and Bills Nation around the country: Go ahead. Burn me in effigy. Get it out of your system, but then please ultimately forgive me. I was just doing my job.

A couple of years later, my office was moved to an area of the building that happened to be next to the Media. Every Wednesday, as per NFL rules, Marv held a press conference in front of about a dozen reporters. During one particular session, multiple media members kept asking the same question – a question which Marv artfully chose not to directly answer as, for competitive advantage reasons, a direct answer would have tipped off that Sunday's opponent about strategy. This press conference reminded me of a Saturday Night Live episode a few years earlier during the first Iraq War when reporters continually asked Defense Secretary Dick Cheney, played by Phil Hartman, questions about his battle strategy which, if answered directly, would have given the enemy valuable information regarding the whereabouts of American troops.

Somehow, some way, I *had* to get a hold of that skit for Marv.

There was no Youtube at the time and coaches certainly were not still up at 11:30pm the night before a game. So, Scott Berchtold, Media Relations VP, used his NBC connections to secure a video tape of that skit which I gave to Marv. He LOVED it! So much so that after showing it to his wife, Fran, he later popped it in to show his assistant coaches during a gathering at his home that following off-season. It made me feel good to know I'd provided Marv with some level of levity.

My Saturday Night Live experience was
about to get a bit more personal.

Late one Friday afternoon in October of 1995, my assistant, Dan Deinzer, informed me that Saturday Night Live was on the phone needing something for a skit – the next night. Dan said, "You'd better take this one."

Sure enough, the SNL staffer nervously asked if we could ship an official NFL Bills sideline jacket, one that only the team carried, to him overnight. I asked what the nature of the skit was, but he wouldn't say. I put him on hold to discuss this most unusual request with Dan. Returning to the call, I insisted that we could only comply if the jacket would be shown in a positive light. Reluctantly, the SNL staffer said that the skit evolved around OJ Simpson and the jacket would be worn by a character playing Marv Levy. Sensing my continued hesitation, he then said, "Trust me – Marv will be portrayed positively and as the reasonable one."

Finally, I said, "OK, I can *sell* you the jacket. At full price. And *you* need to pay the overnight shipping charge."

"Done." he said, as he began reading their corporate credit card number.

The next night, I made sure to stay up to 11:30pm for the episode. *Yikes! It's the opening scene.* Sure enough, there's the jacket worn by then relatively unknown Will Ferrell playing Marv Levy being interviewed by Tim Meadows as OJ Simpson. As promised, the Marv character came off as the reasonable character, politely dismissing the OJ character's bizarre line of questioning about the Bills "murdering" the Jets and ultimately spelling out "I did it" on a football play teleprompter. Very funny, actually, and I was extremely relieved about how Marv was portrayed. For the record, hypothetically, even if I didn't personally like our Head Coach, I'd have been just as protective of our team brand - but, did my personal affection for Marv weigh more heavily into my hope that the scene was above board? *Sure it did.*

In the mid-90's Marv was diagnosed with cancer. Thankfully, it could be treated, but it meant he would take a leave of absence for three weeks during the regular season so Marv chose Running Backs Coach Eli Pitts to serve as interim Head Coach until his return. Roswell Park, a proud Buffalo Cancer Treatment Center who had just treated General Norman Schwarzkopf with the same cancer, took great care of Marv – as they do every patient. When Marv left Roswell, he couldn't yet be at the office so the team asked me to drive Bills practice film to his house. I was prepared to leave the film at his doorstep, but Marv and Fran insisted that I come in for a visit. Marv took me from room to room, proudly showing pictures of his father who was a military war hero.

What a privilege for me (fourth row from bottom, second from left) to have played even a small role in this dynasty. If only I could have prepared better for my luggage speech.

Marv retired as Head Coach from the Bills after the 1997 season. *What a career.* There was no doubt he would be elected into the Pro Football Hall of Fame - it was just a matter of how many others from that great team would follow. The Football Writers of America rightly voted in six more from Marv's team, including owner Ralph C. Wilson, Jr., and there may be more. Marv, as always, led the way.

In 2006, the Tom Donohoe era as President and GM ended. Despite his battles with the press and a management style that worked for some, I experienced my greatest professional growth during Tom's tenure and will always be thankful for how he saw my value with the organization. He is now a consultant with the Eagles who earned a Super Bowl ring and I've since shared my appreciation of his support with him. Replacing Tom would not be easy, so Mr. Wilson asked his trusted friend, Marv, to help with the search. As the intensive search unfolded, Mr. Wilson, asked "Hey, Marv, what about *you?*" After much contemplation, including a serious conversation with Fran, Marv accepted.

How great to have him back in the organization!

Given his humility, Marv's ability to recognize and recruit talent was one of his few personal qualities he'd openly speak about. He often publicly praised his assistant coaches during his incredible Head Coaching run in the 1990's and arriving at One Bills Drive for a different role in 2006, he immediately did the same. Recognizing that Jim Overdorf was one of the best Salary Cap managers in the league in his role as VP of Football Administration, he quickly established that Jim would continue in that role.

Marv's first order of business as GM was to select a Head Coach and make sure he was surrounded by the best football minds available. He ultimately decided on Dick Jauron who held a similar temperament and led the Chicago Bears to a 13-3 record for the proud franchise's biggest turnaround in team history, while also winning AP's Coach of the Year award.

After checking that huge box, Team Treasurer (and Mr. Wilson's most trusted financial man) Jeff Littmann requested a meeting with Marv, Jim Overdorf, John Guy, Kevin Meganck, and me to discuss a critically important salary cap plan going forward. The meeting was in Mr. Wilson's office, so it felt even *more* important. Jeff was way ahead of the game in many regards; he actually chaired League committees and was highly respected around the NFL, including by owners. Jeff was already preparing the team for a possible work stoppage **five years** in advance, when in 2011, an Owner's Lockout did occur. Thanks to Jeff, the Bills were financially prepared – with the salary cap and on the business side. Perhaps where Jeff's intelligence is both a blessing and curse is his unawareness of how far ahead he is than his audience. Being less than fully prepared for a work-related conversation with Jeff was not pleasant as I found out the hard way a couple of times. Put it this way - in 2015, Linebacker IK Enemkpali was cut by the Jets for breaking his own starting quarterback, Geno Smith's, jaw after a locker room argument over a few hundred dollars. Our new Head Coach, Rex Ryan, snatched him up off the waiver wire in a blink - having coached him at the Jets a year before. The signing was legitimate, the guy could play, but it also clearly served as some type of message, the exact message about which I won't speculate, to the Jets and the rest of the League. The next day, IK sat across my desk in my office guest chair, stone-cold silent with an icy stare, as I helped him with some financials. But, I was ten times happier dealing with a situation like that than getting caught flat-footed with Jeff. On the flip side, some of my most rewarding moments were annual budget meetings with Jeff when my mastery of the numbers provided a level of comfort that even injecting some humor seemed appropriate and appreciated by him. (And for the record, while all I knew about IK up to that Day was about his infamous incident at the Jets, he later turned out to be a pleasant, easy-going guy)

When Jeff went deep "into the weeds" in this meeting, there was a lot of polite head-nodding but a gap of full understanding on our parts. Jim grasped most just fine because Jeff was not only "speaking his language," Jeff actually *invented* the language. After a very detail-heavy 90-minutes, we took a much needed bathroom break. Upon return, with all present, Marv asked Jeff, "Ok, can we start all over again at '*This* is the Salary Cap'?" Just one of countless examples of Marv's lightning quick wit.

While he grasped far more than he let on, his point was well-taken and it prompted him to ask Jim Overdorf, "Jim, you've got this, right?"

To which Jim replied, "I absolutely do, Marv. And I'll always show you the bottom line about how much a player will cost and affect our cap. Then you decide from there."

It was a solid, efficient formula that played to everyone's strengths and bandwidth. Marv also often publicly praised Jim's handling of the Salary Cap on television and radio which was gratifying to hear as I saw first-hand, daily, how hard Jim worked at his craft.

Marv's "2ⁿᵈ Act" with the Bills, now as General Manager, had him serving in a less visible, but no less important role than he did nine years earlier as Head Coach. Interestingly, it paralleled one of his own historical idols, Winston Churchill, who served a 2ⁿᵈ term in Britain after the Second World War. During the Covid-19 Pandemic of 2020, Amy found *The Crown* on Netflix which I enjoyed far more than I expected to. The series featured many of the tough decisions Churchill faced as Prime Minister that he needed to coordinate with Queen Elizabeth. The political calculations were extremely complex. Likewise, the most successful teams almost always need the GM and Head Coach, the 1 and 1A, working in harmony as was the case with the 1990's Bills. In his new role, fans didn't see him working the refs on the sidelines or rallying the team, but as GM, he helped *build* the team. Although the decisions he made as GM were different than the ones he made as Head Coach almost a decade earlier, he made them from his same core set of values. Character was very important to him, but he also recognized the premium to be paid for the most skilled players. He once shared a joke with a few of us in the office, something along the lines of,

> *When I was Head Coach, a Scout came back to tell us about this gritty college player he watched who would get knocked down but then get right up and fight. Got knocked down again, but rose quickly to keep fighting. So I finally said to the Scout, "Go get us the guy that keeps knocking him down."*

Classic, and as an aside - knocking down *your own quarterback in a locker room fistfight* was not the type of knocking down Marv was referring to.

> *"Then there are those who are closest to me who sustained and encouraged me, even during moments of searing disappointment. My precious wife Frannie, the happiest when we won, the saddest when we lost, the quickest to shed a tear or to wipe away one of mine. She has brought me love and joy. [...]*
>
> *My family, all girls, is here. Someone once lamented that given my enthrallment with this game, it is a shame that I never had a son. Well, he was wrong. He was wrong. Don't tell me I never had a son. I've had thousands of them, of every size, shape, color, faith, and temperament, and I loved them, every one.*

[...] And because of them I still hear echoes from those sounds which glorify this game."[11]

I was privileged to be assigned to sit with Marv on game days in an executive booth. Before the games even started, he observed and commented on how the wind was swirling in the stadium - he was keenly aware of how the wind affected passing, kicking, and field position, always wanting our offense to have the wind at their backs in the fourth quarter. This was just one of *so* many facets of the game he took into account; clearly it takes more than knowing Xs and Os to earn a place in Canton, Ohio's Pro Football Hall of Fame.

During the 2007 Draft, I was fortunate enough to be in the "War Room." My duties on Draft Weekend didn't kick in until the end of the 7th Round when I was responsible for handling the written correspondence with Agents whose players we signed as Rookie Free Agents. It was a frenzied two hours that resemble what Wall Street trading looks like on TV. So typically, I wouldn't go in that room for the first two days, but for the 2007 Draft the room was open so I sat in the back with Fran.

Marv's wife, Fran, is about the sweetest lady you'll ever meet. She's also an excellent complement to Marv socially - together they collectively remember an astonishing number of people, by name, that they've networked with over the years.

Prior to the start, we were chatting and Fran asked me who I thought we'd select - I didn't know for sure, but would have correctly guessed Marshawn Lynch. I jokingly responded, "I think we'll select a punter in the First Round."

Just then, Marv came to the back of the room to say hello to Fran. Right away, Fran said to Marv, "Don said we're drafting a punter in the First Round."

Marv immediately smirked and said, "Uh oh. Let me go tell Mr. Wilson and the staff about this change of plans."

Following the first-round selection of Lynch, we went upstairs to the cafeteria for lunch. A contingent of decision-makers always remain in the room in the event of trade talks. Fran sat with me, College Scouting Coordinator Doug Majeski, and some others. Doug asked Fran if she planned to go back to the Draft Room for the 2nd Round selection. She said, in a whisper, "No, I'm going to catch a movie at the theatre."

Doug naturally followed up with, "What are you going to see?" We assumed she'd be seeing something with a thought-provoking, perhaps mysterious plot, but no. Her answer was far more "crowd pleasing" for this lunch crew.

"Blades of Glory," she divulged with a sly smile.

Oh man. That answer made our day. We certainly had not pegged Fran as a Will Ferrell fan. Weeks later, I asked what she thought of Blades of Glory. "I laughed until I cried," she said. *Perfect.*

During the time of the storm in 2006, a close friend of mine and former Bills player, Brad Lamb, was enduring a very difficult personal storm of his own in Charlotte, NC. When I informed Marv about the legal trouble Brad was facing, Marv asked what he could do. Brad knew he'd messed up, but it was also easy to empathize with the extraordinary circumstances, the perfect personal storm, that surrounded his unfortunate business decisions that led to him owing a substantial amount to the IRS. He faced a possible sentence that everyone familiar with Brad's circumstances deemed grossly disproportionate to his misdoings. This included prison time and worse, leaving his wonderful wife, Angela, and their five beautiful children without him for a few years. Initially, I couldn't think of anything Marv could do, but after speaking with Brad, he suggested perhaps a letter to someone with some influence over his situation. He then immediately drafted a most moving, well-worded, sensible letter to North Carolina Senator Elizabeth Dole, asking for legal leniency.

It wasn't a one-and-done. Marv followed up, often asking how

Brad, his wife Angela, and their five children were doing as Brad was in Federal Prison in Morgantown, West Virginia. One of Marv's calls to me came just days before I visited Brad in prison so naturally I informed him of this early in our conversation. A friend Brad had made in prison overheard me telling Brad that Marv called to ask about him. It was funny to hear that friend jump in and ask, "Wait, did you just say that Marv Levy - the coach - called about *this* Brad, right here? Brad nodded nonchalantly, but this apparent non-chalantness was not to be confused with deep appreciation as Brad smiled as his eyes filled up with tears: it meant the world to him. Brad offers up, in his own words:

> *Coach Levy was not only an awesome coach but a great friend. I will always remember his genuine nature and how he truly cared about his players. This was not just words from Coach Levy but he followed it up with actions. During one of the most trying times of our family's lives, Coach Levy showed why we, as players, loved him so much. It was after I had been done playing in the NFL for over ten years. I found myself in hot water with a business that I owned. I made a few bad decisions and [...] I was facing a prison sentence of fifty-seven months and having to leave my wife and five kids alone to fend for themselves. I remember my great and long time friend Don Purdy called me and asked if it would be ok for him to share my dilemma with Coach Levy. As embarrassed as I was for being in this position, I said that would be fine. Once Coach Levy knew I immediately received letters from him and Bill Polian (who Marv made aware of my situation) while I served my time at Morgantown. I can't put into words what those letters meant to me.*

When you are in a place like that you feel a sense of hopelessness and of no worth. Their letters with their encouraging words brought back hope and allowed me to believe that I was still a good person. I remember two things in the letters that have left a lifelong impression on me: Coach Levy reiterated that he believed in me and my character and that is one reason they drafted me in the first place, and it would be a reason I would come out of this situation a better person. He encouraged me to make the best of a bad situation. (I remember making a decision that I would not get bitter but better during this time!) My GM when I played at Buffalo, Bill Polian, reminded me that I beat the odds in making it in the NFL and he believed 100% I would beat this and come out better and even more successful than before all of this. Coach Levy also called my wife, Angela, on several occasions during this time just to check on her and the family. This probably meant more to me than just about anything. For them to take the time out of their busy schedules for a former player and his family just goes to show you the kind of people they are and we will forever hold them close to our hearts!"

Being copied on the letters, I marveled at Marv and Bill's choice of words. Just one more example of Marv and Bill's like-mindedness and compatibility. It was a small window into how they collaborated to make decisions and masterfully lead one of the best teams the NFL would ever see – the Buffalo Bills of the early 90's. During the course of fulfilling Workers Compensation duties, I was often subpoenaed to produce copies of **all** records for former players including medical records and contracts. Whenever it involved a player from the early 90's the files included letters that

Bill Polian wrote during the off-season following Super Bowl losses. After reading some of them, I thought, *"No wonder* these players came back the next season hungrier than ever." The letters were so powerful, so true, and so inspiring that it prompted me to reach out to Bill one day to simply compliment him on works that the public would never see. Bill humbly thanked me for this observation and, of course, deflected the praise back toward the "team effort."

Days after I was released from the Bills in 2017, a couple of calls came up on my cell phone with a Chicago area code. I mistakenly thought it was a rather high-maintenance Assistant Coach that I'd been helping with relocation. Finally, I checked the voicemail and it was Marv. I felt terrible for deliberately not answering and called him back right away. Both he and Fran told me how sorry they were, how much I'd contributed to the Bills organization, and most importantly – how fine I'd be in the next chapter of my life. Little did I know at the time I'd be writing a book that featured him.

Marv Levy was inducted into the Football Hall of Fame on August 4, 2001 in hallowed Canton, Ohio. As timing would have it, the Bills had scheduled a three-day scrimmage versus the Browns during that same time at Edinboro University in Pennsylvania – about ninety miles from Buffalo and Cleveland. (Incidentally, my daughter, Anna, would attend Edinboro eleven years later on a partial lacrosse scholarship where she had a very positive experience and established life-long friendships).

As much as I wanted to be in Canton for Marv's big weekend, I was privileged to be assigned oversight and operational responsibilities at our scrimmage in Edinboro which would require me to stay until the very end to "turn the lights out", as they say, from the Bills end. It was fulfilling in a vicarious way, though, to know that, not surprisingly, a huge Buffalo contingent, along with so many of his players and fellow coaches, traveled to Canton to support Marv, Fran, and their family.

At the outset of my drive home from Edinboro, I found an ESPN radio station that was recapping the Hall of Fame weekend. The announcer chose one speech to play in its entirety. With all due respect to the fine speeches given by the other worthy members, including my childhood hero Lynn Swann, one can easily guess which speech they chose.

Following Bill Polian's crowd-pleasing introduction and presentation, Marv's speech fully lived up to his own high standards. Dare I say, I was moved to tears as I drove. With humor and humility, Marv spoke about what a privilege it was to coach in the NFL. For me, what a privilege just to know such a legend.

Thanks in great part to Marv Levy, I own four AFC Championship rings and can reflect on a rich NFL Front Office career. History will remember how Marv managed one of the NFL's greatest core of talent, along with their egos, to such heights.

When I asked Marv for his thoughts about the 2006 October Storm, within one day, he came through once more with words that serve as the excellent foreword for this book - for which I will always be grateful.

Finally, to the reader, thank you for following along with this non storm-related diversion. I truly hope you enjoyed learning more about the great Marv Levy and his wonderful wife, Fran!

> *"And finally, I hear words spoken to me more than 50 years ago by a man whose memory I cherish. He was my basketball coach and my track coach at Coe College. His name was Harris Lamb. And I will conclude my remarks today by repeating for you what he said to me*

so many years ago: "To know the game is great. To play the game is greater. But to love the game is the greatest of them all."[11]

Circa 1992. After many requests, I finally agreed to allow Marv to have his picture taken with me.

FIFTEEN
THERE IS TROUBLE WITH THE TREES

During a drive to Speculator, NY, to visit my parents in the Fall of 2020, Amy was cruising the web on her tablet when she came across the web site, Re-TreeWNY.org. - a grassroots program started by a gentleman named Paul Maurer who recruited forty volunteers in November 2006 to replace 30,000 trees lost in the most heavily populated parts of Western New York. They then worked with local authorities to get the remaining 30,000 trees planted by the municipalities themselves.

Given that we were still in the due diligence phase of the book, it was an exciting find. While we were pleased with our running narrative alongside the interesting and entertaining accounts we'd accumulated from the Bills, Sabres, Meteorologists, Radio professionals, Police, and others, we still lacked an environmental element that detailed the rebuild of Buffalo's beautiful tree landscape; a prime cause of the widespread damage during this storm, officially dubbed "Aphid" by the National Weather Center, was the trees. Likewise, anecdotally, we have heard through many stories shared that (falling) trees were the major source of the power outages, as well as home, property, and car damages. They were even the source of the most unsettling sounds - like "bones breaking" as Kevin Sylvester characterized, or like "gun shots" as Anna described; a case could be made, fairly or not, that thus far in our story, the trees have essentially played the role of a *villain*.

While Paul and the Re-Tree folks - which sounds like a 60's band but definitely is not - would certainly concede that the Storm used trees as weapons, they also correctly contend that the trees themselves were a *victim* of Lake Storm Aphid and defiantly, like Lieutenant Dan, Paul was not going to sit idly by and let the situation go unchallenged. We knew that if Re-Tree's efforts were still ongoing these fourteen years later, we *needed* to speak with them. So we left a voicemail with the Founder of Re-Tree WNY, Paul Maurer - and he did not disappoint.

Paul promptly returned our call to proudly report that they were indeed still operational having reached one goal but seeking to reach further goals. Secondly, he enthusiastically agreed to partner with us on this section of the book in an arrangement that was mutually beneficial. In addition to raising further awareness of Re-Tree's extraordinary accomplishments, we volunteered to channel a portion of our proceeds to their ongoing campaign, in addition to what we agreed upon with Marv Levy to donate to St. Jude's Children's Research Hospital. In exchange, Paul graciously offered us some of the mind-blowing pictures featured here along with fascinating facts that he'd gathered during his own research, and, most enjoyably, his stories from the experiences of bringing Buffalo's natural beauty back.

With so much to unpack from that conversation and his website, we set up a Zoom meeting about a week later; what we learned in that hour-plus long meeting was pure gold. Ironically, we joked with Paul, "And we thought we were almost done writing."[13]

As mentioned earlier, Paul's experience with the October Storm and his subsequent Re-Tree work began with his involvement the Eastern Hills Mall parking lot when it became the largest of the

---

[13] Highlights of this actual Zoom interview can be found on our website ThunderSnowOfBuffalo.com.

"command centrals" for the hundreds of trucks that came from out-of-state to help restore Buffalo's electric lines; Paul and 97 Rock's (96.9 WGR FM), DJ Dave Jickster answered the call by providing coffee and donuts to the weary electricians. While New York State and Erie County were supplying the trucks with the necessary fuel to keep going, Paul, Jickster, and many other good samaritan Buffalonians were keeping the *truckers and workers* fueled up and energized to help restore Western New York's power. The efforts of these essential workers truly inspired Paul to do more.

So his Re-Tree story begins here:

Naturally, we wanted to start at the origins of the movement; Paul was quick to credit the generosity of the late Stan Lipsey, former publisher of the Buffalo News, who, with the blessing of Buffalo News Owner Warren Buffett, got the ball rolling with much needed funding. He correctly pointed out that most successful operations need some initial capital and Stan Lipsey stepped up big time! Paul then lauded the Horticultural and Engineering prowess of Art Traver, Buffalo's Head Forester, and Ed Dore from Dore Landscaping who, among other things, helped gather supplies and planned the ultra efficient and easily teachable operation.

Paul made clear that he was not an arborist, which may technically be true as he wasn't a practicing tree surgeon, however, the dozens of fascinating facts about trees and about the organization's charitable efforts that he floated so effortlessly convinced us of two things: he had at least *become* an expert on trees and he was a humble man and the perfect leader for this community volunteer campaign.

The charity Green Goal joined Paul's movement as well; President Jim Pavel in a 2011 interview with Paul on Channel 2 remarked, "When we first surveyed the street [after the storm], it was enough to make any sane person cry." He then, rather prophetically declared, "We were determined to *make the communities healthy again.*"

The actual tree re-planting began in April of 2007, just six months after the Storm and the earliest possible opportunity after organizing, arranging funding, and waiting for the appropriate weather conditions for the soil to be fertile enough for growth. After the volunteers received some training sessions led by Dave Colligan, the first area targeted was the hard hit, downtown Buffalo "Fruit Belt" - many of the streets bearing the names *Elm, Oak, Maple, Cherry,* and so on. These inner city neighborhoods didn't initially trust the program or feel the need to maintain the trees once replaced, so Paul and his team quickly reached out and connected with prominent community members in each of the replanted areas to help build the pride in rebeautifying their own communities. After the utility company marked the gas and water lines, the remains of the old trees were removed, including the stump grind, which is very dusty and loud, not to mention costly. After eventually seeing the trees take hold and their landscape being aesthetically restored, the Fruit Belt neighborhood ultimately did embrace the effort, even taking ownership and subsequent great care of trees.

Re-Tree then focused their attention on the also hard hit areas of the Tonawandas and Cheektowaga. The resident volunteers used their own crews to plant and even started their own Tree farms. Kenmore and Williamsville/Snyder were next. (At this point we'll stop describing these areas as "hard hit" because *all* the targeted areas were.)

Another plus was that most of the trees came from nearby Springville, NY, only about thirty miles away. Schichtel's Nursery had a system, with the help of very good soil, of growing trees sturdy enough to be transported, but also supple enough to be pulled straight out from the ground to engage in this quick turnover. In 2009, Dore Landscaping, a Tree Farm, was established on 14th Street in downtown Buffalo; much like Schichtel's and Chestnut Ridge Nursery in Orchard Park, Dore Landscaping also provided trees for Re-Tree's work at very good prices and even produced over seventy-five different species which became especially important as

Re-Tree sought to replace trees lost with as similar as possible, if not the same, type of trees in each respective neighborhood. Many of these trees were even donated in various ways according to Paul, all of which he remains very grateful for in making Re-Tree's endeavor even more successful and achievable.

While Paul was not surprised by the interest this project generated, he was very surprised by the sheer *numbers* of volunteers - at times, he had more than he could even use. As much as he hated to, Paul sometimes needed to turn people away, but he always told them to follow up and keep themselves available, if possible, for upcoming bigger projects, like the one at University Heights where, in 2016, they planted 175 trees on *just <u>one</u> Saturday!* In addition to their work, many of the University of Buffalo students created a fantastic promotional powerpoint to help raise funds as Paul's deal that he made with most of the impacted communities and entities like University Heights was that if they paid for and planted 50% of the trees that area lost, he expected the other side to put up the same. Paul felt like this was a fair and balanced agreement that most towns and organizations he worked with were eager to utilize as "any help is great help!"

One unanticipated issue was the enormous weight of the trees. While the volunteers were willing and energetic, they were not the Offensive Line of the Buffalo Bills. Fortunately, a most innovative method of transporting and planting, developed by Nina Bassuk of Cornell University, saved the day. Nina's invention, "Bare Root Tree Planting", involves first severing the tree root, then dipping it into a hydrogel, and finally wrapping it in burlap. This makes it possible for the tree to be transported light, not wet, and without soil - making the transport so much easier. Then, once the tree is transported and planted, the hydrogel-wrapped root can, like a diaper, absorb a huge amount of water - up to one-hundred times its own weight - once in the ground to help keep the newly planted tree hydrated.

Another problem that arose was the emergence of the Ash Borer, a small green beetle that came from China and wreaked havoc on the newly planted Ash trees. Their damage also hurt the furniture industry as major local manufacturers, like Crawford Furniture, rely on Ash wood for much of their quality pieces. This wasn't the first tree plague that affected the downtown area as Dutch Elm Disease started wiping out many trees years before leading to groups like Leaf a Legacy Project, PLANT WNY, Buffalo Green Fund, and, of course, Re-Tree joining forces to address this problem, including re-planting, with an approximate $75,000 price tag according to an article written by Connie Oswald Stofko, editor and publisher of Buffalo-NiagaraGardening.com.

Filling out a trifecta of problems was one that was simple and fixable, but perhaps most avoided: water. Once the trees were planted, some started dying during the hot, dry summer to follow. While volunteers were plentiful for the plantings of the trees, usually on weekends, these folks had real jobs and demands on their time; it was now mainly up to residents to keep up the watering, but they needed to be made aware of how they could keep the trees alive and well. This is where two Re-Tree volunteers, Connie Trisk and Patty Ralabate, stepped in and took on this mission. In addition to filling and dumping five-gallon buckets of water on the trees, they made an effort to educate the residents along the way. Buffalo's Channel 4 (WIVB) News did their part to feature this story as well; the message seemed to catch on as while some trees did die, many were saved through this endeavor.

Aside from these problems that were being addressed, momentum was clearly taking hold: Buffalo companies like National Grid, National Fuel, and Moog stepped up to help with supplies, labor, and funding; Fisher Price, even though they were based in East Aurora which was not at all affected by the Storm, still offered money and resources for the planting up in Amherst. Other organizations like Blue Cross/Blue Shield of WNY, Resurgence Brewery, Home Depot,

97 Rock Radio, the Erie County Fair, the Buffalo Zoo, Buffalo Sabres, Buffalo Bisons, and even the Girl Scouts provided venues for fundraisers and events to promote Re-Tree WNY. Even ABC's Extreme Home Makeover got in on the act when they were working on an episode for a local deserving family. (*Incidentally, as wonderful as this show is, could they at least have the folks throw in a "Please" before the demand of "Move that bus!"? That always bothered me. So correctable. In defense of Extreme Home Makeover, "Move that bus!" is not as harsh as the over-a-century old, "Bring us some figgy pudding and **bring it right here!**" Or, "**We won't go until we get some!**" from Bing Crosby's 1962 version of "We Wish You A Merry Christmas", It sounds more like a ransom than a Christmas song, but I digress.*)

Entercom Radio, with Tim Wenger at the helm, donated WBEN Air time; they were joined by aforementioned WGR 550 Sports Radio and five other stations. Forest Lawn Cemetery launched a "Return the Forest to Forest Lawn" campaign; South Park and McKinley High Schools raised money along with the John O'Shei Foundation, Seneca Nation, and Garden Walk of Buffalo. The Buffalo News raised over $600,000 from their readers alone!

Hillary Clinton, then Senator of New York, having learned of the project connected with Re-Tree and asked how her office could help; she was so impressed by the organization that she continued to send Buffalo area staffers to their meetings to keep her appraised and aware of the progress. She, along with Mayor Byron Brown, also appeared at a photo-op at City Honors High School where she signed a shovel for Paul.

The 10,000th tree was planted in honor of "Buffalo's Favorite Son," Tim Russert. As a fellow alumnus of Canisius High School, Tim Russert's legacy was often lauded throughout Billy's education and experiences at 1180 Delaware so it was no surprise that he was honored in this way; aside from serving as Buffalo's greatest ambassador for the Bills, Sabres, and the region in general on the national news stage, perhaps no news anchor was more synonymous with being both hard-hitting and fair - a true rarity in today's politically charged environment.

Paul found himself in high demand from local media. Local TV stations couldn't get enough of this story. He was even booked on "Hot Sauce - Kitchen World", a show that, as the title suggests, had *nothing* to do with trees. At this point, he'd become a celebrity. It got to a point during research that I'd half expect to see him hosting The Price is Right or in the hot seat on The View. (By the way, Paul, you can now add "publicized in a book" to your impressive media resume!)

Re-Tree didn't seek the credit, only the results. Funds were allocated strictly and solely toward trees, stakes, ties, and other tree-related items. Not a penny went toward labor, which even all these years later is a tribute to the work and steadfast focus of Paul and his team. Civic pride and sacrifice drove these folks. Many planters shared that they would later drive their kids to show which trees they'd planted.

When we asked Paul who he might consider Re-Tree's "unsung heroes" he sighed and said, "Oh man, there are too many to name, but since you're pressing me to, I'll name just a few." Paul first mentioned Tim Finnell, an Alumni of the Park School and skilled organizer; as the beautiful campus of the Park School was slammed by the Storm, Tim took particular interest in its restoration and arranged for classrooms there to be opened up and used to train the Re-Tree volunteers, including in the cutting edge bare root method developed by the aforementioned Nina Bassuk at Cornell University.

In addition, Stephanie Berghash, who resides near Kleinhans Music Hall, is one that Paul kept included on as many plantings as possible. According to Paul, to say she loves trees is an understatement - perhaps "spiritual" better fits the bill as Stephanie was known to even talk with the trees, something we came to find out is much more common than either of us thought! Paul couldn't say enough about how hard she worked and how much she cared about Re-Tree's restoration drive; while he said there were many passionate people who cared, Stephanie was most driven.

Another unsung hero he felt compelled to mention was Linda Garwol who's known locally for her extraordinary work in the "Buffalo in Bloom" and "Master Gardeners"groups; it wasn't surprising to Paul that Linda would embrace Re-Tree as she, the Chairperson of "Buffalo in Bloom", leads the annual efforts to liven up summers at Niagara Square and other parts of downtown Buffalo with colorful flower gardens.

In 2008, Tim Finnell nominated Re-Tree for the National Arbor Day Foundation Award which was held in Lincoln, Nebraska. Paul and Co-Chair, David Colligan, traveled to Nebraska to officially receive the award and, despite being aware of Buffalo's massive tree re-planting effort, Paul and David were blown away by the disparity in numbers. There were several categories awarded - one group won their category for planting five trees. Another group received their category's prize for planting a dozen. When it was Re-Tree's turn to accept their award, they reported that, *so far*, they'd planted **EIGHT THOUSAND** trees! Attendees and presenters looked around as if to say, "You've gotta be kidding me." *Heck yeah, Buffalo! You've done it again.*

This example further reinforces Buffalo's reputation as a giving community, much like the generosity of Bills fans giving to Cincinnati Bengals Quarterback Andy Dalton's charity after his game winning touchdown pass over the Ravens sent the Bills to the playoffs, ending their playoff drought on January 3, 2018. When Dalton spoke at the 2019 Annual Athlete's in Action Breakfast at Buffalo's Hyatt Regency, hosted by Fred Raines and Frank Reich, he recounted how every time he re-freshed his screen he and his wife high-fived each other as the dollar numbers climbed to unimaginable amounts. Dalton and his wife were simply blown away by the generosity of Western New Yorkers. In 2020, in the face of a resurgence of the Covid-19 virus, Bills fans once again stepped up to donate to

Buffalo's own O'Shei Children's Hospital in response to the death of the grandmother of Bills Quarterback, Josh Allen. Within a month of Patricia Allen's passing, over $700,000 was donated, often in $17 increments as a nod to Josh Allen's uniform number; according to the Bills Organization, "The Patricia Allen Fund will directly support the hospital's pediatric critical care team, which provides life-saving care to pediatric patients."[14] There are countless other examples of this type of kindness, but, as Paul summarized it to us, "Buffalo eats this stuff up!"

When we informed Paul that local weather icon, Don Paul, had granted us an extensive interview, Paul lit up saying, "Love that guy!" They serve together on a Board of - you guessed it - Weather; the idea originated with then Congresswoman and current Lieutenant Governor Kathy Hochul asking Don Paul to start a Museum of Winter or even a World Weather Center as no such Museum exists in North America and, given its reputation for weather, *why* **not** *Buffalo?* We humbly requested that the museum include a book store.

Our Zoom meeting closed with Paul assuring us that Re-Tree would keep planting every spring and fall although until the funds and resources dry up. While there are some "ghost" or anonymous donors who continue to finance the group, Paul wished us well and expressed gratitude for our attention to his cause. More importantly, he kept the lines open for follow-up correspondence and delivered on every subsequent question we could throw at him.

A week or so after our interview, Paul arranged to meet and lend us some storm-related material he'd collected. We would have grabbed a cup of coffee, but indoor dining was still prohibited - just

---

[14] LaBarber, Jourdon. "Donations to 'Patricia Allen Fund' at Oishei Children's Hospital Eclipse $700,000." *Bills Mafia Continues to Donate to Honor the Passing of Josh Allen's Grandmother*, Buffalo Bills, 4 Dec. 2020, www.buffalobills.com/news/donations-to-patricia-allen-fund-at-oishei-children-s-hospital-eclipse-700-000.

one more joy of the 2020 Covid-19 Pandemic. So deep in the parking lot corner, with Denny's employees looking on from their break spot, Paul unloaded the contents of his car, mostly envelopes and generic cases, into mine. I wish we'd given this operation some cool code name as, from the perspective of the suspicious on-lookers, there certainly appeared to be some sort of "deal going down." And just as Paul more-than-delivered in his interview, so too did the amount of pictures, articles, and other materials that we feverishly tried to compile here.

After having met Paul and absorbing such great information, we simply could not imagine this book without Re-Tree WNY and him as a part of it. What's amazing is that as thorough as we attempted to be covering this incredible campaign, including the near 90-minute interview and follow-up emails, phone calls, texts, and even in-person meetings, there's even more out there that the reader can find online.

Cavalry of trucks arrives to help Buffalo's
best re-connect the region.

Paul with one of his ace crews at the Teddy Roosevelt site. L to R: David Colligan (pounding stake), Molly Quackenbush (CEO, Theodore Roosevelt Inaugural Site), unknown person, Laura Krolczyk (Chief of Staff for then Sen. Hillary Clinton), unknown person, Art Traver (acting City of Buffalo Forester, Re-Tree board member - in vest), Paul D. Maurer

Award to Stan Lipsey, publisher of the Buffalo News, the biggest supporter of Re-Tree. Left to right: Paul Maurer (Co-chair, Re-tree), Cindy Sterner Kincaide (Buffalo News Promotions Dept.), Judith Lipsey (wife of Stan), Stanford Lipsey, David Colligan (Co-Chair, Re-Tree). This was a fundraiser held at First Presbyterian Church, Symphony Circle, Buffalo.

Re-Tree Founder Paul Maurer speaking at City Honors
High School in Buffalo where Re-Tree, with support from
then-Senator Hillary Clinton and Mayor Byron Brown,
planted new trees at one of Buffalo's oldest schools.

One of Re-tree's "Unsung Heros," Stephanie Berghash (far
right) with Katie Istas, Randy Sheehan, and Dan Istas.

Next time you drive through downtown Buffalo or nearby affected areas and admire the beautiful landscape, be sure to remind yourself that those trees didn't just grow - OK, yes, they grew, but they had to be planted and maintained and now you've met the incredible folks who made much of that return to Buffalo.

"And the trees were all kept equal
By hatchet, axe, and saw... [And Aphid.]"
- "The Trees", Rush (1978)

SIXTEEN
CARVINGS FOR A CAUSE

Given that "Carvings for a Cause" is the name of the organization founded by **Therese Forton-Barnes**, about whom this chapter features, this title might seem lazy. Not for lack of trying, but neither Billy or I could come up with anything close to *this* good. While Paul Maurer and Re-Tree WNY masterfully solved how to replace the damaged trees taken by Aphid, Therese discovered a way to take those fallen, damaged, often centuries-old tree carcasses and have them transformed into art by her friend Rick Pratt and his chainsaw.

So, one may begin to wonder as we head into a second chapter about trees, "Why are trees so important?" For those unfamiliar with the greenspaces in Buffalo, thankfully we learned that there were still plenty who remembered the origins of these beautiful trees that came down in 2006, especially the ones in the Olmsted Park System of Buffalo. The Buffalo Olmsted Park System is made up of six parks, seven parkways, eight circles and other small spaces, all designed in the vision of landscape architect Frederick Law Olmsted. According to the Buffalo Olmsted Parks Conservancy, the original plan was to link a park system of six main with "tree-lined parkways and avenues" that were "designed to allow visitors to travel from one park to another without leaving the serenity of these green spaces."[15] The Buffalo Olmsted Park System was the first system of parks, parkways and circles in the United States and stretches from Riverside Park up in the Black Rock area, down to Delaware park in downtown Buffalo, and Cazenovia Park and South Park in South Buffalo, as well as various circles and parkways like Soldiers Circle, McKinley Parkway, and Red Jacket Parkway along the way.

Frederick Law Olmsted proudly stated in 1876 that Buffalo was "the best planned city [...] in the United States, if not the world," which it could not have been were it not for his vision of making Buffalo "more park-like than town-like."[15] As a result of its origin history and excellence of its execution, the Buffalo Olmsted Park System was added to the National Register of Historic Places in 1982. With all of this history, it made sense that when we talked with Therese, she could become emotional about the trees and parks given how they are a big part of what helped shape the City of Buffalo; part of Buffalo's lost beauty came from when these parkways and circles were paved or lost to development and progress, trading function and practically for the beauty of the greenspaces. Re-Tree WNY and Carvings for a Cause shared a similar mission: to make sure that Buffalo regained its beauty and that the trees that were lost were memorialized in another way...

Just days before we were ready to go to potential publishers, I was speaking by phone with friend and former Bills colleague, Scott Berchtold. Having served as VP of Media Relations, Scott was a gifted communicator, so I asked for his expert opinion about a phrase in the foreword (specifically *my* tweaks, none of Marv's gold). As a reminder, Scott was also the one who needed to call his wife Pam to remind her what a hot shower in Detroit felt like while she was still digging out in Buffalo. After helping with my wording

---

[15] "Our History: Buffalo Olmsted Parks Conservancy - His Legacy. Our Inheritance." *Buffalo Olmsted Parks*, Buffalo Olmsted Parks Conservancy, 28 Apr. 2020, www.bfloparks.org/history/.

issue, Scott asked, out of the blue, "Hey, have you spoken with Therese Forton-Barnes for your book?"

I was not yet familiar with Therese, so I had not, but this would soon seem crazy after discovering that we had sixty-four common connections on LinkedIn. Billy and I were vaguely familiar with Carving for a Cause as Paul had mentioned the movement in his interview, but we hadn't yet fully reviewed our notes from that lengthy chat which felt like being blasted with an information fire hose. I'd like to believe that we'd have eventually reached out to Therese based on that, but Scott's call ensured that it wasn't left to chance.

Scott added, "Oh, Donny, you've GOT to speak with her. Your book won't be complete without her story. But before you meet, do an online search for the New York Times article about her. And after you talk with her, call me and I'll share my role in the Thurman story."

Intrigued for sure. And as promised, Scott made the connection, then Therese and I spoke by phone and she was more than agreeable to "carve out" some time for a Zoom meeting with us. (My attempt at this lame pun bombed other than a polite, courtesy laugh from Therese and a laughable groan from Billy with the agreement that it would need to be included here - my apologies to all.)

In the meantime, Billy and I read Ken Belson's *New York Times* article from 2007. Another article by Doug Stitler in *Buffalo Rising* indicated that Therese and Rick were also covered by *USAToday* and Monday Night Football. From these articles alone, we were amazed at how well Carving for a Cause reinforced the "Civic Pride" narrative that Mayor Brown had emailed just one day earlier. In essence, while most of the damaged trees found their way to serve a practical purpose via a wood chipper, for paper or mulch, or to wood splitters for firewood, **some** of these massive, over 200-year-old downed Maple, Oak, or Ash trees were destined for a different fate.

Meeting with Therese was not only a pleasure, but a breeze;

Therese sported a cool, long- sleeved pullover proudly featuring their artfully designed "Carving for a Cause" logo, with the added bonus of their innuendo catch-phrase underneath that signaled an immediate comfort level with us. (Let's just say that it broke the ice and Billy laughed so hard he almost couldn't breathe for about ten seconds. He has gone on to share their informal "motto" with several friends and family members, but for Pastor Jerry Gillis' sake and others, Billy has offered to tell it to whomever would like to hear it so we don't have to put it in print...)

Before we went any further, we asked Therese how we could help her and/or Carving for a Cause in exchange for her granting us this interview; she, without hesitation, replied, "No, no, nothing. Please. I do not want to re-energize this, trust me." She clarified that the charity had served its purpose well, in its own time, which has now run its proper course. It was also a *lot* of work and she has no trouble staying busy owning and running three businesses – Green Living Gurus, Events to a Tee, and Matchmaking to a Tee. On top of that, she also authored two Children's books, *Zaki and Venus Go to the Beach* and *Zaki and Venus Get Married*, both adorable characterizations of her own dogs that brings their personalities to life.

She was clear, however, that just because she considered *this* organization's work complete, mostly because there are no more tree carcasses left from 2006, she still really enjoyed sharing 'Carving' stories, including, thankfully, with us. So we got right into the *Times* story, which Therese said that writer Ken Belson wrote most thoroughly about, but she quickly pivoted to say that media coverage was not at all what she was seeking. She then took us back to her own personal experience on that fateful Thursday night, October 12, 2006; she got choked up talking about first hearing the frightening breaking of the trees, then seeing the carnage outside her downtown Buffalo home near Soldier's Circle, part of the Olmsted Park and

Parkway System, that Friday morning. "We wondered if *any* of these trees could be saved," Therese noted while holding back tears.

One week after the Storm, while driving Eastbound on NYS Thruway I-90 to a wedding in Albany, Therese and her husband Tom saw an endless army of trucks coming the other way, Westbound, on I-90 toward Buffalo; she said they both noted it was *only trucks* - no other passenger cars were knowingly heading into Arborgeddon. Therese agreed that these were just a small fraction of the convoy that originated even before reaching the Eastern Hills Mall parking lot. In the meantime, she lent her downtown home, which miraculously had power, to friends from the suburbs who did not, including when she left!

Upon arriving in Albany, they walked into the log cabin home of her husband's friend and marveled at the huge wood carvings strategically placed around the property. The virtual light bulbs went off over Therese's head and, you guessed it, the concept for Carvings for a Cause was conceived. In fact, details about *how* she could make this happen materialized before she even left Albany as Tom's friend, the log cabin owner, knew of an artist/carver who lived in Rochester. As we learned from our interview from Therese, she doesn't hesitate to pursue a goal without procrastination, so we were not surprised to learn that she called Rick on the way back from the wedding to propose the idea to him. Rick's response? "I'm in. Let's do this."

Planning and execution was the next step, but Therese was already on it: *Tree supply? No problem.* Sadly, as we know, there was an abundance of huge, downed trees in the area.

Statue ideas? Easy. Therese was a one-woman preservation committee with historical knowledge of many famous Buffalonians worthy of statues, including but not limited to: US Presidents Grover Cleveland, William McKinley, and Millard Fillmore; Architects Frank Lloyd Wright and Fredrick Law Olmsted, the latter of which is a natural choice due to his vision to "refresh and delight the eye and through the eye, mind and spirit. Upon touring the City of

Buffalo in 1868, he convinced the city's leaders that not one park – as in New York City's Central Park – but multiple parks would better serve Buffalo's needs."[15]

Entertainment icons were also chosen including, but not limited to, Buffalo Bob Smith (of *Howdy Doody* fame), Marlon Perkins (*Mutual of Omaha's Wild Kingdom*), Chris Berman (*ESPN*), James Whitmore (Academy Award winning Actor appearing in over thirty films, including my favorite, *Shawshank Redemption*) and of course, the Pride of South Buffalo, Tim Russert (of NBC's *Meet the Press*). The Father of the Erie Canal, Governor DeWitt Clinton, and Author Joyce Carol Oates also made the list along with Buffalo Braves NBA star Bob McAdoo and Bills legends Jim Kelly, Andre Reed, and Thurman Thomas. Lou Billittier Sr.'s statue still makes his presence felt in the lobby of Chef's Restaurant and the late Teressa Bellissimo's statue at The Anchor Bar still reminds Americans who invented the Buffalo Chicken Wing. Up to thirty-three carvings were ultimately created from the fallen remnants of Aphid - an amazing tribute to not only those who help bring pride and fame to the region, but once again the resiliency of Buffalonians to take something challenging and turn it into something we embrace and elevate.

So, what about other locals or other famous or influential Bills players like OJ Simpson, one might ask? Narrowing down the list was not easy, and while OJ's name remains prominently affixed on the Stadium's Wall of Fame for his record-setting rushing yards, Therese understandably didn't feel a need to go down that controversial path. Incidentally, with NBC sending OJ to Buffalo regularly to cover the Bills in the early 1990's, he almost became a regular in our buildings on Friday afternoons before home games - and some of my encounters with him were rather colorful, which I'll save for another time.

Now that the easy parts were over, the real work was about to begin: although Rick had graciously agreed to help, as well as accept a significantly "less than his normal" rate, he still needed to be paid *something* for the very long hours and creative energy spent that he'd otherwise be working for regular pay. A typical carving took Rick an average of five full days to complete. Therefore, Therese needed to start to solicit sponsors to fund each carving - and with her appealing solicitation, and Buffalo's generosity, it was just a matter of connecting the dots until they eventually fell into place.

Therese noted that the hardest part was either finding a place to carve; whether it was where the trees already were or if it would require them to pick up and move the massive trees to a sufficient work area. We've already learned that even a rugged Subaru cannot transport a 600-pound transformer so naturally, neither could it transport a three-ton tree. There was no amount of "bare-rooting" that would help move these massive beasts. So Therese sought out as many resources as she could, even going to Mayor Byron Brown for assistance because, in her search for the biggest trunks available, she found herself "getting in the way a little bit."

Having become friends with Jim Kelly from managing some of his events, including his wedding, retirement party, golf tournaments, and other fundraisers, she asked Jim if he knew anyone willing to help. Being an avid outdoorsman with a huge network, it was no surprise that he did. To the rescue came Jim's friend, David Arnts, president of Twin Lakes Concrete in Lockport; Dave provided his trucks, built to transport concrete slabs, to Therese *for free!* The trucks even had a mechanical arm that picked up the carved and uncarved trees and loaded them onto the truck bed. "He was my life saver!" remarked Therese. Not only did Dave help move the trees, he provided the cement slabs, elevating them off the ground, preventing water damage from underneath, which stabilized and helped preserve the statues.

We were also fascinated to learn that statues were not the only artwork created from the "storm wood"; during their collection of tree carcases, remnants of the best woods like Cherry and Maple that were not big enough for statues but too good to throw away were also scooped up. So, Therese opportunistically held fundraisers selling beautiful household items such as salad and fruit bowls that had been carved from these trees, including one she proudly showed us in our interview, made from a downed locust tree on the University of Buffalo campus - *it even still had the bark edge.* These carved items last longer than the statues, forever actually, and to create these pieces, she found a local group, led by a gentleman named Patrick DelMonte, who regularly gathered to carve wood with a lathe and other instruments to craft these more day-to-day items. Some of these prime (Cherry and Maple) storm wood remnants not big enough for statues were carved into park benches and Therese and her husband used the trunks of downed trees from near their home on Soldiers Circle to construct tables that they have proudly displayed in their home.

Coincidentally, my friends Frank Garrigues and Tom Orser (both "Weekenders") just purchased lathes and have really invested themselves into the hobby. They send pictures back and forth of awesome items they've made - almost like a competition. *Oh yeah? Well, I just made this!* Frank even made a set of drums sticks for me and a corkscrew and bottle opener for Amy. Better yet, he created them from a piece of the Giant Oak we had taken down in our front yard to make room for the new septic system that Amy and I "gifted" to each other in the summer of 2020 – *Yippee!* Of even more relevance, it's the same tree that split in half and landed on our house that fateful Thursday night - making them meaningful *(and expensive)* gifts to us in several ways.

For Therese, this wood carving venture proved to be a fine fundraiser and, more importantly, a way to make sure that these lost trees were not lost in vain, but she didn't want to make a business out of it.

So, long story short, the fundraisers were enough to cover costs and with that final piece of the puzzle figured out, Therese, Rick, and now Dave were on a roll. Therese and Rick appeared on some local shows, such as with Linda Pelligrino on Channel 7 to make a soft appeal for sponsors while showing Rick carve an Eagle on live television. *Oh, how we could have used a "Chainsaw Wizard" like Rick for our October Weekend cleanup!* It was a proven system that was churning out awesome statues and gaining much local and even national praise at the same time. But then, as it often does, the other shoe dropped.

Just outside Ralph Wilson Stadium, before a Bills home game versus the Cleveland Browns, a ceremony sponsored by Sahlens officially presented the carved statue of newly inducted Hall of Fame Running Back Thurman Thomas. Therese and Dave were on hand, along with DJ Jickster of 97 Rock and Andre Reed, as Jim Kelly delivered words of praise for his good friend before the statue was unveiled. The pre-game event was clearly the highlight of the afternoon as the Bills suffered an ugly 6-3 loss inside. (Coincidentally, this game also happened to be our 2009 "October Weekend" so, likewise, our tailgate was the highlight that day - but this isn't about that story and, little did they know at the time, this story was just beginning.)

Following the game, Therese and company upon walking back to the parking lot where the tents were set up discovered that the Thurman statue was gone. *Stolen.* An investigation began immediately, though they knew immediately that they had made a mistake, the fatal error was not so much that the statue was left alone during the game, but rather that this statue was carved from pine. Therese noted that while most of the statues are made from heavier woods, Thurman had been carved from the much lighter pine, making it easier to lift and transport by even the most - ahem - *lubricated* Bills fans.

On the following Monday morning, Therese received a call from Fox News asking her to share her story with the nation. More calls came flooding in from other major media outlets asking her to appear. Caught completely off guard, she reached out to Bills VP of Media Relations Scott Berchtold and media friend and journalist Doug Sitler to handle the heat, lending herself to a select few interviews.

The prominent question posed to Therese by the media was, "Are you going to press charges upon finding out who did this?" to which she wisely responded that she would not, so as not to deter the culprit(s), who were undoubtedly still sobering up, from confessing and hopefully returning it.

Her tactic worked as Therese received an anonymous call from a fan claiming that he had first-hand knowledge it had been smuggled into Canada. Somehow, while my wife, Amy, was once grilled by agents for inadvertently having an apple in her car while crossing the border, two fans successfully circumvented International Federal Law by carrying a huge wooden statue in an open-bed pickup truck across country lines, claiming that "they do it all the time and it was their good luck charm."

The fan's story proved to be legit, including the current, accurate whereabouts of the statue. He agreed to meet Therese "at a bar around the back" to arrange the specifics of the Wooden Thurman's return. So, Therese accepted the offer to drive up to the Great White North – Welland, Ontario, and retrieve the statue. But it wouldn't be as easy as just popping up to Canada and making a quick drive back…

While her friend, Amy, agreed to drive the car, Therese needed to, once again, recruit Dave to follow her in his concrete truck. Dreading having to make a bizarre appeal at the border, Therese caught a big break when a company who assists Americans seeking to cross the border with unusual circumstances, heard her story on a television news report and offered their help.

The stealth operation ended up not being so stealth as one media outlet followed her north to try and capture the reunification. They actually did meet "the perps" at the bar who were initially very nervous, but after realizing that Therese's singular goal was to retrieve the statue with zero intent to hold anything against them, legally or otherwise, they were able to share some laughs, then go rescue Wooden Thurman.

While Therese completely forgave the culprits, she didn't forget – in a good way – as she had the foresight to have her friend, Amy, record parts of the trip.[16] And upon returning to Buffalo following a mission that went as well as could be hoped, another press conference awaited with Thurman present to express his relief at his wooden likeness's return. This too made (even more) national news - a fun three-and-a-half minute video of this adventure from Therese's perspective can be found on YouTube by searching, "Carving Adventure Thurman."

As promised, I called Scott Berchtold after our great Zoom call with Therese to hear about his part in the story; according to Scott, Thurman was (naturally) perplexed, and directed some of that anger at Scott, mostly because he was excited to display his replica at the Sahlen's Sports Park in Elma where he ran a training program. Scott, as a lifelong professional master of spin AND having worked with the out-spoken Thurman during his playing days, responded, "Hey, Thurm, look at the bright side: at least your statue was worthy of being stolen." *Rich.*

While most of the money raised was used to pay for the work that Carvings for a Cause did, the remaining proceeds were generously donated to Paul Maurer's Re-Tree WNY program, once again reinforcing Therese's civic-mindedness and love for Buffalo. Nearing the end of the interview, I found myself, somewhat reluctantly, employing my own "Roy Firestone moment" as made famous in the movie *Jerry Maguire* when the ESPN Reporter's signature goal was getting the subject to cry. Given that our goal was ultimately to discuss the Storm, I went back to the well one more time, sensing that Therese had more to share about that fateful night of October 12, 2006. She absolutely did. Therese's home was very close to the Olmsted Parkway system where the trees were re-planted in 1983 after the originals were all lost to the Dutch

---

[16] These along with pictures of many of the statues and our interview with Therese can be found on our website, (you know it by now, right?) ThunderSnowOfBuffalo.com.

Elm Disease. For people who purchased homes around those streets, the canopy of trees was a major draw. Moreover, Therese had been part of a $40,000 fund raising effort that planted ornamental pear trees in Soldiers Circle just a few years earlier. Therese shared her heartbreak at her efforts being destroyed by the Storm saying, "So all you could hear was cracking and everything breaking. It was a war zone. The storm ruined it all." But, as one not to wring her hands or dwell in self-pity, Therese then noted that Mother Nature was just doing its job by pruning and noted that Re-Tree specifically targeted that area for repair, for which she was deeply grateful.

Therese also appreciated Re-Tree's efforts to replant at the devastated Forest Lawn area where she has fond memories of riding her bike as a young girl. Forest Lawn Cemetery reciprocated by requesting (and receiving) a statue to be built of Chief Red Jacket, who despite leading battles against settlers in Western New York, received a Medal of Peace from George Washington, and is buried on the grounds of Forest Lawn.

The background of Therese's home during the zoom call looked like a greenhouse, lush with plants that were clearly well-nurtured. Outdoor living was in her DNA as she "reminded" us that it was World Soil Day, at which point Billy and I apologized to each other for not exchanging gifts. She recommended to us that we use the opportunity of this holiday to watch the movie, Kiss the Ground, about how important healthy soil is to the food growing cycle and how innovative farming methods improve the process. And the movie prompted her to *somewhat* forgive Tom Brady, featured in the movie, for his years of tormenting her Bills.

A point she wanted to make before we concluded was that, as Re-Tree dedicated their 10,000[th] tree to Tim Russert, Carvings for a Cause honored him with a statue in 2007, one year before he died, so Tim did know about it. After his passing, Ken Belson of the New York Times reached out to a shocked Therese for a comment for which she obliged.

The carvings were very personal for Rick as well. On one local TV program while performing a live demonstration of his work, he noted, "If these trees could talk, they'd each tell a story. For example, it is possible that the tree used to carve Fredrick Law Olmsted may have been planted by Olmsted himself."

On a lighter note, one funny memory she left us with was when the Buffalo News featured her in an article about Carvings for a Cause. She gladly conceded that she'd become known as the "Tree Lady" but didn't feel a need to be seen stereotypically hugging a tree. When the photographer asked her to stand next to the tree, the picture on the front page the next day showed her, of course, hugging the tree.

Therese Forton-Barnes, founder of Carvings for Cause, grants an interview to the New York Times. Below, Therese is surveying tree carcasses for her carvings just next door to the future site of Buffalo RiverWorks in the Old First Ward.

Rick Pratt demonstrating his chainsaw
wizardry on one of the carvings.

The plaque at the base of Tim Russert's statue. Therese
takes solace in knowing that "Buffalo's Favorite
Son" saw the statue before passing far too soon.

The Carving of Thurman Thomas, ominously unsupervised at one point during the game. Below, however, are Thurman Thomas, Jim Kelly, and Therese Forton-Barnes posing with 'Wooded Thurman' before it was stolen and taken away to an undisclosed hideaway in Canada.

As it pertains to this storm and our story, thanks to Paul and Therese, we've seen trees go from Villain to Victim to spectacular works of art - something that we feel is not often recognized as much as it should be.

SEVENTEEN
ONE FOR THE BOOKS, NUMERICALLY SPEAKING

It has been said that unless you're speaking with an accountant, statistician, or mathematician, a story-teller can lose their audience pretty quickly if they dwell on numbers for too long. We knew this would be a challenge, but we also knew that the numbers were just as much a part of this story needed to be told. There are some staggering statistics involving the October Surprise Storm of 2006 that surely merit at least a mention, including some that may be hard for some readers, including deaths. Unfortunately with any major storm or event of this magnitude, deaths can be a saddening result; we recognize that not mentioning those that were lost in this storm is a far greater disservice than honoring them here:

PEOPLE:

- Deaths; reports range from 11 to 20 people depending on the source, but the official NWS report stated:
    - "One death was directly attributed to the Storm. In Amherst, a man was clearing snow in his driveway when a tree limb broke off, fell and crushed him. Fourteen other deaths were indirectly storm-related. This number includes four people who died from carbon monoxide

poisoning from the improper use of generators and kerosene heaters."[1]

- In fact, during the week of the Storm, as the reports of these deaths and illnesses began rolling in, Billy's neighbors began keeping an eye on one of their elders who was also one of the original homeowners on his street *"who lived across the street had a gas powered generator that she had been running in her garage. We started to hear reports on the radio of people dying or getting very, very ill from Carbon Monoxide poisoning so we were all very quick to remind her to leave her garage door open, it was also our way to start asking if we could start running extension cords across the street to run some of our basics. We didn't do this at first because we all recognized that everyone had needs and that local officials were suggesting against it for safety reasons, but as things started to get better and this became a more and more common practice in neighborhoods like ours, everyone got a little more flexible with those types of rules. This was especially true when, a week after the storm, our power eventually did come back on, but only half of our house came on; we began running cords for our neighbors who were not as fortunate as we were for the brief duration before theirs came on a few hours later."*

- Hospitalizations:
  - 200+ people were treated for exposure to carbon monoxide[17, 1]
  - "17 were treated for hypothermia"[1]

---

[17] Owen, Chris. *14 Years Ago Today: The October Surprise Storm.* 12 Oct. 2020, wyrk.com/14-years-ago-today-the-october-surprise-storm-photos/.

- Number of households that lost power, some for only 2 days: 100,000[18]
- Number of people without power for up to 2 days: 400,000[19]
- Number of people without power for up to 7 days: 100,000[20]
- Number of fans that attended the Sabres game just two days after the start of the Storm: 18,690[20]

SCHOOLS:

- Most schools resumed on October 23rd, ten days after the initial storm and six snow days; this was the first Monday after most people got power back[20]
- Number of weeks Amherst & Hamburg schools closed[20]: Two
  - Amherst schools returned on October 26th; Hamburg Schools returned the next day on October 27th
  - Hamburg was delayed due to damage to the buildings and power causing delays to this work
  - Spring breaks for many school districts were taken away due to so many snow days

---

[18] Pignataro, T.J., and Janice L. Habuda. "Area Slammed Hard by Snow Thousands In Region Without Power 'Enormous Amount of Physical Damage'." *The Buffalo News*, 13 Oct. 2006, buffalonews.com/news/area-slammed-hard-by-snow-thousands-in-region-without-power-enormous-amount-of-physical-damage/article_85108f62-0742-58e2-8321-6a1d40e16771.html.

[19] Contributors to Wikimedia. "Buffalo, New York Snow Storm Closes Schools, Leaves Nearly 400,000 without Power." *Wikinews, the Free News Source*, Wikimedia Foundation, Inc., 13 Oct. 2006, en.wikinews.org/wiki/Buffalo,_New_York_snow_storm_closes_schools,_leaves_nearly_400,000_without_power.

[20] "Lake Storm 'Aphid.'" *Wikipedia*, Wikimedia Foundation, 21 June 2020, en.wikipedia.org/wiki/Lake_Storm_"Aphid."

SNOW STATS:

- Lightest possible snow to rain ratio[21]: 1" of rain = 22" of snow
- This is type of Powder Snow that skiers love
- Heaviest possible snow to rain ratio: 1" of rain = 6" of snow[2]
- Ratio of October Storm: 1" of rain = 6" of snow[2]
- Miles, in width, of the weather band: 10[2]
- "Heavy Hitters" aka the areas with the most snowfall from the Storm[17]:
  - Depew - 24 inches
  - Alden - 24 inches
  - Cheektowaga - 22 inches
  - North Buffalo - 20 inches
  - "Parts of Amherst saw upwards of 20-22 inches, while other parts saw 14 inches. Many suburbs saw at least 10-12 inches of snow."

TREES[22]:

- Trees Lost to the October Storm: 55,000 - 60,000
  - Percentage of trees damaged or "in need of care" in the City of Buffalo: 90%[23]
- Trees Replanted by Re-Tree WNY: 30,000
- Trees Replanted by Cities, Towns, Municipalities and Organizations to match Re-Tree's donations: 30,000
- Number of Re-Tree WNY volunteers: 1,500
- Numbers of Service Hours Logged by Re-Tree WNY volunteers: 5,000

---

[21] Paul, Don. Interview. By Don Purdy. 15 Oct 2020.

[22] Maurer, Paul. Interview. By Don Purdy and Billy Klun. 13 Nov 2020.

[23] Thompson, Caroline. "Early Snowstorm Battered Buffalo's Historic Parks, Trees." *USAToday*, 20 Oct. 2006.

- Number of Trees Refurbished by Carving for a Cause: "32 or 33"[24]

DAMAGE & IMPACT:

- Cubic yards of debris caused by storm: 8-10 million[25]
- Dollars needed just for initial cleanup: $135 million[25]
- Number of Miles of New York State Thruway shut down, including a significant stretch by Mike Nigrelli: 105[26]
- Distance needed to drive from Buffalo to purchase a generator in the immediate aftermath of the Storm: 130 miles
  - Rochester, Syracuse, and Erie, PA were all sold out
- Number of Insurance claims that would be considered a "good month" at Erie Insurance: 30 - 45 claims[27]
- Number of Claims to Erie Insurance on Friday the 13th, 2006: **hundreds** of claims *per hour*[27]

UTILITIES:

- Number of line crews required to repair damage: 423[28]

---

[24] Forton-Barnes, Therese. Interview. By Don Purdy and Billy Klun. 5 Dec 2020.
[25] Beebe, Michael, et al. "Storm Reimbursement Cloudy FEMA Won't Predict Chance of Disaster Decree by Bush." *The Buffalo News*, 21 Oct. 2006, buffalonews. com/news/storm-reimbursement-cloudy-fema-wont-predict-chance-of-disaster-decree-by-bush/article_2c00923b-d1c9-5922-a1b2-1681fe68aeb3.html.
[26] New York State, 2006, p. 1
[27] Sirianni, Michael. Interview. By Don Purdy and Billy Klun. 12 Dec 2020.
[28] New York State, 2006, p. 10

- Number of **National Grid** field workers who did the work: 3,700[29]
- Number of Electric Trucks brought in from outside of WNY that called the Eastern Hills Mall homebase: "multiple news stories quote that there were around 500 vehicles [...] for electrical repair", per Paul Maurer and his contacts at **National Grid**[30]
- Number of Hotel Rooms needed and used by said crews: 465[31]
- Number of Places Crews Traveled in From: at least seven States and one Canadian Province
  - "Crews traveled from as far a way as Kentucky, Maryland, North Carolina, Virginia, West Virginia, Michigan, Texas, and New Brunswick, Canada"[28]
- *"Figure 2"*[32]

	NYSEG	**National Grid**
Circuits Affected	138	257
Circuit Lockouts	69	403
Poles Broken	289	600
Transformers Replaced *[including ones that exploded in blue fireworks!]*	84	300
Services Repaired	1,432	10,000
Number of Customers out of Service on Friday, October 13th, 2006	261,000	135,000

[29] Reilly, E. (2016, October 7). *Remember Oct. 2006? Lessons learned will apply to Hurricane Matthew.* https://www.wkbw.com/news/remember-oct-2006-lessons-learned-will-apply-to-hurricane-matthew.
[30] Paul Maurer, email message to the authors, February 25, 2021.
[31] New York State, 2006, p. 21
[32] New York State, 2006, p. 5

- Amount of Wire Needed by **National Grid** for repairs: 1.5 *Million* feet[29]
- Number of surveyors utilized during restoration: 321[33]
- Number of customers identified by **National Grid** "as having life support equipment [that] were initially contacted by the Company at the beginning of the storm and every day thereafter until the storm restoration was complete": 148[34]
- Number of **National Grid**'s "Critical Care" customers: 250, who were contacted "according to the procedures in its emergency plans, [...] each of which were given the highest priority."[34]
- Total Utility Calls during Lake Storm Aphid:
  - **National Grid**: 208,856 calls[35]
  - **NYSEG**: another 60,049 calls[36]
  - **Verizon**: 93,00 "trouble tickets"[37]
    - "74,000 trouble reports were from customers and approximately 19,500 [were] troubles reported by field technicians found while working on other troubles. Nearly half of the reported troubles were related to drop wire damage."[33]
  - **Time Warner:** "sustained over 149,000 outage or service affecting conditions"[38]
- Number of poles "replaced, reattached, or repaired" by **Verizon** during the course of the restoration: approximately 350[39]

---

[33] New York State, 2006, p. 8
[34] New York State, 2006, p. 16
[35] New York State, 2006, p. 17
[36] New York State, 2006, p. 28
[37] New York State, 2006, p. 6
[38] New York State, 2006, p. 30-31
[39] New York State, 2006, p. 40

- Number of dropped wires "repaired, replaced or removed" by **Time Warner**: over 46,000[38]
- Amount of Dry Ice Distributed by **NYSEG** to residents: 74 tons[36]
- Number of Bottles of Water Distributed by **NYSEG** to residents: 310,000[36]
  - **NYSEG** did so at "three distribution centers and by delivery to shut-in customers throughout the affected areas"; "distribution centers for dry ice and drinking water were set up at locations in the most severely affected areas."[36]
- **"Verizon** reported at the beginning of this event that it had lost commercial power in 15 of its central offices, however all but one continued running on backup power generation without interruption until commercial power was restored."[40]

MISCELLANEOUS MULTIPLES:

- How much longer the Bills' team Doctor's commute home was than usual: 24x
- How many more trees planted by Re-Tree than the 2nd place winner at the National Arbor Day Awards in Nebraska: 666x more
  - *Yikes. Paul, couldn't you guys have planted a couple more?*
- Pounds, according to the owner's manual, that a Subaru is recommended not to exceed carrying in its interior: 900
  - *So while perhaps the car was designed with the ability to carry a 600 lb. transformer, the designers probably didn't mean concentrated in one place, but more likely spread throughout the car as passengers. Thus, Amy made the right*

---

[40] New York State, 2006, p. 33

call to wait one more day for NYSEG to deliver it properly in their truck.

- Number of Miles Therese Forton-Barnes drove to reclaim the Wooden Thurman Thomas: 26.6 (unless she went the long way).

  - After this comprehensive Numbers chapter, please excuse us for calculating here exclusively in *miles* rather than by miles to the border and kilometers in the Great White North - we figured everyone could do the math if they so choose.

EIGHTEEN
"I MOWED THE LAWN"

On November 7th, about three weeks after the Storm and its aftermath, I sent an email to my "Weekend" Friends and some others. The subject line, "I mowed the lawn", resonated with them big time. When each had departed Buffalo on Sunday, October 22nd, their final, lasting vision of our property was of a wall of tree branches along the street (that they had dragged there themselves) about ten-feet high and thirty-feet long - almost the size of a school bus. There was another huge pile of chain-saw cut, burnable logs stacked closer to the house. This scene was replicated at house after house after house all the way back to the airport for them to scan over and over. These images were indelibly burned in their brains.

My friends, along with Amy, Anna, Claire, and I, had tackled the *macro* that weekend. I still needed those next three weeks to address the *micro*, which culminated in mowing the lawn, something that seemed inconceivable just three weeks ago, in the 2nd week of November. While there were craters everywhere from the fallen limbs that had plunged into the earth, never had such a mundane task seemed so triumphant let alone worthy of an email subject line.

Now, with our yard *and* our elderly neighbor's yard cleared, Amy and I gladly helped our friends, John and Lori Jakiel, drag trees off their large West Seneca yard. Amy and Lori laughed again thinking about how they were planning to spend that "snow day" having lunch at a restaurant somewhere – a novelty that teachers can rarely partake in during the school year on non-holiday weekdays that just feels like a sinful treat. John and Lori kept thanking us, but they have always been quick to help us with anything, too.

A few months later in February of 2007, our family traveled to the Bahamas, fulfilling a year-long planned vacation. Ironically, Buffalo had experienced an easy winter up to that point - aside from the October Storm which technically had happened in autumn. In fact, we were actually disappointed in how little snow had fallen. I had purchased season passes for Anna and me at Holiday Valley, the fabulous ski resort in Ellicottville where we have skied every winter since she was six years old. The break-even point to make the season pass worthwhile was nine ski days, but at that point in February, we had gone only twice because January had been so warm with so little snow. While this may not seem like a big deal - or really a small deal - to many, in Western New York this is a rare feat.

Anyway, the Bahamas provided a much-welcomed getaway for us. I won't go so far as to say we "deserved" it, but we had saved, budgeted, and planned a solid year in advance. Just seeing and feeling the sun's rays, trading coats and boots for shorts and sandals felt heavenly, and it never fails - whenever we go south for vacation, we run into people from Buffalo. Anyone wearing a Bills hat, a Sabres shirt, Canisius College alumni gear, or someone proudly representing their Sweet Home High School might as well be walking around with a huge sign that reads: *Please come talk to me if you're from Buffalo.* Typically, the conversation then goes something like:

> *"Hey, are you from Buffalo?"*
> *"Yeah, you?"*
> *"Yeah."*
> *"Cool. Where in Buffalo?*
> *"Orchard Park."*
> *"All right! I'm from Tonawanda!"*

DON PURDY & BILLY KLUN

"How 'bout those Bills?"
"I know, right? How 'bout those Sabres?"

Then inevitably, depending on how long they speak, which is usually directly proportionate to how much drink is left in their glass, we will discover a person, first or second-hand, that we both know back in Buffalo.

But in February of 2007, just four months after, the conversation went more like this:

"Cool. Where in Buffalo?
"Orchard Park."
"All right! I'm from Tonawanda!"
"How did you make out in the storm?"

Boom. **Second** question!

Billy would like to quickly note that while many, if not all, Buffalonians are guilty of this, his Uncle Dan who lives down the street from us is always the one who not only finds all of the self-advertising Buffalonians, and Ohio State Alumni, he is also "that guy" that always knows someone anywhere they go - including but certainly not limited to: halfway up the 252 foot Pilgrim Tower in Provincetown, MA, at a random bar in St. Kitts, and the main terminal of the Manchester Airport in Manchester, England, just to name a few. But we digress, again...

In April of 2007, using the $12,000 of insurance and FEMA money, we had our roof repaired, fences rebuilt, and basement walls and floors repainted with a waterproof, DryLok paint. In May, two truckloads of topsoil arrived to fill in the craters on our front lawn so well that it would make the moon jealous. The $12,000 seemed like a fair amount given that it covered these repairs at market prices, but Amy's "never let a crisis go to waste" instincts kicked in regarding the roof: our claim covered only the one-hundred square foot area affected by the fallen tree, but we ended up having the *entire* roof stripped and re-shingled, which we were within just a few years of needing anyway, however this was at *our expense.*

A professional investment friend of ours who lived down the street, found a clause in his insurance policy that unequivocally and legitimately promised to pay an amount TEN TIMES what they'd initially quoted. Upon bringing the clause to the Claims Adjuster's attention, our financially savvy friend responded simply, "I didn't write the policy, *you* did." Lesson being, reading the fine print is sometimes very much worth the time. Also being a family friend of Billy's as his aunt and uncle, who also live on Don's street, about halfway through the week of no power, Billy's uncle, Dan Marren, had a chainsaw that he was going from yard to yard helping to cut up trees and share the workload, accompanied by this same friend. According to Billy,

> *We eventually made it up on the priority list - again, as we knew the tree in our yard wasn't causing any damage or any safety concerns at that point - so we finally were able to start to get to cutting. Much to my chagrin at 14-years-old, I was not allowed to do any of the cutting, but I was told that I was allowed to stack all of the wood on the opposite side of the yard from where the tree was - needless to say I was less than ecstatic. (The fact that my Uncle Dan not only owned but was operating a chainsaw was a fun family joke at the time because, despite being one of my own personal idols and role models, he has never been the handiest of men so him wielding a chainsaw made several of us laugh, though I don't believe my Aunt Pattie was one of the ones laughing...)*

Later that month, Anna and her friend, Stephanie Szeluga, volunteered to rake our elderly widow neighbor's yard for an 8th grade community initiative. Not only was it a legitimate venture, I suggested they might be underestimating the challenge and commended them for taking it on. From personal experience with "The Weekend" friends, we had tackled the macro last fall, the raking was micro – under normal circumstances. After a few hours of seeing their exasperation at what they perceived as a lack of progress despite their hard work, I joined to help them cross the finish line. Had it been just raking leaves, pine cones, and acorns it would have been no problem, but when writing their summary report for the school project, they were sure to *emphasize* that they cleared a great deal of broken tree debris "and stuff" that remained from the October Storm the previous fall.

A few months later, on a warm, sunny June day, a huge, twenty-foot branch crashed on our front yard with a booming thud that shook the ground. It was a dangler, an unknown Widowmaker, from the tree that split in half and landed on our roof eight months earlier. With the trees having filled out with leaves, it was harder now to spot these danglers lurking up in the shadows, but they were all too plentiful. It was almost as if the October Storm was saying, *Don't forget about me yet!* All these years later, I can attest that we haven't. On the plus side, our backyard and pool are now splashed with sunshine in previously shady areas as the tree line is now missing huge, jagged gaps of green, almost like a jigsaw puzzle with a couple of key, green pieces gone.

In November of 2016, Frank Garrigues (my old college roommate and fellow "Weekender") came to our house, along with his wife Roxanne, to help me take down a tall pine tree that Amy and I noticed leaning - little by little, year by year - toward the pool. Having seen the remarkably small bases that pine trees have from falling after major wind storms, I wanted to catch this one before it caught us. (Let's just call that being proactive in hindsight to a traumatic event...) Upon walking into the backyard, Frank said to Roxanne, "Here we are - the scene of the crime. You wouldn't believe what this yard looked like after the storm they had a few years back", which at that point was ten. Frank was right. After he perfectly dropped the eighty-foot pine, we cut it up and dragged the logs and branches to the curb for the town to feed into their wood chipper for mulch. Another reminder of ten years prior, but on a much smaller, and strategically planned, scale.

In September of 2017, I traveled to Orlando, Florida, for the funeral for my very first boss at the Bills, Jerry Foran. Seeing his wife June and the Foran Family (Joe, Kim, and their now grown-up, impressive sons) again brought back a flood of memories about our "glory days" of the 1990's - naturally, I wish it were under different circumstances. Following the service, I finally met some of June and Jerry's Chicago Cubs "family" who I'd heard so much about over the years; it was also nice to reconnect with Bob Schultz and his wife, Becky, at the luncheon afterward and reflect about our "Bills Family" that we shared with Jerry and June - a sentiment that the Forans embodied. The night before the services, I stayed in the Apopka home of my cousin Doug (not only a "Weekender", but the one who prompted the whole idea), his wife Jaime, and their daughter, Avery. I arrived at about 8:00 pm and before we knew it, after a few cold ones and a couple cigars it was 2:00 am already; we got the full scoop on Avery's softball team, then reminisced about our Camp-of-the-Woods days and our October Weekends. At sunrise the next morning, only about five hours after going to bed, I noticed something huge that I'd missed the night before: in front of theirs and every other house in the neighborhood were ten-foot high, thirty-foot wide piles of tree limbs and trunks - the result of

Hurricane Irma ripping through Central Florida a month earlier. Doug turned to me and asked rhetorically, "Look familiar?"

Other than these being mostly palm trees, the scene was eerily similar to the tree piles we'd stacked during the October Weekend after our storm. "The difference," Doug noted, "is that WE stacked these trees *before* you came - and NO stinking carpet!" *Touché*.

The hurricane comparison, while somewhat apples to oranges, is an interesting one: A Bills Offensive Coach who had been with the Saints the season prior, in 2005, the year Hurricane Katrina hit Louisiana, told us that while the damage was different - winds and street flooding versus thunder, snow, basement flooding, and falling trees - the *fear* during the storms was very similar. In both cases, there was a feeling of helplessness during the dark night as nature unleashed massive forces of peril and threat. This coach admitted that the sights and sounds, as Kevin Sylvester so perfectly described about the early morning hours of Friday the 13th, absolutely did remind him of his experience with Hurricane Katrina one year earlier.

Likewise, a Bills Veteran Running Back who grew up in Louisiana, had seen his share of hurricanes ravage the bayou, but Buffalo's October Storm was definitely the worst storm of *any* kind he'd ever experienced. "A bunch of guys on the team lost power at their homes. Somehow, we didn't lose power at our apartments, so when guys heard that, they all came over to hang out at my place. And I'll *never* forget practicing with those huge construction lights."

It has been established that, among other notables such as wings and beef on weck, the proximity to Canada, and being the hometown of icons like Tim Russert, Buffalo is known for two other major topics: the Buffalo Bills and snow. Over the half century since the Bills joined the AFL (the predecessor of the NFL) in 1960, there have been numerous games that were played before, during, and after snowstorms. Images of near whiteout conditions fill the minds of many - some of whom have never even experienced it first hand envision footage of such games and naturally assume that could only happen in a place like Buffalo, NY and while those people may be correct, there is one game that stands out amongst the rest: the 2017 "Snow Bowl" against the Indianapolis Colts.

Three years earlier, the 2014 Snowvember Storm dumped *seven* feet of snow on the then Ralph Wilson Stadium causing a game against the New York Jets to be rescheduled to a later date (to their advantage trouncing the Jets 38-3 in Detroit), however the Colts were not as fortunate - *they had to play through it*. During the game, both the Bills and the Colts would have to cope with eight to nine inches of snow falling during the game alone, totalling almost seventeen inches when the Lake Effect Event was done.[41] The conditions would prove so bad that CBS struggled to televise the game and broadcaster Jim Cornell would describe it as "worse than what you saw on television" and Steve Tasker, former Wide Receiver for the Bills turned Sportscaster, said that despite his eleven years playing with the Bills in addition to his years of reporting on them, he had "never seen the franchise play a game in these conditions."[42] This included not even being able to see the yard-markers, or in some cases entire players; while the Bills were clad in their, then newer, bright and bold **red** uniforms, the Colts players were practically invisible, only recognizable by their blue numbers and logos as the *white* jerseys blended right in with the snow.

---

[41] US Department of Commerce, NOAA. "Lake Effect Snow Event Archive: Dec 10 2017 to Dec 11 2017." *National Weather Service*, NOAA's National Weather Service, https://www.weather.gov/buf/lesEventArchive?season=2017-2018&event=C.

[42] Deitsch, R. (2017, December 11). 'Once In A Lifetime Conditions': A Closer Look At CBS's Terrific Broadcast of Bills-Colts Snow Game. Retrieved January 05, 2021, from https://www.si.com/media/2017/12/11/bills-colts-snow-game-cbs-broadcast

Much like Marv Levy has been known to say, "When it's too tough for them, it's just right for us" - this proved true as the Bills would not only beat the Colts 13-7, but this win would also help them clinch their place in the playoffs for the first time in eighteen years, the last being just a few after Marv left his coaching position with the Bills. Even in this storm, a storm that in any other place would be considered "the Storm of the Century" was just another inconvenient snowy Sunday in November in Buffalo, NY.

The magnitude of the October Storm has resonated all these years later, so much so that no matter when it comes up, even when reaching out to begin compiling these stories, people come out of the woodwork to share their own experiences - and while many start to sound alike, everyone still listens because they remember what it was like in their own home. One such account not shared until now is from **Chris Brown,** Lead Reporter and host of "One Bills Live" - which, as a side note, is a wicked balancing act of a job being paid by the team, but portrayed by the public as striving to be objective - and whose storm story is remarkably similar to my own:

> *First and foremost, I remember as the snow was piling up on the tree branches that still had plenty of leaves on them that I had a major risk issue in my backyard. My 150-year old elm tree, which had somehow escaped Dutch elm disease, was the only tree I genuinely worried about dropping large branches on my home. It was 125 feet tall, but it was only about 50 feet from my home.*
>
> *Hearing branches snapping under the weight of the snow had me on edge. So, sleep wasn't really happening through the course of the night. The three feet of wet snow we had in Lancaster was also melting at the ground level, since the ground was warmer than the air, and my sump pump was filling up fast. With no*

power I was reduced to bailing the sump pump, well, every hour on the hour throughout the night. Fun!

Through my brother in law, I had arranged to have his brother, who lived in Binghamton [about 200 miles and a little over 3 hours], drive up portable generators to power the essentials in the house since there was no word on when we'd be getting power back. We had a gas insert fireplace so we could keep the home relatively warm, but keeping the food in the refrigerator from spoiling and having a couple of lights was necessary.

The worst part was that Saturday around 1:00 pm, I was scheduled to leave Buffalo to fly to Detroit to cover the Bills game against the Lions.

My generator arrived from Binghamton around 12:15 pm. I hooked it up to everything that was essential, ran to the gas station to fill my five-gallon gas can and brought it home. I then gave instructions to my poor wife on keeping the gas tank full and not closing the garage door with the generator running. With two kids ages 2 and 4, my poor wife was literally left holding the bag for two days while I traveled with the Bills to Detroit where we roomed at the Ritz-Carlton in Dearborn. To say that I was racked with guilt would be an understatement.

The power didn't come back on for my wife and kids until late Sunday afternoon. They slept in the living room in front of the fireplace on Saturday night. When I came home Sunday evening, while they were happy to see me, I think they felt I had gotten out of the harrowing experience. They were right. I did (and I still feel guilty today). Suffice to say a stand-by generator was purchased a week later!

The huge tree in the front yard; not sleeping; bailing water from the basement; a brother-in-law bringing a generator; traveling to Detroit; the great hotel; feeling guilty about leaving the family behind. *Hard to believe we didn't have this conversation while I was still at the Bills.*

Eclips Hair Salon ("Salon" being very overqualified for my simple haircut) in West Seneca, is owned by Sue Beres - who we have become friends with as our daughters, Kelsey and Claire, played college lacrosse at Medaille together. During a recent haircut, and without hesitation, Sue rattled off her memory of the Storm – one that has her "still eating crow to this day – fourteen years later." She and her husband Joe built their house in the year of the Storm, 2006. Joe very much wanted to include a built-in backup generator, but Sue didn't want to spend the $5,000. *Oops...* Despite this regret, Sue had no problem sharing this story as she's a good sport and no doubt wins more arguments than she loses.

Across Seneca Street, from the "Hair Chair" to the Dental Chair, memories were just as clear. Tracy, the Dental Hygienist at Dr. Thomas Augustine's office in West Seneca, remembers being paid that Thursday afternoon, but then unable to cash her paycheck because her bank lost power. Once back to her also powerless apartment, she was able to borrow cash from the candy bar drive her kids had just completed. Having lost heat, they actually felt fortunate to finally benefit from the 90 year-old lady in the apartment below who always cranked her thermostat to 85 degrees. That Thursday night, after creating a "Snow Fridge" on the balcony for their perishables, Tracy and her family played games by candlelight and creatively tried to make Jiffy Pop popcorn with candles - a cooking practice she doubts you'll ever see Martha Stewart or Guy Fieri promoting. These activities helped create a diversion from the terrible, scary noises happening outside. On Friday, after surveying the damage, they found an open Wegmans in the Southtowns where they waited

two hours for coffee - just another person agreeing that my Airplane 2 coffee reference is a very accurate placement.

When the guys from Pools Unlimited came to close our pool in 2020, something my friends in the south like to remind me they do *not* need to do, I ran my now normal storm inquiry past them. Dave instantly remarked, "Blue Lightning! Will never forget seeing blue lightning and hope to never effin' see it again." Incidentally, the date we closed the pool was October 15th, which just goes to show that the weather is still rather nice in Buffalo in mid-October, sometimes. Full disclosure, I hadn't been in it for about a month, but *technically* I could have if I *wanted* to. (Billy shared that since moving out of his Mom's house, Kate has chosen to close it earlier in September now that Billy isn't *insisting* that he will still use it "on the nice days.")

A former Bills colleague and friend, Julie Lantaff, shared with me by phone just the other day, as many of us re-connected to discuss how well the Bills were playing in 2020, that her daughter brought her premature baby to her Williamsville home that had no power. Obviously with special needs that required electricity and heat, Julie immediately brought her daughter and grandchild thirty miles south to her unaffected home in North Collins.

When I recently popped into Bank on Buffalo in Orchard Park to establish the DBA for Thunder Snow of Buffalo, Vice President Kathy Barry Kane, without hesitation, shared her personal Storm remembrance. On that Friday the 13th, after walking her dog on the green lawn of her East Aurora home, Kathy drove fifteen minutes north to West Seneca to watch her sister, Karen's, boys because they had no power. Kathy was shocked to suddenly find herself in a "war zone." She then turned her attention to her Orchard Park HSBC branch (where she served as a Manager) that borders West Seneca where there was big trouble there, too. Kathy remembers, "The branch closed for two days, then re-opened on a Sunday, which is unheard of in the banking business, made possible only by the power of generators."

A Property Manager who I worked closely with at the Bills said that his mother happened to be visiting him from Israel and did not expect her limited time in Buffalo to be so restricted. His wife, who was about to fly home from some time in California with friends, ignored his plea to stay a couple of extra days until things cleared up. Unable to fly into Buffalo, she and her friends were diverted to Rochester where they took a taxi home. With the NYS Thruway still closed, they found themselves stuck in a cab near Batavia for several hours *with no winter clothes!* Oh, and the cost of said taxi ride with the hold up in Batavia? ***Five hundred dollars!***

Conner Gallagher-Von, just nine years-old at the time, fell asleep that Thursday night of 10/12 along with the rest of his family in West Seneca before the Storm kicked into full gear. BUT, at 3:00 am, he awoke to a terrifying sound similar to a gunshot or explosion. While it was neither, it was still a big problem. Through flashes of blue lightning, Conner saw that a tree had split and fallen on top of his mother's car, the crushing of the metal and glass more than explained that startling boom.

Just the other day during our weekly garage band session, where I play drums (bass on one and three, snare on two and four, with eighth notes on the hi-hat cymbal and an occasional fill covers about every tune we play), I mentioned the Storm and this subsequent book odyssey to my fellow bandmates. Our lead man Phil was quick to state, "That storm is the reason *everyone* in Buffalo has a generator," which is *so true.* When the power goes out in our neighborhood now, the hum of generators kicking on is much faster and much louder than it was in 2006. Phil went on to describe how he used his truck to attach a rope to pull a fallen tree off Pete and Marcia Laforce's house next door. Not only that, it was on the same day, while I was in Detroit, that Tony and Joy were surgically removing the one on our house. As mentioned, at any neighborhood gathering, like the ones at Jason and Janelle Millard's incredible Tiki Bar across the street, someone brings up the October Storm and the stories start flying - which is both a tribute to our experiences as well as reason to have them all anthologized here.

For many Bills fans, their recollections of the 2006 season likely blurred into other seasons where the 7-9 record simply isn't that memorable, but I'd contend that the team was "in the hunt" for the playoffs, a familiar position during that era. This is not to mention how many times we have seen a team sneak into the playoffs as a 6th seed, healthy and hot, to go an a playoff run and even win the Super Bowl; that's how teams *must* think until they're mathematically eliminated from playoff contention. Perhaps Offensive Lineman, Brad Butler, sums the mentality up best. "I still had a job to do and did not have time to take in the magnitude of the storm until after the season. We had to play the Detroit Lions that weekend and I had my complete focus on defeating them."

In 2020, Amy and I were forced to replace our septic system. *Ugh. Of course this too would happen in 2020.* Never had we spent that amount of money on something that offered so little new in return, at least so little that we could *see*. To provide the space needed to be compliant with Erie County code, we needed to have a water line moved and a huge Oak tree taken down. During the estimate, the folks from Premier Skid Works, looking strangely at the tree, asked "What happened to this tree?" Answer: *The October Storm*. More specifically, and sentimentally, it was the giant Oak that split in half and crashed on our roof fourteen years earlier! Naturally, Amy cried when they had to take it down. It had charm, provided some privacy, and as we all now know, the dozens of other benefits trees provide.

As Don Paul aptly pointed out, the Buffalo Storm
it resembled most occurred in 1906 –
exactly one hundred years earlier.

Tim Wenger said it forever changed how radio
would cover such a paralyzing storm.
The National Weather Center officially called it *Lake Storm Aphid.*
Others, less formally, call it *Arborgeddon.*
But most Buffalonians know it simply as the *October Surprise.*

It would be our privilege for this collection of tales chronicled
in "Thunder Snow of Buffalo" to be woven into the fabric of the
Storm's lore, after all, it was The Storm of the Ages.

*Above: Hi view Terrace on 10/13/06 (notice
the car in lower left corner). Below: Eight
months later from the same exact spot.*

AFTERWORD

REFLECTIONS ON THE REFLECTIONS OF THE OCTOBER SURPRISE STORM OF 2006

First and foremost we want to thank our families - telling them about our decision to re-open this project and dive back into something that we had not meaningfully touched in a decade seemed a bit crazy, but we are so appreciative of their unwavering love and support throughout this endeavor - even in the midst of a once in a lifetime pandemic.

To Amy, Anna, and Claire: *Ladies, thanks for putting up with what must have seemed like an obsession for that several month stretch in 2020 and into 2021. If somehow able to see myself on video rewind, like the movie "Click", I'd surely be embarrassed by how often you were speaking to me while I was on the computer only to solicit a lame response of "uh huh." Catching myself in those moments, I hope I made a decent recovery to ask you to repeat yourself so I could listen better. Amy, you found this to be the case in the mornings and evenings. Claire you dealt with it during the day. Anna, you wisely got your own apartment in Orchard Park, then your own house in West Seneca. Ha!*

And upon reading the book (you did read it, didn't you?) you have surely discovered two things. First, those many hours, at 5:00 am or 10:00 pm, when you saw me pounding away at the keyboard, you now know that I wasn't just writing "All work and no play makes Don a dull boy." Secondly, you also found yourselves to be actual characters in the running narrative. Attempting to pull off the balancing act of making you all real to the readers while not crossing a line of privacy, please know that when on the fence, I opted for the latter. Perhaps the downside is that readers could never know how truly special you all are, but I do!

To Lenni & Mom: *Thank you for never having doubts in this endeavor or me - or at least never letting me know that you did! Your love and motivation helped me rejoin Don in pursuing this old, familiar dream of mine and made me feel so much more capable and able to pursue this - I could not have done this without your help. 2020 was a challenging year for everybody, and our family was not only no exception to that, but it certainly felt like 2020 had it out for us; this book came at the very end of a very tough run, but I hope now the time and work put into it can be appreciated - and maybe every considered worth it!*

From Don:

Writing this book was a joyful grind, if that makes sense. Not to get too deep into the anatomy of the book, it was more of a compilation of stories that we composed. This has afforded me the freedom to brag like crazy as, while my story about the tree falling on house and the Bills and Weekend stuff certainly served as a running narrative, most of the words were other peoples'! As Billy's title "Reflections of the Reflections" suggests, our goal was to provide the "story behind the stories." A "Bookumentary?" (Hey, I finally got in my Spinal Tap reference - where Rob Reiner introduces the movie, as a "Rockumentary.") Sidenote: Given my several movie references, you might assume I'm a huge movie buff. Not really. I probably rate at about five out of ten for overall movie fanship, but the movies I do like, I *really* like; I will watch them repeatedly, to a fault, and remember much of them – the profound and the trivial, much to Amy's chagrin when something more important is forgotten! If it's a Tuesday night and I'm just going to bed, then I see *Shawshank* or *Jaws, Hoosiers, Remember the Titans* or a handful of others are on

TV, I <u>must</u> stay up and watch the end. *Again.* Also, if you thought I was heavy on the movie references, be thankful for what I left on the cutting room floor. You don't think I was tempted to suggest that "Aphid" was actually "an old, old, wooden ship?"

While compiling stories of others certainly helped with content, it presented unique challenges. One being that when Billy was in full edit mode he had to restrain from changing words actually spoken; I did as well, often telling myself, *No. That's what they said and that's how they said it. Why should I think I could say it any better?* So, in those cases, we put on the brakes, for the sake of integrity, to leave those words alone - and the book is better for it.

There's plenty online about the October Storm, but it's a bit like herding cats. Another major goal was for <u>Thunder Snow of Buffalo</u> to be a one-stop shop or a Greatest Hits. Again, that is certainly not to suggest the book contains everything there is to know about the October Storm as Billy and I are merely a sample of two. But, combined with intensive years-long research and accounts from a wide range of <u>over fifty</u> outstanding story-tellers, we felt good about the level of comprehension the book ultimately contained. It's one reason why I also aggressively, short of restraining orders, pursued the Meteorologists from ALL THREE networks - with Billy's securing Chesley McNeil years ago as a bonus. We wanted to hear, then share, their own words - and their own personal experiences; that's a chapter I'm especially proud of.

Billy was exceptionally skilled at compiling, then composing the raw interviews that I'd compiled in their various forms (ie. emails, notes from phone calls and in-person conversations, voice memos, and Zoom calls). Never again will I read a book and not appreciate the investment of effort, time, and sweat equity required by the author, publisher, editor, artist, and others, but I must admit adding "Author" to my LinkedIn profile was deeply gratifying – a lifelong dream actually.

When my parents attended a Parent-Teacher Conference with

my 6th grade teacher, Mr. Virgil, he told them I was underachieving in Reading and Writing, which I did not disagree with. Reading traditional books was just not my thing, but knowing that I loved sports, he encouraged me to read sports magazines and newspaper articles - and he was right. (The only person this would negatively impact would be my poor sister Tracy as I used to give her sports quizzes as if she could flick a switch and love sports the way I did.) My parents purchased me a *Sports Illustrated* subscription and I often purchased the now defunct *SPORT* magazine, especially when any Steeler, Yankee, or Sixer was featured on their awesome covers; my source was always our local *Charlie Johns Grocery Store*. Shortly thereafter, following Yankee box scores and accompanying recaps in the local *Leader Herald Newspaper* became a daily habit that one could argue was the first tangible sign that sports were always going to be in my life and my career. So I wouldn't go so far as to say Mr. Virgil and my other Lake Pleasant Central School teachers are surprised that I now *read* books, but they're surely surprised that I'm *writing* one. I've now been cast in this unlikely role indeed.

Knowing Billy, as a neighbor, since he was in Junior High School, I could tell early on that he was a gifted communicator. His aunt, uncle, and cousins live on our street so he'd cut through our yard from his house on Treehaven often. Sometimes while hosting gatherings in our backyard in the summer with friends and family, he'd stay for a few minutes and say hello, knowing he had an open invitation. He conversed comfortably with my friends and family on an adult level, even holding court with some of the funniest things you'd ever hear from someone that age. As an ambitious high schooler, conversations about the October Storm morphed into a flippant book-writing idea, but it turned real enough that we started this book about a year after the Storm, back in 2007. We started compiling some stories from family, friends, and work colleagues, but then... life happened. We ended up unofficially shelving the project simply for the lack of time.

Late in the summer of 2020, I was going through some old files and came across some old material. As I started reading it, I thought to myself: *This was good. Really good. Maybe I'll dust it off and try again since 2021 would be the 15ᵗʰ anniversary.* I called Billy and, without hesitation, he was back in. And I truly could not have produced a book of this level without him!

It gained serious traction when prominent professionals like Tim Wenger, Mike Schopp, Pastor Jerry Gillis, Patrick Hammer, Aaron Mentkowski, and Don Paul, none of whom we knew, showed such willingness and eagerness to share their memories. Then personal colleagues like Mike Nigrelli, John Guy, Bob Schultz, Deb Driscoll, Joe Frandina, Perry Dix along with players and coaches I worked with solidified and added such color and context to the project. Paul Maurer, Therese Forton-Barnes, and Mike Sirianni were icing on the cake. And the degree to which having Marv's foreword further legitimized our efforts in ways that can never be quantified. Finally, we much appreciated Mayor Byron Brown's contributing statement as it surely added an element that moved us closer to our goal of being "the official book of the October Storm."

Above and beyond this all-star lineup, which felt like an embarrassment of riches both in terms of quantity and quality, we continued to almost inadvertently compile unique fascinating stories during the normal course of life by simply bringing up our book during haircuts, dental checkups, pool closings, banking transactions, and other routine errands or phone calls - most of which are featured in Chapter Eighteen.

Perhaps one the most gratifying aspects of this experience has been finishing what we started. My humble advice to those out there wrestling with crossing the finish line on something meaningful, **make the time**!

Before we went to print, we sought out a demographic range of friends and family for their honest critique. My top candidate was

Teri (DeGlopper) Martin, Amy's close friend who also happened to be Claire's first grade teacher and a super knowledgeable Bills and Sabres fan. Upon informing Billy about Teri, he said, "That's Miss DeGlopper! I had her in Fourth Grade at West - that was the year of 9/11 and I remember her being pulled out of class when they were telling the teachers." Teri was even more excited to learn that one of her prized students had become an author. Wow, again, *that* is Buffalo for you.

Joy and Tony also read the book and gave me excellent suggestions. My Mom, who vowed to not read it until the finished product came out in print, finally caved and not only read the book, but also offered surgical ideas about re-phrasing certain parts.

This book journey also provided an opportunity and reason (not that a reason should always be needed) to reconnect with former colleagues and friends that I hadn't spoken with for a while, years in some cases. Sure, we stayed in contact by occasional text messages and on social media, but it's not like hearing someone's voice. I recall one the LinkedIn post of one of my former Bills colleagues, Marc Honan, that was so simple, but equally true: PICK UP THE PHONE AND CALL SOMEONE. These phone calls were so great! Not only did people gladly share their "storm stories", but we went down many other memory lanes. Getting together in person is even better, but much of my writing occurred during the 2020 Covid-19 Pandemic, which made that a bit more challenging. But thankfully, everyone's eagerness to share their storm memories for this book were heartening, even if virtual and from afar. Marc also helped me to "think big." Speaking of which, please check out our website, thundersnowofbuffalo.com and check out some of our promotions, including select merchandise!

The Bills material served multiple purposes. First of all, while the book is primarily about the October Storm, it couldn't be "all storm, all the time." If the movie, "Titanic", was solely about the boat sinking, *"When the vessel's speed increased from 15 to 20 knotts going*

North, North East with a slight southerly wind toward the iceberg..." *No, thank you.* Personal stories are needed in the context of a central catastrophe to resonate. Working for the Bills was where I happened to be in 2006. So, at a basic level, I simply asked my colleagues about their storm experiences - and they came through *big time!* This also meant that they became characters in the book, so naturally I shared supporting (and true) stories about them to help make them more real. A prevailing reaction from friends and family after reading this book will be, "Hey man, you've been holding back all these years." *Yes. Guilty as charged.* Some of my Bills stories were simply too good *not* to share and while I might have told one of these stories to one person, a different one to another, never have I shared so many of my actual Bills experiences in one place, at one time, like this. Again, to the reader, thanks for obliging!

The cover, which is clearly "coffee-table worthy" is another source of pride for us - evolving through a series of revisions, edits, and "shower thoughts." Given that many people told us that blue lightning was so prevalent in their storm memories, we had toyed with the idea of "Thunder Snow and Blue Lightning" as a title, but *Thunder Snow of Buffalo* worked better for it's flow and quite frankly, having Buffalo in the title made it all the better to us. So we eventually settled on making "Thunder Snow and Blue Lightning" a chapter title, while Tom subsequently worked some blue lighting into the cover to convey that aspect pictorially. Incidentally, to have another young neighbor friend, Tom Cavanagh - who was at the game when Kevin Everett was injured - design the cover was a special part of this adventure, too. If you like the cover - and how could you NOT? - you can find Tom's work at cavanaghdesign.com. But get your requests in early, because he's got a long list of clients! - so thanks to Tom for his time, patience, and efforts!

On May 30, 2017 my long career with the Bills came to an unexpected end. The new General Manager, Brandon Beane, sat down with me in Jim Overdorf's office to explain how the football side of the Front Office would be moving forward without me. I respected Brandon's decision and appreciated the manner in which Brandon, Jim, and HR Director Barb Evans handled the meeting. The Bills organization also helped me, financially and otherwise, bridge to the next stage of my life. In my remaining last couple of hours in the building, while packing up my office, Jim Overdorf stopped by again to express his appreciation for my years of service under him. Kevin Meganck came by next - including a visit to my house a few days later with some items I'd left behind. Other colleagues including Julie Lantaff, Amanda (Shevchuk) Schwartz, Gail Zielinski, Toni Addeo, and my favorite Finance Team gang (who still owe me a lunch) did the same. With Julie and Amanda, I tried to break the ice by reaching under my desk to present them each with Vitamin D sun lamps - the source of an inside joke as a former Bills executive had been issuing them to players, then turning over the mundane, methodical inventory and payroll-deduct duties to us. Before leaving the building, I purposefully detoured to the VP of IT, Dan Evan's office, expecting perhaps one last prank (his legendary pranks on me alone could constitute their own chapter). No pranks that day. Instead, Dan and Kevin organized a farewell Happy Hour for me the next week. My next stop was down to the Weight Room to thank Eric Ciano, Hal Luther, and their Strength team whom I'd worked closely with. After one last visit to the Training Room where Bud Carpenter, Shone Gipson, Chris Fischetti, and Greg McMillen had helped make my Worker's Compensation duties less miserable over the years, I finished my "tour" at the Security corner where VP of Security Chris Clark, along with Bob Schatz, and Marty McLaughlin bid me farewell and already talked about meeting for lunch in the near future. Chris graciously told me to take my time and he'd leave my credential active for the whole day in case I needed to come back for anything, which I did not. Phone calls followed - starting with my great Ticket Office friends like Karen

Renzi, Sharon Hart, and Deb Cummins, who were my first office mates during my 1988 internship and subsequent early years.

Correspondence with all these folks was special, even if expected as I'd worked with each of them for years, but the one encounter that remains perhaps most meaningful and unexpected was the very last one with our new Team Chaplain, Len Vanden Bos. I'd only known Len a few months, mostly by handling his relocation as he joined the team in March having come from the Baltimore Ravens. Once we settled his relocation, I didn't see Len often during the course of a normal day, except for an occasional lunch in the team cafeteria so quite honestly, he's not a person that I sought out during my final few hours in the building. I'd planned to maybe shoot him a text days after my release – truth be told, "planning" during those hours were sketchy as I was both numb and hypersensitized at the same time, if that's possible, but as I walked out of the building for the last time in twenty-seven years, his office, near the Security exit, became an unexpected final stop. Seeing me walk by without any knowledge of my release, Len called me in. Sensing that something was different, he inquired, so I told him. Len shut the door and shared a quick story:

> *Don, after being with a church for twenty years, one day out of the blue, the HR person presented me with a dismissal letter. I didn't know what would happen next, but God did. He was already there. I found myself next in the NFL with the Chicago Bears – fulfilling a lifelong dream. Don, you surely don't know what's next for you, but God does. He's already there.*

That encounter and those words were exactly what I needed in that moment; it instantly provided a sense of peace that has stuck with me ever since. In a text exchange and phone call with Head

Coach Sean McDermott some weeks later, Sean shared how he too was moved by Len's words to me that day.

During our impromptu farewell meeting, Len also gave me a book, <u>All the Places to Go</u>, by John Ortberg about God opening and closing doors which I carelessly misplaced during my "new life overhaul." That book resurfaced in my basement on Sunday morning, January 24, 2021 during a time when some doubt crept in my mind about our own book-writing journey due to some unexpected hurdles. I texted Len that Sunday morning about the book resurfacing as he was in the hotel in Kansas City with the Bills where they were to play the Chiefs in the AFC Championship game that evening. He was where he was supposed to be. And so was I.

So many unexpected things happened that year. Having left the Bills after twenty-seven years, I couldn't envision a scenario that would ever bring me back to the stadium. Amazingly, later that fall, our West Seneca West Indians High School Football team went on a magical run. Amy had taught several of the players when they were in 6th grade and we were friends with Assistant Coaches, Matt Marinaro and Rob Lares, who had each also coached Anna and Claire in lacrosse and basketball years earlier. A pivotal Sectional playoff game was played at Bills Stadium (then New Era Field) where, like the Simpsons, the *whole town* attended (or so it felt) and cheered the team onto a comeback win over South Park. A couple of weeks later, the town of West Seneca took over the Thruway (I-90 East) to the Syracuse Carrier Dome where the team won the State Championship! The whole experience was unexpected and fulfilling - especially watching the Fire Department give the team buses a parade upon returning home on all the local news stations. And there was my "football fix."

The opportunity to work with the wonderful folks at Avrij Analytics, a leader in AI technology for scouting and hiring, and having the chance to stay in professional sports, has been a true blessing. <u>So too has the journey of writing this book with Billy Klun.</u>

I am convinced that this most fulfilling bucket list experience was, at least in part, *exactly* what Len meant about God's plan for my future.

Major thanks to Archway Publishing, especially Morgan Judy, for patiently working with a couple of rookies!

Kudos also to Bills Alumni Director Jeremy Kelley who helped reconnect with several players from that 2006 team that we'd interviewed, but then lost contact with during the *DECADE* that our book was on the shelf before we resurrected the project.

Finally and most importantly, to the reader - thank you for taking this journey with us. Above and beyond your monetary investment, you invested your valuable time into a fairly non-traditional book, one that can't be put (figuratively) into a box. We truly hope your reading experience approaches how rewarding our writing experience has been. And let us ask you one more favor - next time someone brings up the October Storm, please say, "Hey, there's a book out about that." *We'd really appreciate it!*

From Billy:

When Don first reached out to me about restarting this project, ironically this was not the first or even second idea I had about why he was reaching out; a collection of stories about a snowstorm almost fifteen years ago did not seem as relevant anymore as it did then - but then I started thinking about it, *talking about it,* **remembering it.** It all came rushing back and I realized that we needed to put this story back into the memories of Western New Yorkers in its rightful place next to the Blizzard of '77, as well as evidently the October Surprise of 1906. With that said, I began to realize that this wasn't going to be a telling about a storm - the Storm itself was only unusual in that it formed how it did when it did; instead this was a telling of *the stories* of the Storm, which suddenly flooded back why we wanted to do this in the first place. I never thought that this collection of stories would lead into us learning so much that we did; from Re-Tree's work, to the Carvings for a Cause, to all of the insurance and damage data; all of this goes above and beyond the expectations I had for where this story was going to develop to. I am so grateful to Don for re-initiating this project and thinking to include me again; as Don said, this journey has been one I will never forget and I remain so thankful for.

For those of us who lived through this storm, all we did for weeks afterwards was talk about our experiences and over time, to Don and I at least, it seemed everyone went through their own personal challenges and triumphs in their own unique ways that deserve to be shared more. We faced an almost insurmountable challenge of deciding *who, what, where, and when* was included in this because we knew not everything could be; this was the hardest part - deciding what would **not** make the book. We thought of all the friends and family that would not have their experiences - good and bad - included, and realized we needed a place to continue this beyond just the book - thus, thundersnowofbuffalo.com where we hope people from all over will come to continue to share their tales as everyone deserves to be heard.

I was fortunate enough to have been taught so much about Buffalo and its history from a very young age - my maternal grandparents grew up in the Old First Ward and the Valley, my Mom in South Buffalo; much of my family and extended family with roots there are still there and I have always loved hearing the stories told. Gramps - who came to stay with us during the Storm - as well as my Grampy, better known as Corky Connors, who both grew up, worked, and lived in these areas were prolific story tellers, a trait I came to admire and idolize and something I hoped to aspire to; my Uncle Dan Marren is also known for his storytelling abilities and ways to capture the attention of an audience which is something I thought about throughout this process as we were so hopeful to appeal to as broad an audience as possible.

Thus, it was important to me to make sure that some of Buffalo's history - both recent and not-so-recent - were a part of this book and that we were telling the stories of the people who lived it, not just the Storm itself; much like Don said, we realized quickly the book couldn't be about a snowstorm - no one cares about that because why would you, but the *people* who were *impacted* by the Storm are the ones we knew everyone would want to hear from and about, as well as relate to on a greater scale.

There has been a part of me that has wanted to be "an author" for years - my Mom will probably say that it stems all the way back to early in my childhood as I was a voracious reader - though not as much as my cousin KC who could always "out-read" me and still can - but I have always found books to be an escape; books were a way for me to see and learn about worlds that I had not yet been able to experience. I think that is the most wonderful part of a book - seeing an event, real or otherwise, from someone else's eyes; it offers a perspective and a world of insights that we are not always privy too. In my work as a Mental Health Therapist, part of my job is to try and help people better understand what is going on inside their own minds, or to try and get them to have this same perspective as when they are reading a book, to see the situation through another person's eyes, but it is not always easy. When I was younger, I was in love with fiction, but as I've grown older my love has shifted more towards historical fiction, fiction rooted in something real that makes it both; I'm sure there is someone psychoanalyzing that much deeper and better than I ever could, but from where I sit, I think historical fiction is a fair way to reflect on ourselves and our histories: we remember all of the details, but not always exactly as they were, but more importantly what they meant to us. Thunder Snow of Buffalo is the same: while people's memories shift and fade after almost fifteen years, what does not change is the memory of how these days, and for some weeks, *felt*. My goal - and I believe Don's as well - was never to get a perfect picture because we knew we couldn't, but what we did want was to give people a space to relive and share how the Storm forever impacted them.

Growing up, I was fortunate enough to go to my fair share of Bills Home Games, that was until my cousins KC and Tom became old enough to enjoy the extra season ticket seat that, their Dad, my Uncle Dan had right on the goal line, ironically not too far from where Don would sit when he was working these games. I was there the day that Jim Kelly was added to the Wall of Fame; I have been at The Ralph - as it was known for most of my life - for exciting wins and devastating losses, something that almost all Bills Fans can relate to. I was raised in the post-Super Bowl era, when the Miami Dolphins were still our love-to-hate rivals, and watching the New England Patriots begin to grow into the empire that Bill Belichick and Tom Brady created, with the funding of Bob Kraft, wishing that Buffalo could be the team that gets that fame next - and now with Josh Allen and Sean McDermott, anything is possible! But growing up in an era of the Bills where they were struggling and fighting for each win, it's inevitable to wonder as a kid, *what brings Bills Fans back every week?* This is one of those questions that people from outside the region ask all the time, but that any true Bills Fan knows the answer to: ***because we genuinely believe that this year could be the year.*** We have to, we have to have the hope because if not, then it's all for naught; this resiliency, I think, comes from years of shoveling the same snow over and over, knowing that no matter what we do it will always come back, but we don't leave, we don't complain, *we just deal with it.* Or something like that.

There's gotta be a reason, *right?*

Although I moved away from Buffalo a few years ago, I remind everyone that #BuffaLove will always be my home; there is no experience like leaving Buffalo knowing that your next visit will only be that, *a visit.* I say this knowing full well that thousands if not millions of people leave their homes and hometowns every year, but Buffalo has always been a unique place to live and love. I will never forget introducing my, now fiancee and (hopefully) future wife Lenni, to Buffalo; as she likes to remind me and everyone else, she never thought she would spend so much time in Buffalo, especially in the winter, but has come to find a love for Buffalo almost as much as the people who call it home. Buffalo offers to all who visit it a type of feeling that words can't really describe - ironically something we have tried to do in the last 80,000 words or so but I guess I still struggle to find - but what makes Buffalo so different is it's people; the people of Buffalo are what everyone who knows I am from Buffalo tell me about their visits there (as well as the wings, obviously). But what outsiders and even some locals don't appreciate is that the people of Buffalo have been shaped by the from generations of hard working immigrants, some who were thwarted by the Great Lakes in their attempts to move West and some who were drawn in by the abundance of factory and labor work in the early to mid-1900s, who knew that to survive the community needed to lean on each other and help each other. In the Covid-19 Pandemic, we saw how communities who work together can be more successful and how divisiveness and focusing on differences can hurt us more; this is what the true Buffalo is about, this is why we all survived and thrived through the 2006 October Surprise Storm, and is also why Buffalo will forever be known as **The City of Good Neighbors.**

WHERE ARE THEY NOW?

(IN ORDER OF APPEARANCE)

Sports Illustrated runs a popular annual issue entitled "Where Are They Now?" that features former stars or memorable characters who have been out of the spotlight since their playing days. Bill O'Reilly in his "Killing" series - Jesus, Lincoln, Kennedy, Patton, Reagan, and others - similarly dedicates a post-story chapter to what ultimately happened to the main and supporting characters. Even some movies that are *based on true events* share what happened to the people-turned-characters, like in *Remember the Titans* and *We Are Marshall*, for example. Since the storm and subsequent events occurred in 2006, many of the key players in our book have entered new chapters of their own lives and we felt it was important for the readers to know just how much everyone *has* thrived.

Marv Levy began coaching in 1951; his professional football career began in 1969 as Kicking Coach with the Philadelphia Eagles; transitioning to a Special Teams Coach for the Los Angeles Rams (1970) and the Washington Redskins (1971 - 1972). He served as Head Coach in the Canadian Football League for the Montreal Alouettes from 1973 to 1977 before returning to the NFL as Head Coach of the Kansas City Chiefs in 1978 where he remained until 1982. Following a two year gap in coaching and one season with the Chicago Blitz (of the USFL), Marv was brought onboard with the

Buffalo Bills mid way into the 1986 season where he would remain, leading the Bills to all four of their charter's AFC Championships, until his *first* retirement in 1997; during this brief retirement, Marv served as an analyst for ESPN and was inducted into the Football Hall of Fame in 2001. In 2006, Marv was *called back to duty* by Mr. Ralph Wilson himself asking him to take on another leadership role with the Bills as General Manager which he accepted in 2006 and stayed on for two seasons. Since then, Marv has written four books, including an autobiography, a football fiction, and a children's book. Marv was also among a small group of people who attended both times the Chicago Cubs were in the World Series, 1945 and 2016; in 1945, Marv was on furlough at the time from the Army Air Force. Just as this book went into print he was, not surprisingly, inducted into the Canadian Football Hall of Fame. Marv and Fran are currently enjoying retired life in the Chicago area.

Mayor Byron Brown is the 62nd Mayor of Buffalo and has been since taking office New Year's Day, 2006; Mayor Brown also served as the Chair of the New York Democratic Party (2016 - 2019) and was a New York Senator for two districts (57th District, 2001 - 2003; 60th District, 2003 - 2005) and as a member of the Buffalo Common Council (1996 - 2001) before becoming Mayor. Once again, we thank the Mayor and his Deputy Director of Communications, Lorey Schultz, for their participation!

Joe Frandina *tried* to retire from the Bills a few years ago. The Bills organization threw an official retirement ceremony with his wife, Linda, and family in attendance. He was presented with a framed Bills #1 Jersey with "Frandina" on the back. Joe was emotional as the retirement was final - he *really* meant it at the time, but after a couple years with Joe away, VP of Business Dave Wheat, begged him to come back and Joe did ultimately negotiate his own terms to rejoin the Bills. Incidentally, Joe's return forced me to breach my own personal Facebook rules. I had vowed not to be Facebook friends with anyone who I *currently* worked with. This was simply perhaps an overly protective measure from my own self-incrimination (was that redundant?). As soon as Joe retired, I sent him an invite, but then he came back. What to do?! I kept him. After being let go myself in 2017, I freely (and happily) became friends with dozens of current Bills employees - which helped Joe "blend in" with the crowd.

Perry Dix, since moving on from the Bills, is now a Construction Inspector with DiDonato Associates. My phone call to Perry about this venture was among my favorite book-related conversations.

Roger Edel continues to serve as Managing Partner at Williams and Williams Workers' Compensation Defense Firm. God bless him! While I do not miss the Worker's Compensation element of my job at the Bills, I very much miss the most pleasant phone conversations with Roger, who does a very difficult job with a smile.

Pete LaForce retired from the Buffalo State College Security team and currently, with wife Marcia, enjoys the heck out of their time with grandkids, Kate and Cole. Pete, given his versatility playing guitar, taking on lead and backup vocals, and rocking the keyboard is known as the "Swiss Army Knife" of our little old Hi View garage band.

Brian Moorman punted for the Buffalo Bills from 2001 to 2012. After playing a year with the Dallas Cowboys, the popular punter returned to the Bills for a final season. Brian still holds the Bills record for the longest punt: 84 yards, earned First Team All-Pro twice, and was voted as the punter for the Buffalo Bills' 50th Anniversary Team. Brian serves today as the founder of the P.U.N.T. Foundation which supports children in Western New York who face life-threatening illnesses. He is also the owner of Sotheby's International Realty in Ponte Vedra Beach, FL. I believe we all just found out that he's also a heckuva writer.

Mike Schopp continues to serve as the co-host of WGR 550's Sports Talk which, together with Chris "The Bulldog" Parker for over ten years, have become the #1 most listened to talk show in all of Western New York and have earned national recognition as well.

John Guy was released by the Bills in 2010 after a Front Office sweep and today splits his time between Charlotte, NC and Tampa, FL serving as Director of Professional Development with Vanguard Sports Group. He is still as stylish as ever!

Tim Wenger continues to serve as Operations Manager/Director of Content & Digital Strategy at Entercom Radio, which includes overseeing operations of NewsRadio 930/107.7 WBEN, WGR SportsRadio 550 and WWKB radio. Days before we went to print, Entercom changed its name to Audacy. I knew this was a serious move when the Radio app on my phone changed to Audacy without any action taken on my part.

Police Commander Mike Nigrelli retired from the New York State Police in 2011 after almost twenty-seven years on the force and he stayed on as security staff with the Buffalo Bills until 2017. Most recently, he has been working as a Confidential Criminal Investigator for the Erie County District Attorney's Office. Mike has also offered excellent advice to our scouting and hiring startup company, Avrij Analytics.

Jim Overdorf, my long-time boss, remains with the Bills as the Salary Cap Wizard and other intangibles. He has seen and dealt with all that can be thrown at an NFL Front Office. When his grandchildren are of age, they'll be treated to NFL stories even better than those in this book.

Dave Beh and his brother, Dean, still serve the Webster, NY community as Chamberlain Septic and Gordon Beh Excavating, with son, Jessie, learning the ropes and ready to run the show when Dave retires to Florida.

Joe Kirchmyer continues to oversee the West Seneca Chamber of Commerce as Director while running his own promotion company, Kirchmyer Media, LLC. If you detected a professional level of writing while describing his quest for a generator and a disaster averted (with his neighbor's gas stove), you would not be mistaken as he wrote for The Buffalo News for over two decades. Joe also still commands the pitching mound in his softball leagues.

Angelo Crowell is a former linebacker for the Buffalo Bills from 2003 to 2008. In the summer of 2006, he was named the starting strong side linebacker and started every game until suffering a late season injury. He went on to play for the Tampa Bay Buccaneers from 2009 to 2010 and the Omaha Nighthawks of the UFL from 2011-2012. Angelo is now President of Fifth Quarter Investments, LLC in Tallahassee, Florida.

Deb Driscoll retired from the Buffalo Bills in 2014 to Bradenton, FL where she and her husband, Mike, proudly run the Fish Hole Miniature Golf Lakewood Ranch. Stop in to relay that you read about her in the book!

Bob Schultz retired from the Bills in March of 2009. Since moving to Florida, Bob now serves as a Lieutenant of the Jupiter/Inlet Police Department. Rumor has it that he now has his *own* driver.

Tom Cavanagh was 14-years-old and a Freshman at West Seneca West High School when the Storm hit. Today, Tom runs his own business, www.cavanaghdesign.com and created the most awesome cover of this book!

Aaron Mentkowski has worked for WKBW in Buffalo as part of their Meteorology team since 2000. He has also acted as a forensic meteorologist for legal cases regarding weather and teaches about "Severe and Unusual Weather" as an adjunct professor at Buffalo State College.

Patrick Hammer was working as a meteorologist at KTSP TV in Minneapolis during the October Storm, however has been at Buffalo's WGRZ since 2015. Patrick has been a meteorologist all over the USA starting with NBC 24 in Chico, CA back in 1996.

Chesley McNeil was a meteorologist at WGRZ in Buffalo during the October Storm in 2006 and remained there until 2009 when he moved to Atlanta to join 11Alive, WXIA where he now hosts his own morning show *"Wake Up With Chesley."*

Don Paul has worked at all four major news networks over his legendary local career dating back to 1984; after working in Detroit, Tampa, Wichita, and Bangor, Don was Chief Meteorologist at WIVB from 1984-88, Chief Meteorologist at WGRZ from 1988-91, and returned to WIVB in 1991where he remained until 2016. After a brief retirement, he returned to WKBW as the Weekend Meteorologist for two more years before retiring again in 2018. Don is still active locally, often contributing to the Buffalo News as well as being featured in spokesperson and voice over roles.

Keith Ellison, former linebacker for the Bills from 2006 to 2010, finished his degree in history after his tenure in Buffalo and returned to his hometown of Redondo Beach, CA where he now teaches World History, Physical Education, and an elective course on developing healthy lifestyles via nutrition, emotional health, and physical fitness at Adams Middle School. After being drafted by the Bills, he was not permitted, by NCAA rules, to partake in Organized Team Activities because Oregon University required him to stay on Campus to complete his Final Exams. But that didn't stop Keith from catching up quickly and earning a starting Linebacker spot. And I'm proud to say I negotiated Keith's first NFL contract!

Ryan Neill was a Defensive End and Long-Snapper for the Bills from 2006 to 2008. He signed as a Free Agent with the St. Louis Rams in 2009 and was nine days into his 2010 contract with the San Diego Chargers when he suffered a leg fracture against the Seattle Seahawks finishing his NFL career on the injured reserve list in 2010. He has since worked as a successful sales representative for a medical technologies company, Stryker. A smart guy, without a doubt.

Bill Kollar was a defensive lineman for the Cincinnati Bengals from 1974 to 1976 and with Tampa Bay Buccaneers (77-81) before becoming a coach. After taking on the role as a Defensive Asst./ Special Teams coach for the Bucs in 1984, he spent four years coaching at Illinois and Purdue before beginning his long career as a Defensive Line Coach for the Atlanta Falcons (1990 - 2000), St. Louis Rams (2001 - 2005), Buffalo Bills (2006 - 2008), Houston Texans (2009 - 2014), and has been with the Denver Broncos since 2015, including for during their victory in Super Bowl 50. Can one imagine how loud his celebration roar was?

Brad Butler, former Guard for the Buffalo Bills from 2006 - 2009, started in 31 out of 33 games he played for the Bills. Today, after earning the Social Impact Award in 2013 at the Kellogg School of Management, Brad remains active in the business and political arenas.

Fred Jackson was a star running back for the Buffalo Bills from 2006 to 2014 before finishing his career in 2015 with the Seattle Seahawks. During his tenure with the Bills, he was the recipient of their prestigious Walter Payton "Man of the Year" Award in 2010 and remains the third-best rusher in Bills history. Since then, Fred has operated the steakhouse SEAR in Buffalo with fellow Bills Alumni Brian Moorman and Terrence McGee; Fred also joined MSG Western New York in 2018 as an analyst for its postgame show, *"Bills Tonight."*

Shane Costa is an NFL Agent and a Sports Marketing Attorney at Generation Sports Group in Buffalo, NY. Knowing his work ethic and integrity first-hand, I'd highly recommend his services to any prospective college athlete with NFL aspirations!

Kevin Everett, drafted by the Buffalo Bills in the 3rd round of 2005, when he suffered a year-ending ACL injury, making 2006 his primary season played; since his career-ending injury in 2007, he has returned to Houston with his family give gratitude to his faith for allowing him to find how way down the path he has led saying, "I got the one year of my dream job - that was what God had planned for me." Kevin famously won the Jimmy V Award for Perseverance at the 2008 ESPY Awards and shared his remarkable story on the Oprah Winfrey program. Today, Kevin enjoys life at home in Houston, TX with his wife, Wiandi, and four daughters while doing some inspirational public speaking.

John DiGiorgio was signed as a Rookie Free Agent Linebacker in 2006 who started thirteen games in 2007. After retiring from the NFL in 2009, John went back to his Alma Mater and earned his

Master's Degree in Principalship. He has been a Physical Education teacher at Chippewa Valley High School in Clinton Township, MI and in 2018 he began working as a real estate agent. From the "it's a small world" category, John's close friend is the nephew of former Bills' Controller in Detroit, Frank Wojnicki.

Ashton Youboty was a cornerback for the Bills from 2006 to 2010 and played his final season (2011) with the Jacksonville Jaguars. After his NFL playing career, he worked as the Quality Control Specialist and then Senior Defensive Assistant for the University of Wisconsin before moving on as the Assistant Cornerbacks Coach at Youngstown State University.

Josh Reed was a wide receiver drafted out of LSU in the 2nd round of 2002 NFL Draft by Bills; he stayed on with the team until 2009 when he became an unrestricted free agent. He was our daughter, Anna's, best buddy when we played basketball across the street at ECC before the trainers (wisely) shut that down after a player sprained an ankle. As much as I liked Josh, I hated running into those sneaky, brick wall picks that he set. Only Travis Henry's were worse.

Lee Evans was the Bills' first round pick for the 2004 Draft, making him the highest drafted wide receiver since 1996. He was traded to the Baltimore Ravens before the 2011 season and stayed on with them until signing with the Jacksonville Jaguars in 2012; after which he retired from the NFL. Since then (and even a little before), Lee has been an owner and investor in real estate and energy companies and projects. In 2016, Lee became a managing partner of quantitative large cap equity funds as well as co-founding the PB2 fund, the first large cap quantitative fund established by current and retired NFL players.

John McCargo, defensive tackle, was a 1ˢᵗ round pick by the Bills in the 2006 NFL Draft; he stayed with the team until 2010, followed by stints with Tampa Bay and Chicago before retiring in 2012. John has since run his own youth football camps and has been active in the business world.

Josh Stamer was a linebacker in the NFL from 2003 through 2010, the Buffalo Bills (2003 - 2007), the Tennessee Titans (2008), and the Cleveland Browns (2009). Since then, he has been a member of the NFL Alumni Association and been working for Lenovo, most recently as Retail Strategy & Operations Officer.

Kevin Sylvester has been a local media icon in Buffalo for many years, prominently known for his years in broadcasting as Host and Executive Producer of Sabres Hockey Hotline, Television/radio Play by Play announcer, and Television Host for the Buffalo Sabres for eleven years. He spent a year hosting *BILLS TONIGHT* post game with Ruben Brown on the Buffalo Bills Network as well as being a play by play announcer for Time Warner Cable from 2012 to 2018. He has hosted a weekly lifestyle television program on WGRZ since 2016 and has been the VP of Sales and Marketing of Logistics Plus, Inc. since 2018. Kevin continues to work as a radio announcer for the PGA Tour Entertainment and PGA Tour Radio, which he has been doing since 2014. Kevin also owns his own Media production company, All Square Media, LLC, as well as being Manager/Co-Owner of Sylvester and Peck Media, LLC. He has also written the "MUST READ book for all men that want to play more golf", *"The Married Man's Guide to Golf."*

George Wilson was signed by the Buffalo Bills in 2004 and played his first game in 2005; he became a team leader and played through the 2012 season, earning honors beyond his time on the field: the President's Volunteer Service Award, given to him by President George W. Bush in 2008, and the Buffalo Bills Walter Payton Man of the

Year Award, not once but twice, in 2009 and 2011. George was signed by the Titans in 2013 and later waived in 2014. George continues his community leadership and volunteer work in so many ways, including his own "George Wilson S.A.F.E.T.Y. Foundation" whose mission is to "Save Adolescents From the Everyday Trials of Youth" by teaching youth in the Buffalo and Paducah, KY School systems life skills to utilize as a tool to survive in different environments. Finally - as a personal message to George - THAT is called "Gettin' er done!"

Rian Lindell, former placekicker for the Seattle Seahawks (2000 - 2002), Buffalo Bills (2003 - 2012), and Tampa Bay Buccaneers (2013). Of note, in 2007 he set the record for the most consecutive field goals made in Bills history and in 2010, he set the NFL record for successful extra points (321) to start a career. Rian is now a Physical Education teacher at Eastlake High School in Sammamish, Washington.

Mike Schneck's career as a long snapper began in 1999 with the Pittsburgh Steelers and was signed as a free agent by the Bills in 2005; he was selected to his first Pro Bowl in 2005 alongside teammate Brian Moorman. He was released by the Bills in 2007 and signed with the Falcons a month later. He announced his retirement in 2010 and became a partner at Altair Management Partner for almost ten years until 2020 when he co-founded and became Managing Partner of his own investment firm, Gridiron Partners in Pittsburgh, PA. When we signed Mike at the Bills, Paul Lancaster, Liz Malstrom (HR), and I asked Mike who handled Player Insurance and 401K at the Steelers, his previous team, as we were already trying to enhance and streamline our best practices. Mike's answer, no lie… "I did." This player was clearly destined to professionally manage other peoples' business and finances.

Jabari Greer signed with the Bills as an undrafted free agent in 2004 and primarily played on special teams until 2008 when he started the ten games of the season at Cornerback until being injured. He was signed by the New Orleans Saints in 2009, where he started and earned a Super Bowl ring, until retiring in 2014. Jabari worked for ESPN as an NFL analyst for a while before starting his role as an NFL Analyst for TSN in Canada in 2016, which he is still doing today.

Perry Fewell was hired as defensive coordinator of the Buffalo Bills in 2006, with the Storm being in his first year with the team. After thirteen years of coaching college football, he joined the Jacksonville Jaguars as Defensive Backs Coach from 1998 - 2002. He held the same post with the St. Louis Rams in 2003 and then with the Chicago Bears from 2004 to 2005. About halfway through the 2009 season, Perry was appointed interim Head Coach of the Bills for the last three games of 2009, before a new staff was brought in by the Bills. Perry moved onto the New York Giants where he earned a Super Bowl ring (XLVI) in 2012. He went on to serve as defensive backs coach for the Washington Redskins for two seasons in 2015 then returned to Jacksonville as the defensive backs coach in 2017. In 2019 he was named the secondary coach of the Carolina Panthers then interim Head Coach before the end of the same year. Today, Perry holds the position of Senior Vice President of Officiating with the National Football League. Talk about taking arrows!

Dave Jickster, aka DJ Jickster, is Marketing & Promotion Director as well as an on-air host for 97 Rock (96.9 FM) in Buffalo and has been for twenty years. He is very involved in local community service works, (including Eric Wood's O'Shei Children's Hospital fundraiser which I've attended multiple times), and is very passionate about serving Buffalo and the WNY region.

Paul Maurer - the easy thing to say here is "See Chapter Fifteen", but we'll still take a shot at summarizing what this incredibly busy and driven man is currently doing. Paul is Principal at PDM Marketing

& Media, Chairman of Buffalo Means Business - an executive networking event, Board Member and Chair of International Weather Experience Center (IWEC), Senior Account Manager for Entercom Radio, and of course - Founder and Chairman of Re-tree WNY. Once again, in addition to sharing his incredible knowledge, Paul also provided pictures and advice - for which we thank him greatly!

Fred Raines has been Director of Pro Ministry for Athletes in Action in Buffalo, NY since 1984. He was Team Chaplain of the Buffalo Bills until 2014 where he helped guide many young men and their families through a major life transition. Fred and his wife, Kathy, have planned, organized, and held the popular annual Call to Courage Breakfast with Frank Reich and featuring recent winners, Andy Dalton, DeMario Davis, along with Kurt Warner, Curtis Martin, and others. On a personal note, our entire family was thrilled to have Fred conduct Anna and Tyler's wedding.

Jerry Gillis is the Senior Pastor at The Chapel Crosspoint in Getzville, NY. Most importantly, as per his own web site, Jerry and his wife, Edie, have two sons and make their home in the suburbs of Buffalo, New York. He loves to watch University of Georgia football, coach his sons in baseball, go for a long run, read a good book, and eat a great meal with his family at the dinner table. It should be noted that he is also a vocal advocate for the Buffalo Bills!

John Murphy followed the legendary Van Miller (who I could write an entire chapter about on his own) as the Radio Voice of the Bills. While their personalities are much different (Van the outgoing, John the subdued) they are both tremendous talents. Bill Mafia will agree that the immediate succession is like Young following Montana, Rodgers following Favre, and Chocolate following Peanut Butter. In May 2019 Murphy was announced as an inductee into the Buffalo

Broadcasters Association's Hall of Fame. John can also be found in a cameo appearance in the movie *Bruce Almighty*.

Brad Lamb and his family currently live in North Carolina where, above and beyond their five beautiful children, became foster parents - even recently adopting one. Brad's wife, Angela, earned her masters degree as a Nurse Practitioner and is currently on track to earn her doctorate by December 2022. Brad went back to school to finish his college degree, graduating with his Bachelor of Arts in 2018. All the while, Brad has been working for a local company in sales for the past nine years and notes, "God is good - all the time."

Incidentally, I still today have Brad and Angela's voicemail saved on my phone from September 15, 2011, informing me that he was walking out of Morgantown Correctional Institution as a free man to meet Angela in the parking lot where she spent the night sleeping in her car. It should be noted that while serving his time there - just as Andy Dufresne built a library and tax center - Brad convinced the institution to transform a large room into a training center where he trained all who wished to participate, guards and inmates alike. He has also been a High School football coach, including for his son, Xander.

Tony (the Barber) Scaccia, now thirty-seven years into the business, will still cut your hair and share great stories as owner of Tony's Hairstyling on 3606 Seneca Street in West Seneca diagonally across from Ferro's Pizza.

Mike Sirianni enters his 15th year as Property Claims Supervisor at Erie Insurance Group. Given his first week at this post was our 2006 October Storm, it clearly was smoother sailing after that "trial by fire" initiation. Billy and I thoroughly enjoyed our most informative zoom call with Mike. Thanks to Martin Shaugnessey for arranging it.

Aaron Schobel ranks 2nd in Bills history in sacks behind just Bruce Smith. He, his wife June, and their family live in Columbus, TX. I can personally attest that this proud Texan managed his money like few players who ever came through One Bills Drive.

"The Weekenders" - Visit our website, www.thundersnowofbuffalo. com to learn more about these life-long friends and see updates as they come along!

Scott Berchtold continues to serve on Special Projects for the Buffalo Bills. He still owns Vince Lombardi's actual desk and is a contributor to some of the most famous speeches ever delivered by Bills' legends. Scott recently gave me one of the most unorthodox compliments I've ever received - one that will remain secret for this book, but that I *might* share personally with some of you.

Therese Forton-Barnes is an Ithaca College Alumni who, above and beyond her aforementioned Carvings for a Cause campaign (Chapter Sixteen), is Owner at Green Living Gurus, Events to a Tee and Matchmaking 2 a Tee. As with Paul, Therese was a top-tier contributor to *Thunder Snow of Buffalo*! She doesn't know it yet, but I have some event ideas for which she's the perfect candidate to oversee.

Sue Beres still owns and operates Eclips Hair Salon on Seneca Street near Southgate Plaza. I don't personally know of a business owner (with co-owner, Marge) who did a better job of operating creatively, safely, and yes, in full compliance of the NY State Covid restrictions, in 2020. Also, as mentioned earlier, our families became friends having our daughters, Kelsey and Claire, attend and play Lacrosse together at Medaille.

Kathy Barry Kane continues to serve as a Vice President at Bank on Buffalo. You've no doubt seen her on a billboard. Incidentally, one of the boys she was watching for her sister, Karen, on October

13, 2006 was Tyler McTigue who is now our son-in-law by virtue of marrying our daughter, Anna.

Chris Brown is the host of the popular daily television program *One Bills Live* and the Lead Journalist for the Bills Insider. As mentioned in Chapter Eighteen, I greatly respect the balancing act that Chris pulls off in his unique role with the Bills.

Don's Family

> **Amy,** my wife: With retirement from the West Seneca School District still a few years away, she remains a great teacher, Mom, and wife who keeps me sharp in every aspect of my life.
>
> **Anna (Purdy) McTigue**, our oldest daughter, is back in Western New York after spending parts of 2019 and 2020 in Sunrise, Florida. She is finally married to Tyler McTigue after their wedding was moved from 2020 to 2021 due to the pandemic. She and Tyler spend most of their free time doting on their beloved pup, Molson.
>
> **Claire,** our youngest daughter is willing to go on the record that we *never* missed another birthday. She's now a proud graduate of Medaille College and will soon enough be a fabulous teacher, just like her mother.

Billy's Mom, Kate retired from Buffalo Public Schools after almost twenty years with the district and although she misses her students, she is now enjoying retirement traveling back and forth to visit Billy, Lenni, & Winston in Boston and Cape Cod as well as in Florida, basically any opportunities she can find to escape the cold winters of Buffalo!

REFERENCES, IN ORDER OF CITATION

1. US Department of Commerce, NOAA. "Lake Effect Snow Event Archive: October 12, 2006 to October 13, 2006." *National Weather Service*, NOAA's National Weather Service, 11 Oct. 2016, www.weather.gov/buf/lesEventArchive2006-2007_a.

2. Paul, Don. "Don Paul remembers the October Storm ... because we forced him to." *Buffalo News, 11 October 2016, https://buffalonews.com/news/local/history/don-paul-remembers-the-october-storm-because-we-forced-him-to/article_a99e47b3-0740-5dbd-b0f4-f28a8835aabf.html. Accessed 22 October 2020.*

3. Hamilton, R. S., D. Zaff, and T. Niziol (2007), A catastrophic lake effect snow storm over Buffalo, NY October 12–13, 2006, paper presented at 22nd Conference on Weather Analysis and Forecasting/18th Conference on Numerical Weather Prediction, Am. Meteorol. Soc., Park City, Utah, 25 – 29 June.

4. Buffalo Enquirer, 1906: "Lives and Property Destroyed!" Oct 11 1906, Pg 1.

5. *Colgan Air Flight 3407 was a connector flight from Newark, NJ to Buffalo, NY which operated as a Continental Connection Flight for Continental Airlines on February 12th, 2009 that subsequently crashed into a home in Clarence Center, NY just*

five miles away from the end of the runway where the plane was headed. It is believed that the cause of the crash was a result of the pilot not responding properly to warnings that the plane was stalling, resulting in the death of all forty-nine people on board, including all passengers and crew, as well as one other person in the house when the plane crashed.

6. New York State, Department of Public Service. October 2006 Western New York Major Snowstorm: A Report On Utility Performance. May 2007. p. 11

7. "Act of god." *Dictionary.com.* Dictionary.com, (n.d.). Accessed 6 Nov 2020.

8. *The Buffalo Braves were a professional basketball franchise of the National Basketball Association (NBA) based in Buffalo from 1970 until 1978. In 1978, Braves owner John Y. Brown Jr. swapped franchises with Irv Levin who owned the Boston Celtics; Levin then moved the team and renamed them the San Diego Clippers until the franchise moved again in 1984 and became how it is now known: the Los Angeles Clippers.*

9. Henry, Michelle. "30,000 homes still without power." *Toronto Star,* 21 October 2006.

10. *The Bible.* Authorized King James Version, Oxford UP, 1998.

11. Levy, Marv. "Marv Levy Enshrinement speech." Pro Football Hall of Fame Induction Ceremony, 4 August 2001, Pro Football Hall of Fame, Canton, OH.

12. "officious." *Oxford Dictionary.* Lexico.com, (n.d.). Accessed 4 Nov 2020.

13. *Highlights of this actual Zoom interview can be found on our website thundersnowofbuffalo.com.*

14. LaBarber, Jourdon. "Donations to 'Patricia Allen Fund' at Oishei Children's Hospital Eclipse $700,000." *Bills Mafia Continues to Donate to Honor the Passing of Josh Allen's Grandmother,* Buffalo Bills, 4 Dec. 2020, www.buffalobills.com/news/donations-to-patricia-allen-fund-at-oishei-children-s-hospital-eclipse-700-000.

15. "Our History: Buffalo Olmsted Parks Conservancy - His Legacy. Our Inheritance." *Buffalo Olmsted Parks*, Buffalo Olmsted Parks Conservancy, 28 Apr. 2020, www.bfloparks.org/history/.

16. *These along with pictures of many of the statues and our interview with Therese can be found on our website, (you know it by now, right?)* *thundersnowofbuffalo.com.*

17. Owen, Chris. *14 Years Ago Today: The October Surprise Storm.* 12 Oct. 2020, wyrk.com/14-years-ago-today-the-october-surprise-storm-photos/.

18. Pignataro, T.J., and Janice L. Habuda. "Area Slammed Hard by Snow Thousands In Region Without Power 'Enormous Amount of Physical Damage'." *The Buffalo News*, 13 Oct. 2006, buffalonews.com/news/area-slammed-hard-by-snow-thousands-in-region-without-power-enormous-amount-of-physical-damage/article_85108f62-0742-58e2-8321-6a1d40e16771.html.

19. Contributors to Wikimedia. "Buffalo, New York Snow Storm Closes Schools, Leaves Nearly 400,000 without Power." *Wikinews, the Free News Source*, Wikimedia Foundation, Inc., 13 Oct. 2006, en.wikinews.org/wiki/Buffalo,_New_York_snow_storm_closes_schools,_leaves_nearly_400,000_without_power.

20. "Lake Storm 'Aphid.'" *Wikipedia*, Wikimedia Foundation, 21 June 2020, en.wikipedia.org/wiki/Lake_Storm_"Aphid."

21. Paul, Don. Interview. By Don Purdy. 15 Oct 2020.

22. Maurer, Paul. Interview. By Don Purdy and Billy Klun. 13 Nov 2020.

23. Thompson, Caroline. "Early Snowstorm Battered Buffalo's Historic Parks, Trees." *USAToday*, 20 Oct. 2006.

24. Forton-Barnes, Therese. Interview. By Don Purdy and Billy Klun. 5 Dec 2020.

25. Beebe, Michael, et al. "Storm Reimbursement Cloudy FEMA Won't Predict Chance of Disaster Decree by Bush." *The Buffalo News*, 21 Oct. 2006, buffalonews.com/news/storm-reimbursement-cloudy-fema-wont-predict-chance-of-disaster-decree-by-bush/article_2c00923b-d1c9-5922-a1b2-1681fe68aeb3.html.
26. New York State, 2006, p. 1
27. Sirianni, Michael. Interview. By Don Purdy and Billy Klun. 12 Dec 2020.
28. New York State, 2006, p. 10
29. Reilly, E. (2016, October 7). *Remember Oct. 2006? Lessons learned will apply to Hurricane Matthew.* https://www.wkbw.com/news/remember-oct-2006-lessons-learned-will-apply-to-hurricane-matthew.
30. Paul Maurer, email message to the authors, February 25, 2021.
31. New York State, 2006, p. 21
32. New York State, 2006, p. 5
33. New York State, 2006, p. 8
34. New York State, 2006, p. 16
35. New York State, 2006, p. 17
36. New York State, 2006, p. 28
37. New York State, 2006, p. 6
38. New York State, 2006, p. 30-31
39. New York State, 2006, p. 40
40. New York State, 2006, p. 33
41. US Department of Commerce, NOAA. "Lake Effect Snow Event Archive: Dec 10 2017 to Dec 11 2017." *National Weather Service*, NOAA's National Weather Service, https://www.weather.gov/buf/lesEventArchive?season=2017-2018&event=C.
42. Deitsch, R. (2017, December 11). 'Once In A Lifetime Conditions': A Closer Look At CBS's Terrific Broadcast of Bills-Colts Snow Game. Retrieved January 05, 2021, from https://www.si.com/media/2017/12/11/bills-colts-snow-game-cbs-broadcast

ABOUT THE AUTHORS

Don Purdy, originally from Speculator, New York in the Adirondacks, served in the front office of the Buffalo Bills for twenty-seven years, with his last and longest role being Director of Football Administration. He saw the Bills through four Super Bowl appearances and managed a twenty-million-dollar budget, including workers' compensation, team travel, and player contracts. Purdy is now Senior Adviser for Avrij Analytics, a leader in AI scouting and hiring platforms and serves on the President's Advisory Board of Houghton College, as an alumni.

Billy Klun is a licensed mental health clinician specializing in addiction, geriatric, and personality disordered populations currently in private practice outside of Boston, Massachusetts. After earning his degree in psychology and English from SUNY at Buffalo, he received his Master of Arts in mental health counseling at the Boston College Lynch School of Education and his second master's degree at UMass Boston in management of aging services.